Bird-Bent Grass

Life Writing Series

In the Life Writing Series, Wilfrid Laurier University Press publishes life writing and new life-writing criticism and theory in order to promote autobiographical accounts, diaries, letters, memoirs, and testimonials written and/or told by women and men whose political, literary, or philosophical purposes are central to their lives. The Series features accounts written in English, or translated into English from French or the languages of the First Nations, or any of the languages of immigration to Canada.

The audience for the series includes scholars, youth, and avid general readers both in Canada and abroad. The Series hopes to continue its work as a leading publisher of life writing of all kinds, as an imprint that aims for scholarly excellence and representing lived experience as tools for both historical and autobiographical research.

We publish original life writing that represents the widest range of experiences of lives lived with integrity. Life Writing also publishes original theoretical investigations about life writing, as long as they are not limited to one author or text.

Series Editor
Marlene Kadar
Humanities, York University

Bird-Bent Grass
A Memoir, in Pieces

KATHLEEN VENEMA

WILFRID LAURIER
UNIVERSITY PRESS

LAURIER
Inspiring Lives.

Wilfrid Laurier University Press acknowledges the support of the Canada Council for the Arts for our publishing program. We acknowledge the financial support of the Government of Canada through the Canada Book Fund for our publishing activities. This work was supported by the Research Support Fund.

Library and Archives Canada Cataloguing in Publication

Venema, Kathleen Rebecca, 1960–, author
Bird-bent grass : a memoir, in pieces / Kathleen Venema.

(Life writing series)
Includes bibliographical references.
ISBN 978-1-77112-290-0 (softcover)

1. Venema, Kathleen Rebecca, 1960–. 2. Venema–de Jong, Geeske. 3. Alzheimer's disease—Patients—Biography. 4. Alzheimer's disease—Patients—Family relationships. 5. Mothers and daughters—Canada—Biography. I. Title. II. Series: Life writing series

RC523.2.V46 2018   362.1968'3110092   C2017-905061-3

Cover images from the author's personal collection (envelope) and iStock/Nicoolay (bird). Cover and interior design by Chris Rowat Design.

© 2018 Wilfrid Laurier University Press
Waterloo, Ontario, Canada
www.wlupress.wlu.ca

This book is printed on FSC® certified paper and is certified Ecologo. It contains post-consumer fibre, is processed chlorine free, and is manufactured using biogas energy.

Printed in Canada

RECYCLED
Paper made from recycled material
FSC® C103567

What are all these fragments for, if not to be knit up finally?
—Marilynne Robinson, *Housekeeping*

Contents

you come home. we need to talk

Late September 1988, Kampala's all brash sunlight, smells of smoke and diesel, moves fast, frenetic by contrast with our sedate village home. I've lived in Uganda for the past twenty-five months as a volunteer for the Mennonite Central Committee (MCC) and I've spent eight of those months struggling with a condition that won't be diagnosed conclusively for another seven years. Dr. B, my aging, cryptic British physician, has helped me research symptoms that he suspects mark the onset of a chronic illness. So I'm surprised when he extends my appointment to ask whether, once I'm "finished with the Mennonites," I could imagine joining the staff of the International School. Dr. B explains that he's on the Board of Governors, they're always looking for good teachers, and he knows that in another year my MCC term will end.

I'm flattered. Even in my unpredictable physical condition, Dr. B considers me a viable candidate for his elite institution. I tell him I'll think about it, though I have no intention of saying yes. I'm engaged in an increasingly affectionate correspondence with a handsome young (Mennonite) man in Canada whom I'm eager to see again in person. Besides which, I miss my family terribly. My mother's already counting the months till I'll be home. In the letter I send my parents a few days later—the seventy-second letter I've written them since reaching Uganda—I report positive medical developments: "Good news on the headache front. Dr. B says they're caused by sinus congestion from my cold. He gave me antibiotics, something stinky for steam inhalations, and an offer to teach at the International School when I'm 'finished with the Mennonites.' 'Doc,' I almost said, 'I'm kind of hoping I won't ever be finished with the Mennonites!'"

My mother's response arrived in her eighty-first letter. "Job offers are always nice," she wrote. "Affirmation of yourself as a productive, worthwhile human being is great, and at the International School yet!? It's wonderful. BUT. You make sure you come home. *We need to talk, right? And talk and talk and talk.*" She underlined the words.

Talk, ongoing and extended, musing, meditative, playful and philosophical, had until then defined my relationship with my mother and would do so for another fifteen years. But in the fall of 2003—just months after my marriage to an even more wonderful (Mennonite) man—it became impossible not to know that my mother was exhibiting symptoms of dementia. It wasn't a surprise by the time Mom's GP diagnosed Alzheimer's in July 2005, but no less devastating for not being a surprise. My mother identified herself with her mind. She knew how Alzheimer's stories end.

I tell an Alzheimer's story in this memoir and I tell a story about my life as it's been intertwined with my mother's, this mostly unknown Canadian immigrant whose spirit was quietly distorted by a sexual predator when she was just a child, and distorted again by the immigration experience that permanently split her life in two; a mostly unknown dreamer, who brought to the work of mothering a weirdly charming awkwardness, sparkling intellect, a spirit of often accidental whimsy, a passionate desire to bring about "a better world," eerie intuition, and radiating empathy that she packed into gloriously dazzling smiles. This is the mother with whom I've navigated distance, time, and, more recently, Alzheimer's, and our stories emerge from several sources, including the two-hundred-plus letters we sent one another while I lived in Uganda; the Friday-afternoon conversations we began recording in 2008; journal entries; email updates; and excerpts from the blog my husband and I began when our baby nephew was diagnosed with cancer.

During the years I lived at Ndejje, my Mom and I both wrote more than we'd ever written before and more than either of us has written since. Mom's half of the correspondence doubles as the only sustained record of her life and (practically miraculously) documents three years of her intellectual prime, a decade before Alzheimer's began its insidious work. Ironically, minus Alzheimer's, I might never have returned to our Ugandan letters. Minus Alzheimer's, I likely wouldn't have spent five years of Friday afternoons in long conversations with my mother. Minus Alzheimer's, I almost certainly wouldn't have written a story about her life. But the world plus Alzheimer's requires new navigational forms. Memories distort in the world plus Alzheimer's, and with memories, language, and with language, precision. Conversations morph to encompass spaces fissured by forgetting, linear time eludes the record, and paranoia lurks. In the world plus Alzheimer's, the work of maintaining relationships—and constructing an intergenerational memoir—folds intricately, repeatedly, unpredictably, inside and out.

And rich parallels suggest themselves, between navigating Alzheimer's and negotiating the challenges of living cross-culturally, especially immediately after a civil war. In the three years I lived at Ndejje, I didn't ever perfect meaningful connection across linguistic and cultural barriers, and I was never entirely comfortable tossing hard-won, handwritten accounts of my life into the unpredictably roiling sea I called the Black Hole of International Post. But the lively record of those challenges corresponds in unexpected ways with the non-linearity of even healthy memories and the fracturing

effects that Alzheimer's has on its sufferers' closest relationships. So I weave my diverse materials discontinuously, quilt-
ing as much as I'm weaving, in order to capture some of the
disorientation of staying connected to my mother over distance and time and dementia.

~~~

Early in my life at Ndejje, I saw a sight I'd often see again and
thrill to every time, a brilliant tiny meadow bird perched on
a blade of elephant grass. I loved the simultaneous serenity
and tension, the compact bundle of bird bones imminently
launched into soaring flight, the robust grass bent under its
weight, capable, in an instant, of miraculous restoration. I hope
that when you read about my mother and me, you'll experience the best of this tension, the powerful, delicate, resilient,
ephemeral, fleeting business of being alive and loving others
in the long or very short time they're ours to hold.

ONE

perfect correspondence

perfect correspondence (1)

Friday 30 September 2011. My mother is having a very bad day, such a bad day that when I email my siblings afterward, I describe her condition as "the worst I've ever seen." Despite the accelerating ravages of Alzheimer's, my mother and I still spend most Friday afternoons in 2011 walking and talking, working on crossword puzzles, singing sometimes, and reading. On this afternoon, though, and for the first time, every one of Mom's attempts to speak ends in nonsense, until—about twenty anguished minutes in—she announces clearly, "Well. That's enough of that. Maybe we should go for a walk." We've walked ten minutes against a surprisingly brittle wind when she turns to me and repeats a question she asked for the first time last week. "You're my daughter," she says, "right?" "I sure *am*, Mom," I answer promptly, pleased when she laughs at my intonation and stopped short by her next question: "So, were you with us when we came to Canada?"

My mother was sixteen in 1952 when she came to Canada from the Netherlands with her parents and eight of her nine siblings. She married six years later, after which my sister and I arrived in modestly quick succession, aware all our lives that *we* are Canadians, our parents are immigrants. I was almost fifty-one in September 2011, Sandy[1] had just turned fifty-two, and we'd been picking up the first hints that our identity as "daughters" was slipping from Mom's cognitive grasp. Several times that summer Mom had expressed amazement or puzzlement or sheer disbelief at the claim that we—together or separately—were her daughters. "How old am *I* then?" she'd asked me on a number of occasions, "if *you're* my daughter?"

"How can I have a *daughter* who's so old?" she'd inquired of Sandy earlier in the spring. Sandy and I speculate that as Mom sinks deeper into memories of her younger self, the concept of "daughters" is increasingly limited to her recollections of "the little kids," "the little girls."

But "Was I with them when they came to Canada?" More than any of dementia's intrusions up to that point, my mother's question unnerves me. "Coming to Canada" has functioned all her life as the dramatic hinge between a wide-open future and the permanent end of cherished dreams, a hinge so powerful that the question casts dementia's erosions into stark relief: if my previously sacrosanct identity as *daughter* is mixed up now in my mother's long memories of emigration trauma, we are further than I'd realized on the way to losing one another completely.

~~~

My mother and I have been exceptionally close all of my life, defined by years of meandering, expansive, intimate, informally cerebral talk. "You are *just* like your mother," friends and family members tell me, disconcerted at the resemblances; even my professional choices inadvertently realize many of my mother's best dreams. By the time my first sabbatical begins, I've had twenty-four months to process the Alzheimer's diagnosis and plan a project that commits my Friday afternoons and Mom's to the work of keeping our conversations going for as long as we possibly can. And so we read out loud to one another on Friday afternoons for the next five years; we discuss the news and retell family stories; we play word games and sometimes I play my parents' dreadful piano and we sing; sometimes we write letters and sometimes we read the letters we wrote in the late 1980s, when we were farther from one another than we'd ever been before.

If immigration to Canada works as a hinge or fold or break in my mother's life, the three years I spent in Uganda in my late twenties function decisively as a hinge in mine. From 1986 to 1989, in the aftermath of a civil war, I lived and taught at Ndejje, a small town in south-central Uganda. Email was seven years in the future and unimaginable; while I lived in Africa, I wrote and received more than eight hundred letters, to and from over sixty correspondents. I saved the letters I received, and most of my correspondents saved and returned the letters I sent. My mother wrote more regularly than anyone else and our two-hundred-plus letters make up almost a quarter of the little archive I created of that time. But archives are notoriously unvisited, and the letters in mine go undisturbed for sixteen years. Then we get my mother's diagnosis.

I know, when I return to the letters, that they'll offer a version of my mother's life and mine that's particular to the years I lived at Ndejje, but they'll also reflect, more generally, the way our lives have been shaped by connection and a desire for connection. I *guess* that the letters will offer a glimpse of my mother's most confident self and of the passions that propelled her. What I *hope* is that the letters will work as memory prompts, to bridge the very different distances opening up between us now. These are high hopes, it turns out, and often thwarted, but stories emerge anyway, about the ways my mother and I have found to find and lose and find one another again.

~~~

I was twenty-five when I moved to Ndejje from Lynn Lake, Manitoba, the nickel- and gold-mining town where I'd spent the previous three years teaching junior high school. At a little more than a thousand kilometres northwest of Winnipeg, Lynn Lake was far from home, though not the farthest I'd been from home. I wrote my family almost every weekend from Lynn Lake and I spent most of my holidays with them in Winnipeg. Otherwise busy with the demands of a first teaching job and the intensity of life as a twentysomething in a small northern town, I paid almost no attention to political events in Uganda. Unaware of my ignorance, I still imagined "Uganda" as more or less equivalent to the infamous "Idi Amin," but I caught myself up in the country's realities in the spring of 1986. I'd accepted a three-year volunteer teaching position with the Mennonite Central Committee (MCC), done some homework, and discovered that Idi Amin had been deposed by Milton Obote in 1979.

The information doubled as a lesson about the West's willfully partial representations of "Africa." The same Western press that loved to frame Amin as a depraved buffoon warmly approved of suit-wearing Obote, despite the fact that Obote's regime was characterized by even more extensive corruption and extrajudicial violence. What came to matter most to me was that after Obote's party won the December 1980 elections, an opposition politician named Yoweri Museveni alleged electoral fraud and declared an armed rebellion against Obote and the Uganda National Liberation Army (UNLA). Museveni and his guerilla fighters, the National Resistance Army (NRA), launched their war against Obote from within an area north of Kampala. Designated "the Luwero Triangle," the region quickly became the target of the UNLA's systematic persecution.

Five years of civil war ensued and Ugandans my age struggled to complete post-secondary training and launch careers in the midst of fighting and infrastructure neglect. And then in January 1986, after half a year of battles outside the capital, Museveni and his National Resistance Movement (NRM) took power in Kampala. I arrived in Uganda seven months later. As I'd dreamed about when I was young, I was finally in Africa. Without the war, though, Ndejje wouldn't have been the kind of "Africa" my younger self could have imagined. Ndejje, at the heart of the Luwero Triangle, was a hub for Church of Uganda religious and educational activities and the site of four schools with national reputations, a far cry from the mud-hut village my child's mind had conjured. Of Ndejje's institutions, Lady Irene College (LIC) had been an especial jewel in the crown, one of the country's premiere institutions for training primary-school teachers (the equivalent of elementary-school teachers in North America). Located high on Ndejje hill, LIC had been occupied in the war's final months by UNLA soldiers who, in their retreat from Museveni's forces, ransacked and vandalized as much of the college as they could.

Rehabilitation was a top priority, the word on everyone's tongue in southern Uganda in the days and months after the war, and Church of Uganda administrators were clear: a functioning college at Ndejje was crucial to restoring the region's morale. Finding teachers—called "tutors"—willing to return to the devastation was just one of the many challenges, and that was where Frances, the other young MCC-er, and I came in. Frances was enlisted to teach English and Social Studies, and, because science instructors were in particularly short supply, I would be LIC's newest tutor for science and mathematics.

I'd first heard about MCC from my mother's father. A passionate amateur theologian and committed socialist, *Pake* [pah' keh] (Grandfather) de Jong had, in one of the many informal sermons he declaimed on Sunday afternoons, declared MCC—the relief, service, and development agency of North America's Mennonite churches—the only development organization worth its salt in integrity. Pake died when I was just twelve, but his endorsement remained indelible. A little more than a decade after his passing, I began applying to do development work and I started with MCC.

MCC had been active in Uganda since 1979 and tuned to events in the Luwero Triangle throughout the war. With the war over, MCC was eager to commit volunteers to the region, even if their official role was to teach. By 1986, MCC was distancing itself from paternalistic development models in which well-meaning people from the global North arrive to "fix problems" in the South. MCC encouraged relationships of "peaceful presence" instead, a dynamic intended to foster mutual relationships and enable lasting positive change. The possibilities of *presence* resonated powerfully for me, and MCC's specific expectations—that its volunteers adhere to local living conditions, act out of pacifist principles, and embody the belief that genuine security is built through mutual friendship, economic development, and equal sharing of global resources—corresponded well with the peculiar ways in which I imagined "doing good."

By 1986, MCC was discouraging teaching assignments, on the grounds that education systems across Africa had been deformed by generations of colonial imposition. The Church of Uganda made a strong case for Ndejje, though, and MCC made the exceptions that set in motion a lifetime for me of pondering the distances between presence and absence, including as Alzheimer's intrudes on my consciousness.

perfect correspondence (2)

As it turned out, our first year at Ndejje was marked by many more stretches of not teaching than of teaching. People were only slowly trickling back into the area, traumatized by the war. On Friday 29 August 1986, fifteen students had returned and Lady Irene's inaugural postwar term began. I'd already written to my family six times.

Letter #1 to Mom and Dad   *16 August 1986*

Scribbling precariously on my table tray, en route to Nairobi, well over thirty thousand feet, and somewhere south of Greece. Mt. Olympus an hour and a half ago on the left, though I couldn't access any of its wisdom: I'm trapped, three seats and an aisle away from a window, and farther from home than I've ever been before. Everything I've done so far I've done before, but from here on in, the world's entirely new. And unlike teaching up in Lynn Lake, I can't come home at Christmas to take stock. [. . .] Our plane was delayed getting out of JFK, so we weren't served supper until 10 p.m.; breakfast followed five hours later in an attempt to convince us that what had just happened was "night," and then it was a four-hour wait in Schiphol (which I used to write to Carla). Now this flight. That bed in Nairobi is going to look awfully good.

I miss you already.

Letter #1 from Mom and Dad   *18 August 1986*

I had a call this morning from MCC to inform me that they had received a telex from Nairobi saying you had arrived safely and everything was going well. I assume you are not yet sure exactly when you will be leaving for Uganda, but I also assume that you will be there by the time this letter arrives. [. . .] Dad had suggested that I start keeping a diary, so I bought a smallish notebook and have scribbled in it a few things every day, beginning on the day you left Winnipeg. I think I mentioned that Kim called, that I gave her your address, and that she will be teaching in Baldur, MB. [. . .]
On Tuesday August 12, I took Beppe to her hairdresser's and while she was there, I went to visit Elke, where it was bedlam as usual, but I guess it's no wonder with three foster children and three of her own. [. . .] Later in the evening I had a long conversation with Sandy. She had been to Stony Mountain Penitentiary to interview two inmates. She's quite busy; I think they really load the articling students down with work. [. . .]
The diary is going to be invaluable. Saturday we had two weddings. The ceremony in Calvary Temple was not very long, a large part of it devoted to the show of the entrance of the attendants. Annette walked into the church on her own, for which she has my respect. I don't think that is the usual thing to do in their circle. We didn't have time to go through the reception line so we just squeezed out of the church and were on our way. [. . .] The second service was very nice and the organ music was beautiful. Carolyn had also various attendants, and she also wore a white dress. [. . .] We miss you very much. We hope all will continue to go well for you. Write soon.

Mom's invaluable diary records a life deeply enmeshed with family. Her beloved father, my *pake* de Jong, had passed away fourteen years earlier, but her mother—whom Mom calls *Beppe* [beh' peh], the Frisian term for grandmother—lived in an apartment nearby. My parents and grandparents were all ethnically Frisian and spoke Frisian as a first language. Frisian is an older language than either Dutch or German, complete with its own long literary history and still spoken by about four hundred thousand people, most of whom live in Fryslân [frēz' læn], one of the Netherlands' twelve provinces.

Beppe appears regularly in Mom's letters, as do Mom's youngest sisters, Gerta and Eta. I didn't usually call Gerta or Eta "Aunt" in either English or Frisian, but I still addressed my mother's closest sister and her husband as *Muoike* [mwoi' keh] Bertha and *Omke* [om' keh] John. Mom's letters reference Bertha and John, her oldest sister Line ("Muoike Line"), and occasionally her brother Louie; and somewhat less frequently, her sisters in British Columbia (Hinke and Jessie) and her brothers Hendrik and Ynse. Not infrequently, as here, my father's sister-in-law appears, Muoike Elke, busy with biological, foster, and adopted children.

My father also emigrated from the Netherlands to Canada, also originally from Fryslân, but he came on his own in 1954 when he was just nineteen. Seduced by the beautiful farms of CPR immigration films, he'd decided against both an obligatory stint in the Dutch army and taking charge of the family's dairy production, in order to pursue his dream of growing golden, windswept wheat on the Canadian prairies. Of his six siblings, only his next oldest brother joined him in Canada. The two young women whose weddings my parents attended on 16 August 1986 are both my first cousins but on different sides of the family, hence the scheduling conflict my mother describes. Mom's report on a call from my university friend Kim was just the first of hundreds of references that would characterize her letters. My mother was almost as attached to my closest friends as I was, and they returned the affection. Zany Tracey M was no exception.

Letter #1 to Tracey   *19 August 1986*

*We were supposed to have left for Kampala this morning
with Jake and Amy, the new MCC Uganda unit leaders, but
I've thrown a wrench into the machinery and we are still in
Nairobi. Had had a bad night Sunday after taking migraine
medication (leaves crazy agitation in place of the headache),
but was so happy not to be in pain by morning, I practically
danced to the washroom. Barely made it there, though,
before I threw up (which at least left me feeling well enough
to shower)(which I certainly needed), then got completely
disoriented by a dizzy spell heading back to our room and
can only remember (i) knowing certainly that Room No. 8
was not our room and (ii) maneuvering my key into
what I certainly believed was the No. 7 lock. Next I knew,
though, I was struggling out of the bed in No. 8 assuring our
startled neighbor that everything was perfectly fine. When I
managed to get the right door open, I collapsed immediately
over top the suitcases and only revived when Frances dragged
me onto my bed.*

The worst part is that my glasses broke in the fall.

I wrote almost constantly to my parents and individually to my
sister, Sandy—recently married to Gary and in her articling
year of law school—and to my brother, Henry, who was about
to start an engineering degree and was dating a woman named
Dana. I wrote less often to numerous other correspondents,
including Lynn Lake colleagues and students, friends from
university and high school and earlier, aunts and uncles, cousins, and people in my parents' church. I saved my best writing energies for my dearest pals: Carla, with whom I'd forged
lifelong bonds in high school; Tracey M and Lil & Roxanne,
who were bosom buddies from university and summer jobs;
and Sharon, so close I called her "my other sister," especially
once we were teaching together in Lynn Lake, where we opened
our circle to include Nathaniel, the young minister in town.

Letter #1 to Tracey [cont.]

Luckily, I was feeling sufficiently better after the others had breakfasted that we were able to get most of our errands done, and an efficient optometrist's shop in downtown Nairobi fixed my glasses in under two hours. [. . .]

20 August. This evening, Busia, a dusty town just short of the Kenya-Uganda border. We're at a curious place for the night, an inn recommended by other MCC-ers, their only criticism having been of the two-hour wait for dinner. Speculating that the chicken for their supper hadn't been killed until after they'd ordered, we requested our meal as soon as we arrived (5:30), to be served at 7:15. And sure enough, only moments after ordering, Jake and Amy found Benson, the receptionist-bellboy-waiter-cook-and-chicken-hunter, plucking a chicken (pronounced "kitchen") behind the kitchen (pronounced "chicken"). [. . .]

Kampala, finally, on Thursday 21 August. Benson's roasted "kitchen" dinner was superb. Jake and Amy are a lot of fun; we laughed till we cried, but that only made me miss you worse. Write as often as you can. Could you also phone my Mom and let her know that I'm definitely not sick anymore and she shouldn't worry?

P.S. I think I have fleas, but please don't tell my mother that.

When Frances and I reached Kampala, we increased the MCC Uganda team by 50 percent. Jake and Amy had recently taken over as Country Representatives. Cindy was halfway through her term as a librarian at Makerere University, having staunchly refused to leave the country, even during the fiercest battles. (Later, when I was ill and often rested at her apartment between medical appointments, Cindy and I became very close.) Luke had been displaced by fighting that continued in the north and the east and was struggling to maintain contact with his primary community. By November it was clear that the work couldn't be resumed safely and his term came to an early end.

Luke and I begin corresponding regularly a year later, but in June 1989, after an exchange of more than forty long and increasingly affectionate letters and just six weeks before I'm scheduled to return to Canada, I'll receive Luke's breezy note letting me know he's met someone else.

Letter #2 to Mom and Dad   *21 August 1986*

So many things to tell you about all at once that words and punctuation are flailing: can you connect enough dots here to see something of what I'm trying to describe? Everything is marvellously "African" and the closer we get to Ndejje, the more thoroughly "African" it feels, which seems to mean magical and otherworldly, which doesn't make sense because what I mean is that what's around me approaches more and more closely what I've been anticipating. The fact is, it's surreal to be in a place you've imagined for months and years. The fact is, if someone offered to reduce my term to just one year, I'd take them up on it in a heartbeat. It's a good thing I didn't know how much I'd miss you or I never would have come. Gone. Come, gone, you know what I mean. "Home" will always mean home with you.

Especially at first, before we'd begun to integrate into the community that was rebuilding at Ndejje, I used almost every moment that I wasn't teaching to write. The ironies of the situation weren't lost on me. I couldn't have completed a handwritten letter (averaging three thousand words) every three days (on average) during my life at Ndejje if I'd been occupied with the considerable work of teaching science and mathematics to three hundred young women in a four-year teaching program at a highly respected teacher training college *and* supervising their teaching practice at various local primary schools. But the war left LIC a ransacked shell and rehabilitation work was slow, and so, ironically, the war that created the conditions to which I had responded in Canada also created conditions in which I could write more, and more constantly, than I'd ever written before.

Letter #2 to Mom and Dad [cont.]

Kampala streets are fantastically atrocious. The city is built on seven hills, like Rome (which, as you know, I've only flown over), so we're always heading up or down steep inclines in our wobbly Daihatsu. Not much fighting happened in Kampala, but years of infrastructure neglect mean some streets are just long potholes held together by strips of tarmac. Despite the neglect, Kampala is like breathing after Nairobi's cosmopolitan throngs and all those Europeans. Here we're emphatically muzungu,[2] the rare sight of other white people already unsettling, as if we're seeing our own misplaced-ness mirrored back to us. The speed with which you can forget yourself. [. . .]

We're hoping to get to Ndejje tomorrow but probably won't stay the night since we need to be in the city to gather supplies for the big move. At this point, Frances and I imagine we'll be in Kampala about twice a month but I don't know if I'll ever be able to phone. Three years is a long time to go without phoning. Write often. (How can I feel so far away when I'm right here?) [. . .]

Sunday 24 August. Ndejje. The last few days have been rough, but today is better because our house is cleaner. I wish you could've seen this place when we arrived. It turns out that the expression "it looks like an army's been through it" means something quite specific when an army has, in fact, been through it. [. . .] Please send Gertie's address. I feel slightly desperate to know that you're thinking of me. I'm certainly thinking of you.

I wrote because I was lonely, and I wrote because almost everything around me was unfamiliar, and sometimes I wrote because I was afraid. I have no way of knowing how close I was to the state my mother would inhabit twenty-five years later, reaching through dementia's fog to ask, "Were you with us when we came to Canada?"

Letter #1 to Lil and Roxanne   *24 August 1986*

Greetings from the land of Gigantic Cockroaches (GCs), where life is a series of Personality-Expanding-Events, not inconsequentially known as PEE. (And lemme tell ya, if the PEE keeps up at its current rate, I'm going to have to buy my personality a seat of its own on the flight home.) You can probably imagine that I hardly have time to write, catching my breath as I am between scheduled rounds of Cockroach Killing and Collecting (CKAC, which helpfully approximates the sound a person makes while thus engaged) and optional activities like Dead Animal Removal (DAR, as in the piratical "ar-be-dar, there's an ex-bird in this cupboard") and Checking the Toilet Tank (CTT, in which the C is pronounced SH for the familiar phrase "merde, that bloody thing is empty again and I'm sure I'm the one who filled it last"). [. . .]

In our cement-block house, we have, for the record: electricity, cold running water, a flush toilet (with manual "fill"), a dining-room table with two chairs, two stools and two beds to go alongside them, enough dirt in the cupboards to grow small but tasty potatoes, and bug carcasses throughout. We may also have fleas. [. . .]

Finishing up. The advantage to owing you as many favours as I do is that if you want to collect, you'll have to keep being my friends until I get back, just two years and fifty-one weeks from now. You think I'm being flippant, but I write with a seriously cold clutch in my guts. Absence makes the heart grow fonder, but out of sight is out of mind.

So write soon. I want to hear all about what's happening in your life/lives (unless it's none of my business, in which case I'm exactly the right distance never to know). (Seriously, write soon.)

I wonder now how afraid my mother was, me so far away in an unimaginable land, and how afraid she's been more recently, dropping inexorably into Alzheimer's dimensionless spaces. I know I've sometimes been afraid. I was certainly wary, that first year, of live grenades and military checkpoints, and I was deeply unsettled several times a day by the piles of skulls retrieved from surrounding swamps and stacked on trestle tables around Ndejje hill, and on the rare occasions that it was necessary, I was fearful of refusing—but determined to refuse—rides to soldiers armed with AK-47s. What terrified me, though, was the possibility that, separated from my friends and family by almost thirteen thousand kilometres and excruciating stretches of postal delays, I wasn't real. Far outside the intimate circle that had surrounded me for years, I began to suspect that I was just a collection of the attributes I loved the most about my friends. Without their presence to draw me out, I regularly wondered how I'd keep being myself. Culture shock, especially in the first year, was a distraction from the unnerving possibility that without my people I no longer existed.

Letter #2 from Mom and Dad   *26 August 1986*

If I'm going to stick to my plan of writing every week, then it's time again. We have not yet heard from you, except for the telex from Nairobi. I'm trying to imagine what it's like for you, everything and almost everybody being unfamiliar, but also fascinating I'm sure. I hope you are adjusting well to it all; I know you're very adaptable.

My mother spent her life self-conscious about many things, including her appalling handwriting. That at least she could blame on the rigid Dutch school system of the 1940s, which forced left-handed children to write (and draw and sew) with their right hands, and she did. The saddest result of the rigidity wasn't Mom's terrible handwriting, though; it was never experiencing writing as pleasure. But she sat down anyway, again and again, at the kitchen table in their little home along the Seine River in Winnipeg, Canada, to pen that week's letter to Ndejje, Uganda.

Letter #2 from Mom and Dad [cont.]

Thursday, they showed the movie Reds on TV. We saw it in the theatre didn't we? It was just as good the second time around. [. . .] This morning, I went to U of Winnipeg to pay my registration fee. My course, Symbolic Dimensions in Religion, starts on September 9. Since I was downtown, I picked up another ball of that purple wool in order to finish the sweater you were knitting for me. I didn't have much heart for knitting lately; I still have to get used to you being all the way in Africa and then I can't knit right away. Maybe that doesn't make much sense; I know I'll get back into it in a little while. [. . .] Did you have a chance to contact Gertie in Nairobi?

Gertie Buis was a few years older than Geeske [gay' skeh] de Jong, but they became close friends soon after meeting in 1952. Both were serious, intellectual young women, though I picture Geeske, who became my mother, as the more outspoken of the two. In 1969, while working as a librarian at the Université de Montréal, Gertie met and later married Gerald Wanjohi, a Kenyan doctoral candidate in philosophy. In 1973, when Gerald had completed his Ph.D., he and Gertie took up permanent residence in Kenya, and I was able to visit them on almost every one of the trips I made to or through Nairobi.

Letter #6 to Mom and Dad   *28 August 1986*

School starts tomorrow, but we haven't yet met the principal, we're not sure exactly what we'll be teaching, and we have no idea what schedule we'll be following, so instead of reading the local blockbuster, Teaching Science in the Elementary School, I'm writing to you.

Please let me know immediately (whatever that means) if three postcards, all sent to your address, arrive safely. After I mailed them, Frances suggested there might be certain things one wouldn't discuss on postcards. I'd expected that and certainly wasn't commenting on government or military matters, though there has been more fighting in the north, which you may not have heard about. We're only affected by the increased security at the roadblocks between Bombo and Kampala, and that's only because Bombo Road heads directly north into the troubled area. Even "increased security" is misleading as we experience it: instead of being questioned politely and waved through, we had to produce our passports yesterday at one of the checkpoints. Not to worry; things would have to deteriorate dramatically before we'd be affected here in the Luwero Triangle.

When I admitted I'd commented on roadblocks, potholes, and dust, I concluded from Frances's skeptical look that she didn't hold out much hope for the postcards' fate. Arghhh, the proverbial labour of love. The one to Sandy is supposed to be particularly funny because it describes my first adventures behind the wheel. [. . .]

By now it's 10:35 p.m. and a choir of insects has taken up its nightly hymn to the gods (in Luganda, so I can't understand a word). We'll be up at 6:30 to be in chapel by 8:00 to help pretend that school is starting, though we only have fifteen students, and the principal and the vice-principal are both away in search of funding. Please write soon. I need terribly to believe that you miss me and are thinking of me the way I miss you and think of you.

Letter #2 from Mom and Dad [cont.]

*August 28th. I hope you are ok. I worry about you
considerably. We think of you very often. If there's anything
we can send you, let us know. Write soon. Much love
from all of us.*

For the first several weeks, neither Frances nor I received any
North American mail. Homesickness felt like amputation, as
if I'd been surgically removed from my own life. Grateful for
a wide circle of friends, I wrote doggedly, selecting stories to
suit the recipient . . .

Letter #1 to Nathaniel   *29 August 1986*

*Am guessing that my "spiritual life" may be a little
haphazard (though that's hardly new), but we had a grand
experience on the trip from Nairobi to Kampala. We were
travelling with Jake and Amy Jessup, who've been MCC
Uganda unit leaders since late July, and had stopped for
the night at a wonderfully shambling inn, arriving in time
for Jake and Amy to get in a run. They set off with most of
the local children jogging alongside and told us later about
their encounter with two men dressed in flowing white robes,
drums and other musical instruments strapped to their
bodies. According to Jake, who conversed with the men in
Swahili, they belong to the "Holy Shipwreck Wilderness."
Naturally we remonstrated. "Jake," I challenged, "that has
to be a loose translation: 'Holy Shipwreck Wilderness'?"
"Ha!" he retorted. "That they said in English."
Apparently the men had asked Jake and Amy if they
worshipped in the Spirit, and when our friends answered in
the affirmative, asked if they thought the Spirit was granted
to all men (their exclusive language, not mine) or just to
some. "A loaded question for sure," said Jake, "which I was
hard pressed to answer. I finally admitted that I couldn't*

*state definitively the Mennonite position" (Jake and I are the
only non-Mennonites in the unit).*

*"Ah," one of the holy men replied, "then you are not
experts in your religion; you are backbenchers." Which I
enjoyed enormously, attributing to Jake the sense of humour
that would translate a Swahili word into "backbencher,"
emphasis on the "ben," and curious to know what the original
word had been. "That was the funniest part," Jake laughed;
"'backbencher' was the only other thing he said in English."*

*Wherever in the world a prophet-man in rural Kenya
would learn the word backbencher, "holy shipwreck" is now
the official MCC Uganda exclamation of astonishment, as
in, "Holy shipwreck, Amy! Did you see how much powdered
milk costs at Nakasero Market?"*

*[. . .] The truth, Rev, is that I feel alone in a world that
has nothing to do with me. I know it's a predictable stage of
culture shock, but it's wracking. I also know that you think
I should be open to a new relationship and you're eager to
hear the details, but honestly, I don't even have the energy to
imagine a close friendship under these conditions. That said,
all the Ugandans I've met so far are as beautiful as I had
expected, by which I think I mean, I feel honoured to meet
specific humans whose experiences have been so different
from mine.*

My friendship with Nathaniel began the moment we met, but
it took me more than a decade to understand that, in the long
conversation we started in Lynn Lake and continued in our letters, we were working out a version of post-colonial theology.

Nathaniel's trick of simultaneous unconditional support
and persistent devil's advocacy kept me aware that I was
bringing a mixed bag of motives into contexts structured
by inequality. Two and a half months later, in my third letter, I wondered again about personal and collective impulses
to "development" and what exactly I was doing in Ndejje,

Uganda. "Surely to God, Nathaniel," I wrote, "it's not to 'help the poor Ugandans.' Every Ugandan I've met will find their way through this as well or better after I'm gone. But if I'm not 'here for them,' I must be here for me, and how (weirdly) self-indulgent is *that*?"

Letter #1 to Nathaniel [cont.]

P.S. Could you phone my parents and let them know that you've received this?

P.P.S. I know: "Lady Irene College" sounds exactly like something the British would've dreamed up, but the college is named for the wife of the last Kabaka, the king of Buganda.

Letter #7 to Mom and Dad   1st September 1986

I hope that by the time you get this, you'll already have had a telegram from me celebrating your anniversary, but I'll have to arrange that through our Kampala connections who probably know as little about local procedures as I do. We're officially into our second day of term, though I haven't yet taught anything, having spent the whole of Friday helping Gordon Read (the other science teacher, a sternly gentle old-school missionary from New Zealand) supervise the students who'd been assigned to clean the science classroom (and keeping them out of the attached storeroom/lab, which is strewn with broken glass and spilled chemicals).

Frances's arrival and mine also increased by half the comple-ment of "Europeans" at Ndejje. Pamela and Gordon Read and Claire and Hugh Fisher were all with the Church Mis-sion Society. Claire and Hugh were nurse and schoolmaster, respectively, and Pamela and Gordon were retired teachers. Gordon certainly looked the part of the quintessential British master, tall and thin and ascetic and stern, but in Pamela's company his quiet kindness and understated humour came alive. Pamela was everything I could have asked for in a fairy godmother: quirky, hilarious, vividly larger than life. Finding a substitute mother turned out to be harder, though, than simply moving in next door. Before a year has elapsed, both the Reads and the Fishers will have left Uganda, the Reads first, after Pamela's stroke; the Fishers, when armed men try to break into the cozy cottage they've rehabilitated at personal expense, an event that occurs just weeks after their new Land Rover's been taken at gunpoint.

Letter #7 to Mom and Dad [cont.]

Imagine a large school complex made up of individual, white-painted, bungalow-sized buildings, set on and around a hilltop. As you approach along the dirt track from the main highway, the overall effect is impressive, of an important place, bright and gleaming in the sun. As you get closer though, the ravages of long neglect and deliberate destruction are increasingly apparent. The area has been at the centre of military disturbances, political uncertainty, and sporadic nighttime killing rampages for so long that, until this past month, it hadn't been possible (counterintuitively) to close the school during regularly scheduled holidays. Since 1982, tensions have consistently been so high that only half the students were sent home at a time because it was too dangerous to leave the college vacant. That changed last September, when, as a kind of culmination to the mounting tension, everyone who was left here "ran."

Uganda is landlocked and exceptionally fertile. Notably well watered, almost one-fifth of the country's total area is open water or swampland. When UNLA soldiers killed tens of thousands of people in nighttime raids throughout the Luwero Triangle, they threw the bodies into nearby swamps. When the fighting ended in early 1986, people returning to the area began the grim work of retrieving neighbours' and family members' remains.

Letter #7 to Mom and Dad [cont.]

*3 September. 10:15 a.m. Back from my one class of the
day. With this small handful of students, we're not exactly
overworked. Gordon and I have divided up the science
curriculum so that I'm responsible for about two-thirds of it,
including a fair bit of the physics, chemistry, human biology
(you'll remember that I've never taken a biology course),
nutrition, and (you're going to love this, Dad) agriculture.
Yes, indeed, your little city girl, with three years' teaching
experience in junior high math and language arts plus
one general science course and one intro physics, is going
to introduce prospective Ugandan teachers to the joys of
seedbed preparation, crop rotation, irrigation, and livestock
management.*

When you've recovered from your collective glee, I'll go on.

Bodies were mostly unidentifiable and for almost two years
after the end of the war, spontaneous, anonymous memori-
als appeared throughout the Luwero Triangle, trestle tables
lined with skulls and surrounded by piles of bones. The forty-
kilometre drive from Kampala to Ndejje took us past three of
them: the first along the Bombo Road just before our turnoff,
one halfway between the turnoff and Ndejje, and one just as
we reached Lady Irene.

Letter #7 to Mom and Dad [cont.]

*4 September. Learned this morning that a live grenade was
discovered and detonated in the midst of yesterday's howling
thunderstorm. I was blithely unaware, but apparently the
explosions caused quite a panic further up the hill. None
of this needs to be worried about; if you were here, you'd
be struck by the tranquility of the place and the slowness
of our lives. The only urgency I feel at the moment involves
finally ending and mailing this letter. Please write. And send
Gertie's address? I'm thinking of you all the time.*

Just a fraction of LIC's former students returned in the first year after the war. We were a small community struggling individually and collectively with what would now be called post-traumatic stress. I was often too immersed in my own forms of shock, especially in that first year, to understand the breadth of challenges my neighbours and our students faced.

Letter #2 to Sharon   *4 September 1986*

Every time I take one of our patented bucket-and-basin "showers" I imagine what I'd say at home if someone poured that amount of water into a tub and told me my bath was ready. We lost power for three days this week, which meant we were relying exclusively on our rain tank, hence made further refinements to our already scrupulous water practices. Luckily we cook on two gas burners, no electricity involved. We've been eating well—or else we're so hungry by the time we sit down that everything tastes gourmet. And even though we're limiting our diets to what we can buy cheaply at the big market in Kampala, we're probably spending six or seven times the money our Uganda colleagues can spare for food. But we're all getting the same international relief aid. Allocated to each of us after last week's staff meeting (only two and a half hours, short by Lynn Lake standards), courtesy of World Vision:

One panga (a long curved slashing knife for clearing fields, which an agricultural expert like me can recognize at quite a distance)(we considered using them to kill cockroaches but realized we'd eventually lose all four of our hands, one digit at a time); one hoe (without a handle); and one woolen blanket. It's rainy season by now and definitely woolen-blanket weather at night, but we'll return ours (with the pangas) so they get to people who need them. Almost everyone who's come back is living in a thatched grass shelter because their concrete-block home was destroyed in a nighttime attack, while we have MCC looking out for everything we need. [. . .]

*P.S. The water here is almost as bad as in Lynn Lake!
(Write again soon.)*

*P.P.S. Is it crazy that I sometimes worry about how much
my mother's worrying about me?*

*P.P.P.S. If you think of it, you might surprise her with a
call. She was really concerned the day I left that she might
not see you either for three years. (Write soon.)*

Letter #3 from Mom and Dad   *7 September 1986*

We've received your first letter!

perfect correspondence (3)

When I reread my mother's letters now and mine, it occurs to me that our correspondence mimics Alzheimer's, with its gaps and its weird delays, its irretrievable losses, its distortions of memory and time's passage. "Write soon," my mother says to end her first letter and she repeats herself in a postscript: "Write soon." Her second letter announces it promptly—they still haven't heard from me, but in that first week, I've written repeatedly, two letters and multiple postcards to my family, and a first letter each to my closest friends, distinct, individual letters with a familiar refrain: "I miss you already"; "write as often as you can"; "it's a good thing I didn't know how much I'd miss you"; "seriously, write soon."

Mom's letters don't mirror my intense homesickness, but they reflect their own peculiar experience of dislocation. Two-thirds of the way through her second letter, she reports that she's registered for another university course and adds, with a poignant and uncharacteristic grammatical slip: "I didn't have much heart for knitting lately; I still have to get used to you being all the way in Africa and then I can't knit right away." Mom and I are so intertwined that she is, in my absence, finding it hard to knit (her second-favourite pastime, after reading), while I task my closest friends with connections I can't accomplish in person. "Could you phone my Mom and let her know I'm definitely not sick anymore?" I suggest to Tracey, and again, to Nathaniel, a week later. Five days elapse and I confide to Sharon that I worry about how much my mother's worrying about me. "If you think of it," I suggest, "you might surprise her with a call."

My mother ends her second letter with the repeated admonition, "Write soon," but ten days later she begins with the jubilant, "We've received your first letter!" It's 7 September and she means the letter that inaugurated our correspondence, the one I wrote on 16 August on the flight to Nairobi. I don't receive her letter telling me it's arrived, though, until 3 October, as I'm finishing my tenth letter to her. My mother and I wrote constantly because we wanted connection, but a closer look at our letters reveals that connection to have often been an exchange of scrambled messages, messages confused in and by space and time, messages that gestured toward, but only rarely achieved, direct communication. And these are the letters I'll use to bridge the distances opening between us now?

"Shall we read the letters we wrote while I was in Uganda and see what that helps us remember?" I ask Mom in the fall of 2007. "Is it okay that I record us talking? Otherwise I'll never remember everything we say." My mother agrees to the project and signs the consent form on a thoroughly lucid afternoon, but when, on subsequent visits, we sit down to record what we read and remember, she frequently surprises me. "These were letters that *I* wrote?" she has sometimes wondered when I've reintroduced the project, and on other afternoons she's asked, "*I* wrote letters?" Once she eyed me skeptically and multiplied the emphases in her question: "*I* wrote *letters* to *you*?"

And my project betrays its multiple origins in desire. There's no capital-A Archive, no capital-M Memory, no isomorphic mapping of one onto the other. Whatever else my archive may do, it will not heal my mother's memory and it will not bring the mother I remember back to me. But I marvel, nevertheless, at the glimpse the letters offer, into my mother's avid reading, her intellectual curiosity, and the liveliness with which she once registered the details of her textured world.

crosswords (2)

Letter #3 from Mom and Dad   *7 September 1986*

*Tracey called last night and told me about the fainting
episode. I hope it was just the arm of your glasses that was
broken and not the lenses. And also that you've been able
to relax more and get more sleep. [. . .] I started doing yoga
exercises in the morning again, and I can already feel that
I'm loosening up. I have every intention of keeping it up so
I'll be in good shape for our visit to Africa. [. . .]
Henry has inquired about the cost of flying to Uganda and
he was poring over travel brochures with Dana. I think he'd
like to visit you next summer, but you'll have to wait for
word from him on that score. [. . .] "Pastor W" and I had a
talk about last week's sermon on Revelation. Walter seems to
be rather fascinated with Revelation. I called him on some of
the things he said. He claims I misunderstood him and that
I should not think of him as a right-wing fundamentalist.
[. . .] Tomorrow is my first class; I'm really curious to find
out what the "Symbolic Dimensions of Religion" are.*

By the fall of 2007, I'm anxious to maintain a connection to
my mother's mind, but time feels scarce. We lose so much
momentum between visits that I wish we could work together
every day. I experiment by reviewing crossword puzzles over
the phone. In the very early stages of Alzheimer's, Mom could
do the daily crossword in fewer than twenty minutes. By 2007,
she struggled for hours. On 15 November, I knew she had the

first and the last letters of 16 Across, an *S* and an *L*. "Mom," I told her enthusiastically, "you'll get *this* one. The clue is 'Dakar is the capital city.'" My brother Henry had been based in Dakar for half a year while he did field research for his master's, and Mom was a whiz at geography. There was no way she could *not* know *Senegal*.

Letter #11 to Mom and Dad   *9 October 1986*

Today is a national holiday to celebrate Ugandan independence from the British, which for us involved sleeping in until 7:30 and a languorous breakfast of pancakes with bananas in fresh orange syrup. Yum. It's ironic: at home, MCC's remuneration structure (more or less zero) seemed to compare unfavourably with other organizations I investigated, but here, living on "maintenance" budgets gives us distinct advantages. Speaking objectively (without, that is, letting any kind of ethical framework contaminate the evaluation), it doesn't matter how outrageously food prices increase, because MCC Nairobi, like a good rich uncle, foots the bill.

But that's not the whole story of course, and there is an ethical framework, and the truth is, I have strongly mixed feelings on the subject.

Unlike international development agencies that paid their workers salaries (usually in American dollars), or faith-based organizations that obliged their workers to raise their own support, MCC committed to what it called its volunteers' "maintenance." The budgets our Country Representatives drew up included housing, food, transportation, and medical costs, all but the last reflecting local conditions as closely as possible. Especially later, when my health faltered, I was grateful for what I jokingly called "Uncle Menno's" commitment to getting and keeping me well.

MCC also paid us a small monthly stipend in American dollars. This was the money we used for stamps, writing paper, pens, long-distance phone calls, clothing, haircuts, and occasional restaurant meals. The intent and the effect was that most MCC volunteers lived simple lives, congruent with the organization's emphasis on *presence*. Dramatically unlike organizations that brought in North American experts, expensive equipment, and impressive budgets, MCC volunteers acted on the belief that lasting change comes about through mutual, cooperative relationships. And we signed on for three full years because building relationships takes time.

In the mid-1980s I was, and I still am, powerfully drawn to MCC's notion of *presence*, although *presence* didn't always work as well "on the ground" as it did in theory. In the MCC context, *presence* was juxtaposed with the active, expert, imposed, and often short-term interventions that characterized other development models. Less than a decade later, I encountered post-structuralist theory in graduate school and I was drawn to that too, with its trenchant critiques of the Western philosophical tradition and its unique perspectives on *presence*. Post-structuralist theories challenge the binary oppositions that structure much of Western thought: "male/female," "white/black," "good/evil," "light/dark," "wealth/poverty," "civilized/uncivilized," "presence/absence," "culture/nature," "human/animal," among a thousand others. A political spin on post-structuralist theory notices that one of the terms in each pair has traditionally been preferred—men over women, white over black, those who are "civilized" over those who are "uncivilized," humans over animals—and that those preferences underpin many of the world's current crises.

A post-structuralist perspective wonders, similarly, about the ways in which Western thought has privileged *presence* over *absence*, and what's been overlooked—what crises have been provoked—as a result. It's not an easy way to think because it requires the paradoxical process of bringing *absence* to consciousness. A conversation with my Mom can help.

Letter #11 to Mom and Dad [cont.]

In the meantime, I'll try to do no more of the swamp aerobatics that puréed the vegetables in the back of the Suzuki on our last trip back from Kampala. Without going too deeply into details (since Gerta may phone with some soon, and I've asked Carla to get you a copy of her Letter #3, the unabridged report), let's just say that, four years since the last time I flipped a vehicle, I thought I'd revive my skills by driving the jeep on its side into a swamp at the bottom of a stupendously muddy hill.

We're fine. Our passengers are fine. The young man hanging off the back of the Suzuki dove clear of the vehicle into the mud and he's fine too, but he needed a wash. We all needed a wash after we'd lumbered ourselves and the Suzuki back onto the track for the final five kilometres home. The Suzuki's back frame is decidedly lopsided and will need some hammering to get it centred again, but we're fine. [. . .]

If I end this now, I can mail it tomorrow, so, quickly: yes, it was the frame of my glasses that broke, and I'm so glad my telegram arrived in time for your anniversary. I sent it from Kampala, which is also where my phone call originated, in the busy, central, downtown post office where I am now a legend in my own time.

I'm often restless on the phone and on 15 November 2007, I find myself in our front hall, low light glowing comfortingly against nightfall. "It's okay, Mom, you know this," I tell her, settling briefly on the landing to the second floor. "It's an African country that starts with S." After a long silence my mother breathes out "essssss" and guesses hesitantly . . .

"Ceylon?"

Letter #10 from Mom and Dad *23 October 1986*

Dear Kathleen,
Yesterday was a windfall day, we received your letters 10 and
11 together. Gerta called me at 10 a.m. also yesterday to tell
me she and the kids also received your letters that morning.

When I visit, Mom and I do crosswords sitting side by side and
I help her locate the correct spaces for the letters, impossible
over a phone line. "No," I tell her, "the first letter of the country's name is an *S. Ceylon* starts with a *C.*" "It's okay, Mom," I
repeat. "You know this."

Letter #10 from Mom and Dad [cont.]

We've had a rather hectic week. Last Wednesday, we received
a call from Dirk Venema who told us that Beppe Venema is
in the hospital, quite seriously ill with a disease of the blood,
not leukemia, but apparently very serious. Dad had to go
to Brandon for a union seminar, but he was home early and
called Holland, talked to Dirk, who didn't come right out
and say it, you know those taciturn Venemas, but gave the
impression that he'd like Dad to come. So the upshot
of the whole story is that Dad is in Holland at
this moment [. . .].
I've just had a call from Dad. He says Beppe's mentally
alert, but looks weak, and asked him why he's come. So I
don't know whether she knows what her exact condition is.
I'm glad your letters came before Dad left. We stopped at the
mailbox on our way out to the airport, and I read both of
them to him as we drove along. [. . .]
I know you're concerned that maybe you're eating
too well. My main concern is that you stay healthy. You
are living with considerable stress as it is, and although
I sympathize with the people amongst whom you live, I
experience considerable anxiety when I think you might

make yourself more vulnerable because you don't eat enough
or not the right quality. You cannot combat the economic
conditions in Uganda single-handedly. I'm one hundred
percent sure that you do not buy luxury foods and don't
waste any of the food you do buy. Just by being there and
living amongst the people, I think you're identifying with
them. You can certainly have the satisfaction that
your presence there does not bring you any
financial gain. [. . .]
I just walked over to the mailbox and found your letter
to Carla and I must say, it's a bit of a hair-raiser, and here
I sit without being able to do anything about it, except to
lamely insist that you please, please be careful! I just
hope the rainy season will be over soon, so that swamp will
dry out and the roads will be safer. I'm glad you sent
Carla's telephone number. I'm going to phone her
soon. [. . .]
Dad called again this morning. The situation with Beppe V.
hasn't changed much, but it also doesn't sound as though she'll
get better and I think she's come to realize that herself. [. . .]
P.S. I hope your language lessons have started; that
should be very interesting.

Tracking my paternal grandmother's illness and death offers a
melancholy glimpse into my strange postal world. My parents
learned about Beppe Venema's illness on 15 October 1986, and
my mother relayed the news on 27 October, in a letter that I
received on 15 November. I mailed my response from Kampala
on 20 November.

Letter #13 to Mom and Dad   *16 November 1986*

Late yesterday, on the front porch to shake out a blanket,
I met a scene that stitched Uganda onto my memory, the
lowering light of the setting sun casting a shadow on the near
slope of the valley and throwing into exquisite relief every

detail of twig and leaf and shade of green on the valley's far side. Just above the hilltops, the faint but perfect circle of tonight's full moon. In the foreground, the delicate bend of a woman in her beans, and nearer yet, alert in the flourishing weeds, one brilliantly serene red flower.

[. . .] After considerable confusion on the subject, the vice-principal announced at last week's staff meeting that there will be a Christmas carol service this year. He subsequently informed the students that they were to prepare a large, though unspecified, number of carols; a carol-service committee has been struck; and that was as much as I knew about what apparently was, traditionally, an affair of considerable proportions.

I thought at first I was pleased not to be involved (none of us science types was drafted), but when I began asking the Year Ones about their carols (they'd been dropping by the house to have me sign their science "schemes," a lovely, sinister word for their student-teaching unit plans, and sometimes more appropriate than it should be), they told me they had no one to advise them. Naturally, I volunteered. They'd picked their songs earlier and because several of them are much more than usually musical (the girls, not the songs), they already sound like angels. Their version of "Mary's Boy Child" is particularly good, and a Lugandan song they drum and then dance to, which promptly makes me want to dance, and that makes them laugh. As seems disturbingly typical, I do almost nothing and in return they've given me some of my happiest moments here.

I was putting in enormous efforts to get to know our students, more of whom were returning each week. LIC's most senior tutors—dignified Janet Nsubuga and Jonathan Ssendawula, one of the community's wise elders—had been among the first back at Ndejje, and they extended collegial support to Frances and me as they were able. William Mutema, our perpetual-motion deputy principal did too, on the rare occasion that he had a moment, but what I needed most (belying my early claim to Nathaniel) was a friend. Beautiful Nakazibwe Cate was near our age and a stellar candidate: smart, sharp, and infectiously funny. But she was Acting Headmistress of Nalinya Girls' Primary School on the other side of Ndejje hill, and scrambling out from under the endless work of rehabilitation every time we met.

Letter #13 to Mom and Dad [cont.]

17 November. I was more than a little distressed to hear of Beppe Venema's illness (though I have to confess, what bothered me most was the thought of Dad in Holland without me knowing). I have a (superstitious) idea that as long as everyone stays close to Winnipeg, my single-minded telepathy will keep you all safe while I'm gone. Having to worry about Dad in Holland instead of at home could strain my powers. I know you'll keep me posted on any and all developments.

Beppe Venema had passed away on 8 November. My father returned to Winnipeg on 14 November, a few days after his mother's funeral, and telephoned the news to the MCC office in Kampala. But Jake and Amy were on a tour of the country, so I didn't get Dad's message until 26 November. One week later, on 3 December, Dad's letter with details of Beppe's final days arrived. On 15 December, my response to the news of Beppe's illness reached my parents.

Letter #13 to Mom and Dad [cont.]

19 November. I discovered late last week that our Year Twos' "mock" national exams will cover the entire curriculum. Holy shipwreck. I finished the unit on Ugandan agriculture but have only just started into Nutrition and Health, and haven't done one iota of hard sciences. Desperately needing

*to get the girls ready, I've allocated all available class time
to reviewing questions from previous exams, as submitted
in advance by students, a poor kind of teaching but
unexpectedly ripe for comedy. I think I wrote to Sandy about
the "r/l" confusion in Luganda, the most frequent instance
of which I experience in my new identity as "Katherine,"
or, more typically, "Miss Katherine"? A brilliant example
arrived yesterday via a previous national science exam
question that reads: "What is morality?"*

*What is morality?! You can imagine my reaction: "I'm a
science teacher; I know nothing about morality," until I did
some fast rearranging and realized that the question intends
to ask "What is molarity?" Aha, a chemistry question, the
number of moles of solute dissolved in one litre of solution, a
purely abstract concept in the absence of specific examples or
appropriate equipment, and that is just one of the beauties
of national %$*#@ exams based on memorization.*

*Not surprisingly, my students know almost nothing
about molarity (and yet far more, I sometimes think, than I
do about morality).*

"S," my mother repeats. "S. And you said it ends with . . .?" "L.
It starts with S and it ends with L. Eight letters in total and you
have an N in the middle." Mom pauses again for a long time.
"It's an African country, Mom," I remind her. "You know this."
"Ess," my mother says then, "Ess. An African country? I don't
think I know any African countries."

Letter #3 to Lil and Roxanne   *23 November 1986*

*Interesting, Rox, that you asked about shelling and food in
the same sentence, almost as if you knew we'd be holding
a farewell dinner yesterday for our Year Four students, our
most overworked students and the ones most grossly under-
taught by virtue of having their education interrupted by a
civil war, currently slaving over their national exams. The*

other students and several of us tutors had worked hard to
decorate one of the classrooms in anticipation of the dinner,
and the effect was gratifyingly festive: great huge bunches
of flowers—poinsettias, roses, bougainvillea, hibiscus,
frangipani—and masses of multicoloured balloons.

All of which should have been only wonderful except that
we decorated in the morning and by hot early afternoon, the
air inside the balloons began doing what hot air does and
the balloons began to burst. Hilarious and frustrating (all
that effort) except that everyone there has just survived two
years of rocket-propelled grenades, mortar shelling, small-
arms exchange and machine-gun fire. The first burst was
decidedly the worst—it took us all a few seconds to connect
the ominous retort with the celebratory balloons and then we
laughed instead of taking cover, but it didn't take long for a
repeat: echoing *k*a*p*o*w*, microsecond of frozen collective
terror, sheepish smiles all around . . .

Nakazibwe Cate (a.k.a. "Beautiful Cate") was most
concerned about the SDA's arrival (our Special District
Administrator, a real live NRA man, an outlaw two years
ago and responsible now for The Country's Future), because
he never moves without two machine-gun-armed soldiers.
Spying his entourage on its way up the hill, she pointed
to the balloons over her head and said, with a look she
has down to perfection, half gravely serious, half devilish
merriment, "If one breaks now, they will shoot at us!"

Letter #14 to Mom and Dad   *24 November 1986*

Our poor Year Fours. They're in the midst of their grueling
three-hour national exam as I write, despite the fact that
there's been a war on for most of their four-year program.
With the high concentration of (then) rebel forces here in
the Luwero Triangle, they've been literally in the thick of it,
until, of course, the college was dramatically evacuated just

*hours before the UNLA forces moved in, after which some
(I gather loosely organized) classes were sometimes held at a
central location in Kampala. Some of the girls have lost more
than a year of formal training, but here they sit regardless,
sweating it out, literally and figuratively, and one of them is
due to deliver her baby today. You can imagine how closely
I'm watching her. I can see my updated resumé now: "East
African agriculturist, rally driver, swamp swimmer, midwife."*

Post-civil-war life, with its palpable sense of a people released
from tyranny, lent Advent 1986 an unusual potency. The possibility that a newborn could arrive promising peace acquired
more joyful symbolism than most festivities can bear. It was
a bittersweet intensity, my first Christmas without my family. In a long letter to my music-loving aunt and uncle, Bertha and John, I recorded the season's highlight, our talented
students' achingly funny, spirit-buoying, extemporaneously
"jazz" nativity play . . .

Letter #16 from Mom and Dad   *19 December 1986*

*Dear Kathleen: It's been mild for this time of year and
tonight it's foggy. I was sitting in the living room just now
with only the Christmas tree lit up, enjoying the peaceful
atmosphere and thinking about you. [. . .]
It's been a veritable avalanche of mail from Africa this
week. On Monday afternoon I went to the mailbox once
more and sure enough, there was your letter #13, the missing
link in the chain, and on Thursday #15 arrived. I hope my
#5 and 6 will arrive yet to you, especially because #6 has also
a letter from Dad for your birthday. It's 9:30 a.m. now, and
I shall write until 10 a.m., because then I have to shape my
dough into loaves. I shall also bake a cake because Mr. and
Mrs. H——are coming over tomorrow after church and that
means I have to bake but also that my house has to be neat*

and clean. I can't let whatever is left of my reputation as a good Dutch housewife fall completely into tatters, so if there is bread dough sticking to this letter or it smells of floor wax, you'll know why. [. . .]

It's now 5:30 p.m., half the house is clean, and the other half is tidy. I'm trying to answer your last three letters in the right sequence but I took them out of their envelopes at once, the pages got mixed up and I had to piece them together again, which procedure has now been successfully completed. [. . .] I'm so glad the singing of the girls has given you so much pleasure. Your description of the scene outside your door was beautiful, a close-up of Africa. [. . .]

This letter cannot possibly smell of floor wax for the simple reason that I didn't wax the floor. Dana convinced me that it looked just fine and I was running short of time. [. . .] I was so curious about the record you mentioned in your letter to Bertha and John that I made Henry drive me to Homemade Music, but they didn't have it. We also stopped at Fellowship Book Centre, but when we saw "Sing-along with Jimmy Swaggart" we beat a hasty retreat!

"Of course you know African countries, Mom," I insist. "You know all kinds of African countries. Remember when you visited me in Africa? This isn't where I was living, or where Gertie is from, but it's where Henry did his master's research. You remember this." I don't say, "Remember when you visited me *in Uganda*," because I don't want to make it too easy.

Letter #16 from Mom and Dad [cont.]

I have done quite well so far on my short assignments, only one B and the rest all A-minus. The prof told us he seldom gives As and never A-pluses, so I'm beginning to be rather pleased with myself, which should be a danger signal, right? I might become complacent, and who knows what kind of

*sloth that would lead to! For your Christmas present I'm
sticking to books, since I didn't want to impose too much
space in Frances's parents' suitcases. (The Robertson Davies
is his latest novel and has had very good reviews. The
Updike one I know nothing about.) It's a rather meager
Christmas present, but be assured it is sent with even more
love than usual, if such a thing is possible I ask myself.
(That's what university has done to me, I'm always asking
myself questions.) In any case, you get my meaning. It's hard
to imagine you won't be at home for Christmas. I hate to
think about it, so I'll just babble on.
When I checked with Nathaniel to ask which books
he had sent you, he told me the things he sent were all
theologically oriented so he classified them as "religious
tracts," which was quite funny I thought. [. . .] It's so
strange not to get ready for you coming home at Christmas
and I know you'll feel something like that too. But think,
Kathleen: if you had stayed in Lynn Lake and everything
had been the same this year as last year that would not have
satisfied you either. [. . .]
Pamela Read sounds like a gem of a woman. Knowing
she's there makes me feel a little better. Tell her that,
being my cautious, Frisian self, I never hurry into love
relationships in a first letter, I always discipline myself to
wait until the second one at least.*

Mom wasted no time extending her affection for my Canadian
friends to everyone I was meeting in Uganda. She regularly sent
greetings to Frances and my LIC colleagues when she wrote,
and had been so relieved to hear about Pamela Read that she
singled her out for special thanks. When I conveyed them,
Pamela responded with a spritely, "Yes, but didn't she say anything about *love*," an exchange that promptly appeared in my
next letter home.

Letter #16 from Mom and Dad [cont.]

We love getting your letters, it's almost like you're here.

〜〜〜

By February, Christmas melancholy had been swept away in the accelerating busyness of LIC's second postwar term. We began with almost fifty students and more appeared every week. Every day I felt incrementally more connected to the community, and every day brought something unexpected.

Letter #18 to Mom and Dad   *13 February 1987*

(At 10 a.m. on Friday the 13th it's a case, so far, of so far so good. Gordon lost his glasses, but that was yesterday, and my back hurts from doing the laundry this morning, but my back always hurts after an hour bent over a laundry tub, so neither counts as bad luck, do they?) As ever, the fun around here slows down but it never really stops. Just yesterday, it was live entertainment, in the form of the motliest collection of dirty muzungu I'd seen for some time . . .

9:15 p.m. Interrupted by today's unexpected variable in the equation-that-is-Ndejje, namely the news that we'll be making a trip into Bombo tomorrow because the meat and matoke[3] for the Reads' farewell dinner didn't arrive as it should have. It shouldn't be too bad a drive: it rained again this afternoon but not endlessly, and it will be a chance to pick up a few more mangoes and bananas. A little more mail wouldn't hurt either, since at least two weeks' worth seems to have gone missing. The last family news came in your #17, Mom, three weeks ago, and in Henry's letter a week later.

"Henry?" Mom asks, puzzled. "In Africa?" "Yeah Mom," I insist, "Henry did his master's research in Africa. And he came back with such funny stories. You *remember* this." "No I don't," Mom says, sounding more certain than she has for the entire conversation.

Letter #18 to Mom and Dad [cont.]

*Let me get back, though, to Thursday's entertainment,
5:30 p.m., and me sneaking in a bit of school work while
preparing our farewell supper for Pam and Gordon, when
Kiyingi Caroline, a bright zing of a student, arrives at the
door whispering apologetically that Mr. Mutema requests
all tutors up in the staff room immediately to meet visitors
to the college.*

*"Pooh," thinks I, "another government committee out
to take the pulse of improvements on Ndejje hill most likely,
but I cannot let William down, so I'd better hop." A quick
mirror check confirms that I'm still wearing my contacts,
which is good since I'm always a little more confident in
my contacts, and I run a brush through my mop of hair.
Nothing remotely stylish left here, but that may never again
be helped. "Just the standard missionary trim," I'll sigh
resignedly in some swanky shop in Nairobi when next we
return to the city of lights. I'm wearing my second-best skirt,
which saves me time dressing and since this is the first day in
the skirt, I'm presentable.*

*And then—because it hasn't rained in days—I put on
leather sandals instead of plastic shoes and don't just feel
presentable, I feel dressed, and I'm off, up the hill, where I
join forces with Pam and Gordon, who are full of stories of
past summonses. They were once told that The President
was waiting to see them. A full-blown ruse, as it turned out,
but an effective one. They're also speculating that it might
be an aid agency. There's a twist. There might be $$$$$
for us in this visit. Maybe I should've changed, but then I'd
have dithered: nicer clothes or rattier clothes, nicer clothes or
rattier clothes?*

*At the staff-room door, I've registered the image of a
philosophy seminar when Pam says conspiratorially, "We
heard they were Canadians." I can feel my skin cool as
my confidence evaporates. Ugandan government officials,*

I'm ready for, or Church of England representatives from
Britain, or even well-meaning Americans, but the possibility
of Canadian visitors prompts a whirl of doubts. "What will
I look like to Canadians?" I wonder instantly; what kind of
me will I look like here to people who could know me? I feel
disconnected, as if someone's pulled my plug, till I tell myself
that I belong here, I've belonged here for the last half year. I
grit my teeth, make a face at Pam, and we stride in grinning.

"Of course you remember this," I contradict Mom, dubiously
convinced that this will be encouraging. "It's where Henry was
the second time he went to Africa, after the first time when he
visited me. You'll laugh when you get it."

Letter #18 to Mom and Dad [cont.]

It's an amenable crowd; there are lots of answering grins
on safari-weary faces. Frances is already ensconced in
unaccustomed attention, and a tall curly-haired man who
looks like someone I went to university with gives me his seat
at the table. "David," he says with a cherubic smile. "Roger,"
says the voice at the end of the thick hand extended on my
left; "Scott"; "Wendy" ("Whoa, Vogue-goes-to-Africa," I
think, glancing again—ineffably chic under the dust, she,
too, looks like someone I went to university with); "Peter";
"Colin"; and it seems I've met them all. I'm starting to relax:
there are two North Americans, but I'm hearing British
accents, too, and something undisguisedly Australian.

When the formal introductions start—"I'm so-and-so
from here-and-there"—the lack of continuity is obvious.
"What the heck are they doing here together and what do
they want from us?" are probably the questions on all our
minds. Hugh finally asks, and the answer is life imitating
art. It's a modern Pilgrim's Progress, no, a Canterbury Tales
for the 1980s. They're each in search of "the real Africa,"
and, each armed with a copy of Africa on a Shoestring,

they've run aground together in a seedy Kampala hotel.
Roger on my left (built like a proverbial brick outhouse and
the only one of the crew who doesn't look like someone I went
to university with) explains that the meeting was almost
inevitable, since the book recommends specific hotels, bus
routes, restaurants, and train trips (all on the same short
string). These six quickly discovered that they shared a desire
to see the Luwero Triangle.

Hmmm. Grim destruction and skulls skulls skulls.
It ain't exactly the south of France. "But why Ndejje in
particular?" Hugh persists. "Or are we in the book too?" I
quip, just ahead of Roger-the-slab. I'm slowly learning what
my Ugandan colleagues find funny; this even made Mrs.
Nsubuga laugh. Somehow this motley crew has persuaded
the SDA's office to spend two days driving them around the
Triangle. It's obvious to us all by now that there's not so
much as a shilling in it for the college, which is all right on
one hand, but also a galling example of what we Westerners
assume about our own importance.

"I don't remember any African countries," my mother says
and tries again. "I don't know, I don't remember. Swaziland?"
"Swaziland is good," I say, "it's close. It's in Africa and it starts
with an S. But this is the country where Henry worked. You
know this, Mom; you can't have forgotten this."

Letter #18 to Mom and Dad [cont.]

I know that each one of the pilgrims is on the string because
s/he hasn't got much cash and, assuredly, because s/he feels
it's an authentic African experience, not the route of luxury
game-park lodges and exotic safari gourmet meals, which is
admirable and courageous in a country just one year past a
brutal civil war. But each one of the pilgrims, even if s/he is
between university and grad school, even if s/he has given
up a job to travel for a year, is infinitely richer than almost

*anyone slowly making their way back to life in the Luwero
Triangle. It makes me angry and oddly nauseous to think
they're wasting six working days (they've enlisted two SDA
guides and a driver) and who knows how much petrol on
what is, essentially, a whim.*

*10:25 p.m., after some reflection. I recoil at the pilgrims'
innocent selfishness but remind myself that they almost
certainly haven't thought through how massively they're
draining a fragile system's resources. In the moment, though,
I can read Pam's irritation with their temerity. "How will you
communicate what you've seen here when you leave?" she
asks them. I think she's also asking, "How will the Triangle
be better for having indulged your whim?" Rog-the-slab is
first off the mark. "We'll each communicate our experiences
in different ways," he begins. "Now, I'm an artist, but I'm not
going to go back home and start doing work that looks like
African art blah blah my Egyptian trip blah blah blah years
later blah blah blah sculpture reflected the images blah blah
blah blah but as a Responsible Artist, I'm travelling around
the world keeping in touch with what's happening."*

*Roger the Responsible Artist. Squeezing his ego out the
double doors later wasn't easy; none of us was sorry to see
him go, and no one's anxious to see his work. Because the
pilgrims are pressed for time and Rog has taken more than
his share, we break into spontaneous conversations with the
people nearest us. I'm grilled by Scott, the one Canadian,
who wants to teach in Africa too but can't imagine surviving
on a local salary. How do we do it? he asks, and I suddenly
feel immensely old letting him in on our little secret, the
full breadth of our parasitic existence hitting me hard. I
can criticize the pilgrims but I can't escape the chasm that
stands between me and whatever "an authentic African
experience" might be . . .*

*And then, as suddenly as the pilgrims have come, they're
gone. We're a nice staff, but we're easily fazed. We stand*

staring down the dusty track until long after the white government Land Rover is out of sight. Blinking.

My mother pauses, and what she says next acquires increasing eeriness every time I think about it. "You say that I still know this," my mother says, "but you have no idea how much I've forgotten."

Letter #18 to Mom and Dad [cont.]

I could go on for pages but if I stop now, Pam and Gordon can mail this from London. [. . .]

P.S. Rest your minds about the bits and drabs of money in my account and the elastic no longer in my underwear: catch-as-catch-can knickers keep me wonderfully humble (like being a pilgrim) and I'll find financial corners to cut.

P.P.S. In the damp weather that inexplicably continues, the skulls are turning green.

It's a terrifying moment on the stairway of our little home in the heart of Winnipeg, much closer to my parents than I've ever been as an adult and, except for my mother's diagnosis, deeply contented with my life. I was certain that evening that an eight-letter word that starts with *S* and ends with *L* and has an *N* in the middle and a capital city called Dakar would resolve itself in my mother's mind as Senegal, the West African country where Henry lived for half a year gathering data for a master's in water systems engineering.

"Senegal!" my mother would exclaim. "Of course it's Senegal." But what she said was "you have no idea how much I've forgotten," as if she's simultaneously losing her memories and keeping an inventory of the losses. She will emphasize this strange loss repeatedly over the coming winter, and every time she does, it seems as if she's fashioned a "bag of memories" that she simultaneously picks up and sets down again. In the moment of insisting that her memories are gone, she seems also to be saying that they're present, but it's an uncanny kind of present—present but not accessible; gone but not (entirely) forgotten; present almost exclusively by being absent.

~~~~

I've been in Uganda barely a day when I begin Letter #2 to my parents. Wracked with homesickness, I believe myself when I insist, "'Home' will always mean home with you." I can't know yet what I continue to discover after returning to Canada—that the next three years will form the critical centre of my identity. I am who I am in great part because, from 1986 to 1989, I lived and taught and learned and got sick and became well again at Ndejje, Uganda. In the fall of 2007, I don't yet know what it means for Alzheimer's to strip my mother's knowledge of me from the world, but I realize for the first time that if my mother can lose *Senegal*, she will soon, despite all our letters, lose *Uganda*.

perfect correspondence (bonus)

By mid-February 1987, I've been in Africa six months, completed one-sixth of my three-year commitment, and written my parents eighteen times. On 11 February 1987, two days before I begin Letter #18 about our motley and unexpected visitors, my mother writes what she calls a "bonus letter" because she's learned she can send me a small package, courtesy of one of Frances's father's colleagues who is travelling to Kampala. She notes that she's in the midst of writing her twenty-first letter, but that that missive can't yet be satisfyingly concluded. "Bonus" is accurate: unlike my mother's #5, 18, 19, 20, and 21, this letter reaches me. When the final tally is in, all 103 of my letters to my parents will have arrived safely in Winnipeg, but 16 of their 105 letters go permanently missing. No one else writes as frequently as my mother, but a proportional number of my other correspondents' letters and packages go missing too, so that, by the time I return to Canada, I've lost approximately one half-year's worth of mail. Because most of us number our letters, we can at least tell when something's lost or arrives out of sequence.

And there are miraculous reappearances. On 15 September 1987, I receive a notice indicating that if I report to the main post office in Kampala, I'll be rewarded with a package addressed to me. This is novel. A number of packages have arrived without any special claiming process. It will also be the first time I'm back at the main post office to do anything besides buy stamps since a memorable phone call on 10 September 1986. On that day, the main post office is packed with people, mostly women, almost all of whom are wearing traditional *busutis*,[4] many of whom are carrying children wrapped onto their backs, and they are waiting six deep in looping queues around the bank of long-distance phones. Frances and I are our customary extraordinary sight. In case we're not already sufficiently visible, I create a bona fide scene: when it's finally my turn at one of the phones, I have to shout to hear myself be heard in Winnipeg; when my mother's voice reaches me, I burst into tears.

Now, almost exactly one year later, I'm directed to another department entirely. I detail the process in Letter #10 to my beloved friend Carla. Suffice it to say that I believe I'm retrieving a single package—an exemplary package no doubt, rating its own claim voucher—but nevertheless, just one package. When I emerge from this damp and cavernous netherworld, however, I am clutching not one but two packages, which together contain books, magazines, a dress shirt, several comical T-shirts, and three long letters, all for me, the earliest of which is dated 10 November 1986.

Subsequent reappearances thrill the imagination. On two separate occasions in July 1988, small packages, both mailed in March, reach me stamped "Missent to Jakarta." Five and a half months later, an airmail letter arrives having been "Missent to Manila." Like the small packages of 1988, Luke's much-awaited and then devastating Dear John letter of February 1989 travels to Jakarta before it makes its way to me in June and is stolen three days later. From an imaginative perspective, though, the greatest treasure I retrieve from what I nickname the Black Hole of International Post (BHOIP) ("and it's *BHOIP*," I gleefully inform my correspondents, "because that's the sound you hear when a letter makes its way out!") has been stamped "Missent to Funafuti."

I speculate that Funafuti may be entirely fantastical, but it is, in fact, the most populated of the six atolls and three reef islands that make up Tuvalu, the island nation halfway between Hawai'i and Australia. With a population of almost eleven thousand, Tuvalu is either the third- or fourth-smallest country in the world, but its exclusive economic zone includes nine hundred thousand square kilometres of ocean. Peer at a map of the Pacific for a glimpse of delicate dots sprinkled onto a vast stretch of otherwise unbroken blue. Howland Island—the refuelling destination that Amelia Earhart missed on her fatal final flight—is almost directly north and considerably larger.

You cannot imagine that an airplane carrying letters to East Africa could find enough land in Tuvalu to land—or take off again with misdirected mail. But Tuvalu has an airport and a capital and a main post office, all on Funafuti. Tuvalu is exquisitely beautiful, the rarest of paradisiacal destinations, and its citizens experience significantly rising sea levels and increasingly more powerful ocean storms. Depending on the politics of your science, you may, like me, believe that rising sea levels and devastating storms are the result of climate change caused by human action. If you do, you may believe, like me, that Tuvalu, and Funafuti with it, could disappear.

Over the course of my three years in Uganda, BHOIP disgorges four letters that reach me—and, later (minus the letter that's subsequently stolen), my informal archive—via exotic locations I may never see myself. If one-sixth of the letters addressed to me at Ndejje never arrive, some may still be in Manila or Jakarta or dozing precariously on an ever-smaller beach on Funafuti. Most likely they were declared "dead" and destroyed years ago, meeting more or less the same fate as the letters that arrived duly at their destinations—Winnipeg, Lynn Lake, Gabarone, Kampala, Brampton, Ndejje, Victoria, Nairobi, Steinbach, Addis Ababa, Bombo—but were misplaced or thrown out with the trash or lost or stolen. I still miss each one.

perfect correspondence (5)

During the winter of 2008, Mom and I quickly discover just how incoherent letters can seem outside of their original context, even when you're not cognitively impaired. On 22 February, though, Mom and I read the three letters her mother wrote me while I was living in Ndejje. Except for a few English phrases, Beppe de Jong wrote to me in Frisian, my mother's mother tongue. Mom begins haltingly—her mother's cramped handwriting presents an understandable challenge—and she shifts in and out, Frisian to English, English to Frisian, forgetting whether she's supposed to be reading or translating, but it doesn't matter: Frisian was my first language too, and I follow my mother's shifts with ease.

As we read, we remember together what my grandmother has written—her warm thanks for the letter I've sent her; how often she's thought of me; how my life in Uganda has put her in mind of her own experiences on first arriving in Canada and what she'd tell people who asked her what she thought of Canada once she was here, namely, "I nearly died of homesickness!" I'm curious about Beppe's use of a rare English sentence and guess that when my grandmother tells this truth, a legend in our family, she tells it in English so that no one can misunderstand: she really did almost die of homesickness.

What she omits, though, and what the letter prompts my mother to remember, is that if Beppe had died of homesickness, it would have been at her own hand. What my mother tells me next is a version of a story she's told many times since we began spending Friday afternoons together: at the point in her life when she would otherwise have followed her dream of studying languages and literature, the sixteen-year-old girl who would become my mother was obliged instead to come to strange, cold Canada and to spend most of her first year here on suicide watch, ensuring that *her* mother didn't carry out what she threatened repeatedly—to drown herself and the two youngest children in the frigid river racing two hundred metres north of their home. Reading both what her mother wrote and what her mother left unsaid prompts *my* mother to echo the threat she's remembered for fifty-six years: "*ik spring 'er sa mar yn, mei de lytse bern.*" The original words make it chillingly clear that the threat can be carried out in an instant: "Just like that, I'll jump in, with the little kids—"

"*De lytse bern,*" Mom says sometimes when she tells this story, "the little kids," and sometimes she says, "*de lytse famkes,*" "the little girls." The point of the story is the ease with which the little girls—now my adult aunts Eta and Gerta—might have disappeared forever. On our afternoon in 2008, Mom reflects on the events and the constraints, the regrets and the unfulfilled dreams of immigration, and then she announces, "Sometimes I think, it never should've happened you know. I really do, the whole thing." "Do you mean emigration?" I ask. "*Jah,*" my Mom says; "It never should've happened." And then she pauses. "Well, anyway," she adds with resignation, "you can't go back in life."

Unexpectedly and only in retrospect, given the genuine fun my mother and I have that day, what can and can't be done with a life becomes a theme for the afternoon. In her second letter, written just a few weeks later, Beppe reflects again on my situation in terms of her own experiences, but this time she goes all the way back to a golden age, the several years before she married, when she lived independently and worked as a nurse in a psychiatric hospital. My grandmother writes about the inevitability, in unfamiliar circumstances, of an adjustment period, but concludes enthusiastically, "*Mar it is ien fen de mooiste tiiden yn myn libben west.*" "It was one of the loveliest times of my life."

This, too, is a crucial part of family mythology, the bliss with which my grandmother recalled those precious years. "She should never have married," my mother and each of her sisters have told me about Beppe on different occasions; "She should never have had children. She should have spent her life with her friends from nursing school. The three of them should've just lived together." My mother had often talked before this afternoon about her mother's two closest friends from nursing, how neither had married, and how they'd arrive together to visit her mother once or twice a year. My mother has talked, too, about how intensely her mother would anticipate those visits, and how, once her friends arrived, they'd get her full attention. On our afternoon in 2008, my mother adds a story I haven't heard before, explaining that one of Beppe's friends was extremely reserved, but that that wasn't surprising because—and here Mom's voice drops as if we're telling secrets—that woman's mother had hanged herself. "It was awful, *awful* you know," my mother emphasizes. "Annie was quite a lively woman, but Tina was—*quiet*." She pauses. "But no wonder, with *that*."

We talk for another ten minutes about various topics and then my mother returns, of her own volition, to the second of Beppe's two best friends. "Yeah," she muses with considerable humour, "*Annie* had pep." Mom laughs, remembering. "She told us a funny story," Mom says. "I think it was Annie, and what was it, I'm a little vague about it, but she was also visiting somebody, a lady, you know, in an old folks' home, and that lady, that woman said, '*Sla mij maar dood!*'" Here my mother switches to Dutch, her second language, to capture precisely what the woman in the care home says to her nurse. "*Sla mij maar dood!*" the woman says, and my mother switches back to English to explain: "Because she didn't want to, she didn't any longer want to"—Mom laughs helplessly—"any longer live, and then that care woman said"—and here Mom shifts back to Dutch: "'*Ja, dat dach je maar: jij lekker in de hemel en ik lev-*

enslang in de gefangenis!'" And my recording of the afternoon captures us laughing uproariously.

A literal translation of *"Sla mij maar dood!"* renders the nonsensical "Hit me then dead!" "Whack me on the head, hard enough to kill me," is semantically strong, and it conveys the request's delicious vulgarity, but it loses the comic effect of the original alliteration, the terrifically efficient syncopation—and I have known my mother's love for languages and their thrilling multiplicities long enough to know that it's precisely the statement's crafty terseness that prompts her helpless laughter. *"Sla mij maar dood!"* the woman in care proposes, as if the act were that simple: "Bop! Dead. Done."

The nurse in the story is equally adept at caustic play with linguistic possibility. "Sure, you go ahead and think that," she responds in crackling Dutch, "you nicely in heaven [by implication, "for all eternity"] and me in jail for the rest of my life!" "I've always found that so hilarious," Mom manages to say through her laughter, and then she adds, "Oh my goodness. I'm lucky. That's one of the things I remember. I don't remember what I did ten minutes ago, but *that* I remember." Despite her multiple cognitive losses, my mother still takes pleasure in the pleasure she takes in linguistic play, the capacity here, of Dutch idioms to celebrate the unsavoury options of tending— or not tending—the near dead. The multilingual capacities that allow my mother to engage simultaneously in literal and semantic translation likely slow the pace at which Alzheimer's predations march through her brain, but what is that prolonging, I wonder: a blessing or a curse? And what about the unpredictable memories that Mom's many languages help her retain; are they similarly mixed, blessing and curse?

As it happens, it won't be long before my mother proposes her own version of "Bop! Dead. Done." In a harrowing coincidence whose resonances emerge months after the fact, my mother and I have our lively conversation on the same afternoon that my brother and sister-in-law race their ten-month-old son to Children's Hospital. My baby nephew Harry has a tumour on his liver, which is confirmed, two days later, to be cancerous, and diagnosed eleven days after that as a "primary rhabdoid tumour," a rare and lethal form of childhood cancer. Harry's journey with cancer comes to take a central place in my story with my mother: from the moment of the diagnosis, even our briefest conversations and every one of my visits with my parents was framed and shaped and saturated by anxiety and love for Harry.

And then Harry died. Held in the fierce and ardent love of his parents and sister, his family, his extended family, and a thousand friends around the world, Harry died. Harry died and I never again read letters with Mom. Cracked with grief, she balked and stomped and stopped, just short of the extra cognitive work that letter reading requires. In the months after Harry's passing, my mother—a long-time advocate of the right to doctor-assisted death—became obsessed with ending her life. I come to dread our conversations that winter. My mother wants to write her own conclusion, but I'm not done yet with our story. I have the law on my side, though, and, ironically, Alzheimer's, so that my mother is alive in September 2011 to pose the question with which I began.

"Were you with us when we came to Canada?" she asks intently, watching my face.

"No, Mom," I wish now I'd answered then, "I was waiting for you here."

TWO

crosswords

crosswords (3)

I wait while Mom finds her place. "Ohhhhhh!" she's exclaimed, laughing, "Listen to this," but it takes several moments before she reads aloud from the notebook we've discovered: *"For the first time in my life I'm going to keep a journal. I am a little nervous about it, but also excited: nervous because I know someone will read what I'm writing and excited because I've often thought about keeping a diary, but nothing ever came of it."* Mom and I are engaged in an impromptu inventory of the Dutch and Frisian books she has piled haphazardly onto shelves and tables and stools in the cramped room at the top of the stairs in my parents' cobbled-together farmhouse. So far, we've found Pake's Dutch translations of *Crime and Punishment*, *Paradise Lost*, *Romeo and Juliet*, and *All Quiet on the Western Front*, plus *Merijntje Gijzens*, the thick Dutch novel Mom reveres. We haven't yet located *"De Krystreis fen Broder Iwersen,"* the Frisian Christmas story she loves beyond all others. It's Friday 12 December 2008 and Mom and I have been exploring her memories for a little over a year.

Mom pauses, then continues reading: *"I did not have to do it. I wonder, will I find enough to write about three times per week?"* The specific concerns Mom reads prompt us to guess that the notebook's a journal she kept for one of her university courses, and we're right: "Advanced Composition, Winter 1983," the cover reads in Mom's unmistakable handwriting. Mom reads silently, laughs, then reads aloud: *"My handwriting tends to become quite scrawly after a while. I always blame that on the fact that I'm left-handed! It says here, I am left-handed, but was forced to write with my right hand in school.*

Having several older brothers and sisters to inform me, I was well aware that once in school, I would be expected to use my right hand for writing. That I do remember very well is an incident connected with my left...left-handedness which happened when I was about five years old."

By late 2008 Mom is having increasing difficulty tracking lines of writing. Often now when she reads out loud, she repeats a line or skips one completely, without registering the effects on narrative logic. Handwriting presents far more difficulty than type does, and Mom's "scrawly" handwriting is its own peculiar impediment. I wait, imagining Alzheimer's plaques encasing the neurons that enable my mother to see. The journal entry reads, "*What* I do remember very well is," and Mom's error presages several anxious minutes as she tries repeatedly to find her place. When the story finally reappears, Mom resumes reading, taking multiple runs at tricky phrases:

"My mother had a friend, an unmarried lady who was a schoolteacher. Most Sundays this lady would visit us after Sunday morning church service, and there I would be, busily scribbling away in the margins of old...of old...of an old...of an old scribbler provided by one of my older siblings, with my left hand...with my left hand of course. I knew she did not approve, as she had made very clear the very first...the very first time she had seen me at it."

"Oh, I know that," Mom says fervently, looking up from the notebook, "I remember that. I didn't like her because of that, you know. 'Oh,' I thought when I saw her coming, 'that was one of Mom's'"—and here she pauses a long time while she searches for the word—"'friends.' *Jah*." And then Mom continues reading and we both laugh: *"Needless to say, I did not like the lady much and as soon as I'd spy her coming, I would either stop writing immediately and leave the room, or hope she...she wouldn't notice me (there were, after all, seven of us kids in the family by that time) and...and con-*

tinue . . . continue writing surrepti . . . surrepti . . . surte . . . jah, surreptisti . . . surreptisteeously."

"Surreptitiously, Mom?" I ask. *"Jah,"* she says, "surreptitiously. Surreptitiously." She pronounces it perfectly both times. "Do you know what it means?" I ask and Mom's response is vividly instant. "Oh yes," she says with considerable delight, "on the sly!"

One of the great pleasures of conversations with my mother has been our shared love of language and wordplay. Eighteen months before this December afternoon, I begin the project by organizing my archived letters into neatly labelled file folders and puzzle over a scrap of orphaned paper that reads, in Mom's handwriting, "Sovereign Almighty, Inscrutable, Immutable, Eternal Ruler of Lady Irene College."

Letter #6 to Carla   *5 March 1987*

This past week has been very hard, including learning from my Mom that you haven't heard from me since December. (Rumours are circulating in Kampala that both in- and outbound mail may be being opened, so if you're not getting my letters and I'm not getting yours, what's to stop me from panicking?) [. . .] Things began with my period bright and unexpected Saturday morning, just in time to drive out to Kalasa to check on the mortar and pestle we'd ordered, and for our car to die. Gargantuan thunderstorm threatening, excruciating cramps, and our car is dead, again. Car gets fixed by a local mechanic who walks the kilometre from his house barefoot, reattaches a wire that's come loose, and says nothing about money. We give him a ride home and the equivalent of three Canadian dollars (a teacher with no experience earns about seventeen dollars Canadian a month), a mere gesture of our gratitude. Car dies two more times on the way home, three times getting into the garage. We're expert by now at reattaching loose wires but cancel plans to drive the archdeacon to Lutete on Sunday. [. . .]

Sunday, rain pelts down. Monday is my first day ever as Duty Tutor and I dutifully hop into my sweats at 6:15 a.m. to tramp around the soaked and smoky college grounds checking on the students who should be out hoeing and slashing. The girls are all still in bed. An attractive idea, but not one I can countenance. "Youdeehoo!" I warble cheerily outside the dorm: "Time to get to work, Year Ones." Twenty of the twenty-two students want to throw sharpened pangas at me. Two of the girls are ill and excused; they can ignore me and they do. The others drift out slowly. New prefects are appointed that morning and my short chat with this week's Head Girl bears discernible fruit: by Tuesday morning, I can account for all but six of the girls.

The week brightens further when the deputy principal leaves for Kampala, pausing long enough to declare me Grande Fromage in his absence. To celebrate, I hoist placards proclaiming myself "Sovereign Almighty, Inscrutable, Immutable, Eternal Ruler of Lady Irene College." No one notices. Tuesday is otherwise a quiet day and so I add, "President for Life, Baby-Kath. Everything here is mine," to the bottom of the placards. Frances tells me I've spelled "immutable" wrong.

Wednesday, in Kampala, after a month of waiting, Frances gets a full metric tonne of Canadian mail. I get letters from Ethiopia and Botswana, but nothing from home. I break my resolve and the bank and phone my mother to cry for fifteen of the most expensive minutes of my life. Friday, a partial lifting of gloom: I catch the Fishers lingering over breakfast and regale them with a week of Duty Tutor stories. By the time I ask if they might detour up to Cindy's with my letters (she'll mail them from Nairobi), they fall over themselves insisting it would be a pleasure. Which frees up my mind for a blissful afternoon catching up with the students who've just started their teaching practice, and that buoys me all the way to here,

hoping #5 has f-i-n-a-l-l-y arrived, sending barrels of love,
and wishing you the happiest of birthdays ever, beloved pal.

My biologist-landscape-architect-artist friend Carla and I have lived in the same city now for over sixteen years and we still craft funny long emails to celebrate our connection and our connection as writers. I depend on Carla's intuitive allegiance with my mother, the two of them acutely sensitive introverts. It's Carla who reads an early version of this manuscript and jots, "That's your mother writing," in the margin. I love the image I can suddenly see, little Geeske scribbling furiously in a sibling's worn-out notebook, five years old, sheltering herself from her mother's friend's scorn, left hand in motion, *no* shame, *no* doubt, *no* hesitation: *writing . . .*

On Friday 12 December 2008, Mom and I are upstairs amongst a jumble of books, notebooks, photograph albums, orphaned pictures, event posters, and political buttons ("I'm already against the *next* war"), because my mother thinks my sister is taking her books. Sandy began cleaning our parents' home a year earlier and her weekly tidying regularly unsettles our increasingly easily confused mother. Alzheimer's incursions prompt many otherwise trusting people to fierce bouts of paranoia, and it's probably not surprising that my mother's fixate on her books. If she can't see her precious books—her *friends* she calls them—she can't be sure they exist. If Mom's books don't exist, she knows she's under threat.

Letter #20 to Mom and Dad   *7 March 1987*

It's hard to know what's worst about these long-distance
calls: the prolonged nausea getting through to the operator;
the creeping panic that he hasn't heard correctly; the split
second in which Mom picks up the phone and I realize I'm
not going to keep from crying; discovering that letters mailed
a month ago haven't yet made it home; knowing that letters
from home aren't arriving here . . .

Mom's pressing concern on 12 December is for "the *Monitors*," by which she means the Canadian Centre for Policy Alternatives (CCPA)'s monthly publications.[1] She insists that it's okay if Sandy takes the older issues, but she's certain the most recent one is gone, too, and that, she tells me emphatically, "is not right." When I find the issue almost without trying, I ask Mom whether it's just these publications she's worried about.

"Well, see," Mom begins and pauses. "I don't know," she says, repeats herself in Frisian, and then switches back to uncharacteristically stilted English to tell me: "I know not all the titles of the books we have." I doubt out loud that Sandy would take Mom's books, but Mom is unconvinced. "I don't know," she says again and switches back to Frisian to tell me, "There are Frisian books that I don't know any more—that I don't *see* anymore," she corrects herself. I repeat my conviction: Sandy knows Mom's books are her treasures. "Why would *Sandy* take your books?" I ask. I sound remarkably patient in the recording; what I remember is irritation, feeling cross at what I think of as wasted time. Mom responds vigorously then, switching rapidly between English and Frisian, playing fast and loose with logic, and inadvertently identifying the cause of her confusion, the disorganization that reigns here now. Before Alzheimer's, my mother kept an impressively orderly home.

"Because it's," she begins energetically, "it's not *tidy*. Because I haven't rea—, organized tidy enough or whatever. But it's all upstairs practically. Well, there's stuff here too, and the stuff that's down here is in a bookcase actually, so that's okay, but there are also books that are lying loose, in piles here and there, you know. So. I don't like it because...I need that because...for my memory! If I don't hear that or see that anymore, then...I'm going to lose it! You know?" "Yeah," I agree, wanting her to say more, "you have to actually *see* it to know it's there, right?"

"Yes," Mom says in precise English. "Yes."

~~~~~~

Before Alzheimer's erosions effect their full obliterating scope, there are spaces and moments in which the past and the present exist simultaneously and bring joy. Mom's first letter calls her diary "invaluable," and it is, because, with the letters it prompted, it forms the most detailed record that exists of my mother's life. The letters the diary made possible reflect the mother I remember, the one propelled by lively passions for formal learning, theological engagement, and progressive political action. The letters evidence too Mom's frequent anxiety about doing things—especially school-related things—well or "right"; her consciousness of being an immigrant; her extreme agitation in test conditions. In their sometimes awkward, long-winded English, that is, they recollect the mother who was mine—the whimsical, generous affection she extended into the world, the way she grounded her being in books, how much she loved to laugh, her propensity for daydreaming, and, again and again, her devotion to me.

crosswords (4)

Letter #3 from Mom and Dad   *7 September 1986*

*Walter seems to be rather fascinated with Revelation. I
called him about some of the things he said. He claims I
misunderstood him and that I should not think of him as a
right-wing fundamentalist. We got to talk about Sojourners
and I brought him a back copy with a sermon called "Being
with the Lamb," which is also on Revelation, but not nearly
so speculative as to the symbolism, and yet in my opinion,
much more to the point.*

My mother shared with her parents and her siblings a fas-
cination with the dynamics of *church*. They approached and
approach biblical texts with a combination of reverence,
curiosity unfettered by excessive piety, and a commitment to
probing questions and careful study. They turned and turn
to trained clergy for existential guidance and intellectual
engagement. But during the years I lived at Ndejje, an interim
minister named Walter D had charge of my parents' church.
Walter D was well intentioned and intellectually lazy, blandly
incurious about the theological questions that burned in my
mother's mind and heart. Walter's leadership left much for
Mom to desire, and her letters chart her stalwart efforts to help
him see that—among other things—Christians must neces-
sarily oppose the nuclear arms race.

As it happened, Mom and Dad's loyalty to the church's
Dutch-immigrant roots didn't survive the American minister

who replaced Walter D and was, by 1990, using the pulpit to rally support for the US Army in the first Gulf War. But in 1987, Mom still believed that "Pastor Walter" might be urged into action, specifically via Richard Mouw's "Being with the Lamb," a compelling argument for Christians to challenge nuclear armament.[2] Mouw, a long-time president of Fuller Theological Seminary, embeds his call to action in an interpretation of the politics of Revelation, a radical reading of the Bible's difficult, final book, and one that directly implicates the American government of the day. "This teaching would not have surprised Christians in biblical times," Mouw insists, and adds, "They were well aware of Jezebel and Ahab, of Herod and Nero. [...] Nor should it surprise us in the light of more recent history, for we too know the likes of Hitler and Stalin and Idi Amin."

More than thirty years later, I'm provoked by Mouw's indirect reference to Uganda and reflect on his examples, each of which functions as a synecdoche, the part standing in for the whole. The *whole* in question is, each time, a version of "pure evil" (itself an oxymoron): "pure evil, Nazi"; "pure evil, Soviet"; "pure evil, African despot." What synecdoches might we add by now: "pure evil, ISIS"; "pure evil, alt-right neo-fascism"; "pure evil, climate-change denial"; "pure evil, anti-taxation, neo-liberal globalization"?

By "we," I mean my mother and I.

My mother first learned English in the 1940s at the M.U.L.O.,[3] the Dutch equivalent to Canadian Grades 7–10, studies she began a year earlier than her age-mates, having skipped a grade. Fluent in both Frisian and Dutch, she particularly enjoyed studying English, French, and German, and dreamed of a career as a language teacher. She was forty-one when she took and passed the Canadian high school equivalency exam, forty-two when she registered for her first university course. She never vanquished her anxieties about writing and speaking "correct" English, but she thrived at university.

Letter #4 from Mom and Dad   *12 September 1986*

Yesterday I went to a lecture on nuclear waste disposal with
Dana. The lecturer's theme was basically that the language
used by the nuclear establishment is designed to obscure
what is really meant and so to deceive the public; he called it
"Nuke Speak."

My brother's girlfriend Dana was smart, sassy, and interested
in many of the issues that invigorated my mother. She was
adventurous, too, eager to trek through Europe with Henry
for three months to reach me in Uganda very near my one-
year anniversary—my first visitors from home. After a week
together at Ndejje, we travelled to a resort on the Kenyan
coast, where, despite my delirious love for the Indian Ocean,
I'm daunted by snorkelling's mechanics. "Dana," I whispered after three attempts to keep my head underwater, "I'm
scared." Her response was prompt, startling for its clarity and
the speed with which it became a family maxim. "Kathleen,"
she announced sternly, "you live in Uganda; you can breathe
through a hose." The first fall I lived at Ndejje, Mom took
a course called "The Symbolic Dimensions of Religion" and
revelled in its challenges.

Letter #7 from Mom and Dad   *1 October 1986*

Sometimes I can still hardly believe that you're all the way
in Africa, but I guess the fact that I'm writing to you is proof
enough. There hasn't been very much news here so I'll tell
you a little about my course. We do not have to write essays,
but every week we have to read an article in a theological
journal and write summaries and responses. I got my first
one back yesterday with an A-minus with which I was
very pleased (CBC is playing music from The Sting right
now!) [. . .]
The prof also shows us slides of paintings and afterward
the symbolism in them is discussed. Now you know how little

I know about art so I haven't ventured any remarks so far, but it's enlightening to hear some people talk. It was almost funny to hear some chap say that he thought the second painting was evil. Another claimed he saw a devil's face and tail in it. The title was The Root of Jesus, by a Japanese artist brought up in a convent, and I can assure you that there was nothing evil or devilish in it. Last class we were shown a Chagall painting, which is "full of religious symbolism," but I don't think I'll see it until it is pointed out to me!

Mom's consciousness of her immigrant status and her distinctly accented English emerges regularly in her letters, especially while she was attending university, where she felt her "outsider" status acutely. But we white people, even if we're anxious, self-conscious, heavily accented immigrants, wake up every day cocooned inside privilege and racism. Mom ends her third letter hoping that the people I'm working with are nice, and she adds, "also the black people." I'm startled, rereading. I want to project back onto my justice-loving mother an exemplary awareness of racism's complexities, and I want to strive to match the example she sets, but I'm reminded how entangled racism is in everything I do and think. Six letters later and probably unintentionally, Mom mitigates the assumption that a black classmate would be "other" to Canada by referencing what she considers her own illegitimate status as non-Canadian-born.

Letter #9 from Mom and Dad   *13 October 1986*

Last week our class went to the Art Gallery to look at a sculpture exhibit, but I don't exactly know what to make of it. They weren't sculptures in the traditional sense of the word. For instance, there was a white painted door with a series of little switches (I think) lengthwise on it and the upper one was a red light bulb. Then there was a white rectangular table with two wooden spools also white on

*which some rope was rolled. I wished I'd had you along
to interpret for me. There's one black man in our class,
probably in his early thirties; I don't know where he's from,
I don't have the nerve yet to ask him. I don't think he was
born in Canada; he says very little. (But then, I don't say
much in class either, maybe because I also wasn't born in
Canada.) [...]
I've finally found a good place to store your
correspondence. It came to me "in a vision." Do you
remember that red tin with the pointed front that came
from our store in Nijemardum? Well, that is where your
letters now repose. The tin itself I have put underneath the
dresswair so that now at least the dinner table is not an
unorganized "jungle" of letters, bills, newspaper articles,
cartoons etc. that I'm saving up to send. (Only the articles
and cartoons, not the bills.)*

According to family legend, Pake and Beppe de Jong got off
the boat from Holland with eighty Canadian dollars; nine of
their ten children; a few items of furniture packed into a crate;
a trunk filled with mattresses, bedding, books, and a paltry
handful of household goods; and three suitcases. Among the
household items was an orange toffee tin about the size of a
breadbox, featuring exotic birds on three of its four sides, and
filled for many years with my letters from Ndejje. The *dresswair*
was the only substantial piece of furniture my grandparents
brought to Canada, a sideboard my Pake had built with his
father in the Netherlands, and which my parents received as
a wedding gift. My mother appreciated the *dresswair,* but she
treasured her intellectual inheritance, the cerebral ferocity
both her parents bestowed—though she was inclined to attri-
bute all her best qualities to her father.

Letter #16 from Mom and Dad   *19 December 1986*

When I checked with Nathaniel to ask which books he had
sent you [. . .] he mentioned that he's just read Not Wanted
on the Voyage, which reminded me to tell you about Answer
to Job, which our prof mentioned, written by Carl Jung. I
found it very interesting and I thought to myself, I'll bet
Timothy Findley is familiar with these ideas about Yahweh.
It certainly reminded me of his book.

Mom accurately intuits Jungian influences in Timothy Findley's controversial novel, *Not Wanted on the Voyage*, which
retells the Genesis flood story with a decided preference for
feminine principles of connection, communion, and reverence for life. Findley's representation of Yahweh as a childish,
depressed old man, dependent on others' adulation and—
crucially—their belief in him, galled some readers. Thirty
years earlier, in *Answer to Job*, Carl Jung had proposed that God
isn't independent of humans and, indeed, requires humans'
engagement to transform and grow. It was a provocation my
mother loved—the possibility that God may not just be *capable*
of change and growth, but *must* transform, and must *continue*
to transform.

Letter #17 from Mom and Dad   *4 January 1987*

My dear daughter, it's high time I catch you up on the latest
happenings here. Our first issue of Sojourners finally came.
Realizing that yours would run out at the end of the year, I
took out two one-year subscriptions, one for ourselves and
one for "Pastor Walter." He told me a few months earlier
that he was familiar with the magazine but could not afford
it. So, thinks I to myself, what better way to radicalize good-
old-Walt. So far I haven't noticed any improvement in his
preaching (style or content), but who knows. We must not
expect instant results, right, that wouldn't be fair?

Church-wise, the de Jongs were, for the time, conventionally observant. What set them apart was their ready engagement in the fine details of theological positions and the political ramifications of those positions. Many family stories feature one or the other of my maternal grandparents taking unconventional and sometimes unpopular theological and political stances, in public church contexts and in personal conversations. Mom's methods were subtler. And if her efforts at radicalizing Walter had stalled, her academic successes were accumulating . . .

Bonus Letter from Mom and Dad   *11 February 1987*

This unnumbered letter is mainly an explanation of the parcel you'll be receiving with it. Because I had not figured out a safe way to send you the requested underwear I had put off buying it. Thus (formal? you bet), when Frances's father told us we could send a care package with his colleague, I did some power shopping. (I was considering finishing Letter #21 and sending it along with the package, but somehow the contents didn't lend themselves to a practical finish; consequently you're getting this extra one.) [. . .] I got my Answer to Job card back with a "wow" on it. Two of my classmates have already asked to read it; it's almost embarrassing.

When it was carried to us directly, mail arrived promptly. Mom's "bonus letter" reaches me just nine days after she's finished it. Likely because I'm missing her four previous letters, I answer more or less instantly.

Letter #19 to Mom and Dad   *20 February 1987*

Have just opened the package delivered by Frances's Dad's colleague: new underwear and such classy underwear I may have to wear it over my clothes for the first few weeks! Plus cartoons, dropkes,[4] and Winnie Mandela's autobiography, all infinitely marvellous. Of the books I'm sending back to you, I've read both Unwinding Threads and So Long a Letter. If you're still looking around for something to read, look around for One Hundred Years of Solitude, Gabriel García Márquez. Weird and wonderful. Mostly wonderful.

perfect correspondence (6)

In the first year that I lived at Ndejje, Mom and I wrote to one another about—and in some cases sent one another copies of—*Lust for Life,* Irving Stone's biography of Vincent Van Gogh; Winnie Mandela's *Part of My Soul Went with Him*; Steve Biko's *I Write What I Like*; Northrop Frye's *The Educated Imagination*; *A Certain Sound,* Cedric Mayson's account of the liberation struggle in South Africa; Robertson Davies's *What's Bred in the Bone*; John Updike's *Roger's Version;* Timothy Findley's *Not Wanted on the Voyage*; Carl Jung's *Answer to Job*; Gabriel Okara's *The Voice;* Gabriel García Márquez's *One Hundred Years of Solitude*; Joy Kogawa's *Obasan*; *Unwinding Threads,* an anthology of short stories by African women writers; Margaret Laurence's first four Canadian novels; Karen Dinesen Blixen's *Out of Africa*; Kenneth Kaunda's *The Riddle of Violence*; Keri Hulme's *The Bone People*; C. S. Lewis's *Perelandra*; and *So Long a Letter,* Mariama Bâ's semi-autobiographical epistolary novel.

Not in that order.

crosswords (5)

Letter #22 from Mom and Dad   *23 February 1987*

I'll report on two peace-related activities in hopes you'll find it interesting.

In my second year of undergraduate studies, I enrolled in Literature of the Bible, a popular religious studies course taught by the legendary professor, Carl Ridd. By asking radical questions about the nature of biblical texts, the course answered deep intellectual longings my mother had experienced most of her life, and she began attending classes with me. Mom and I were powerfully influenced, too, by the connections Carl was drawing between biblical theology and social engagement, and we joined an action-study group that Carl and his wife Bev and several others had formed one year earlier. For the first few years, we called ourselves "the Stella group," because we met at the United Church's Stella Mission in Winnipeg's historic North End. Later we renamed ourselves R.A.R., for "reflection-action-reflection." As other such groups did at the time, we engaged in study and action on nuclear disarmament, anti-apartheid efforts, the US-fuelled conflict in Central America, child poverty in Canada's inner cities, and suburban sprawl, with its untrammelled use of non-renewable resources and its corollary, the de-development of urban cores.

Over the years, several R.A.R. group members took peace-making as their particular focus and in 1983 formed Project Peacemakers, a local organization patterned after Ottawa's

Project Ploughshares.[5] Mom volunteered at Project Peace-makers for years in various capacities, including a stint on the board of directors.

Letter #22 from Mom and Dad [cont.]

1. About two weeks ago I received a chain letter from a woman unknown to me. It was written in a rather clumsy hand, but I couldn't ignore its appeal. It's in support of the women at Greenham Common and was requesting the recipient to send two postcards with the words: "Women Demand Peace For The World."[6] One to be sent to a woman on the list they included and one to Margaret Thatcher of Prime Minister fame. (This pen is awful, it makes my handwriting look worse.) Also, we were asked to send the letter on to six other women friends. At first I was sure I could never come up with six names, but I did, including your very own Sharon!

Until Alzheimer's robbed her of the ability to voice them, Mom recounted graphic memories of the terror she felt as a child, eager to finally join her siblings at school but acutely aware that she'd be forced to use her right hand when she got there. As we sit among her beloved books on 12 December 2008, she reads her certainty from twenty-six years earlier, that *"educators are more enlightened now and don't force all kids into the same mould for fear of causing trauma."* And then she reiterates a theory she fondly maintains, despite my logical rejoinders. "I actually... actually, I think sometimes, you know, if I hadn't... if nobody had forced me to read with my right hand... *write* with my right hand... maybe I wouldn't have Alzheimer's!?"

Letter #22 from Mom and Dad [cont.]

*The second thing I did was ask G.O. (Good Old) Walter
for permission to use the poster "A Modest Proposal for
Peace" as an insert in our bulletin. Permission was duly
given and they were inserted last Sunday and now the
question is, how many people bothered to read it, let alone
think about it. I find it rather strange that G.O. has not yet
mentioned anything to me about Sojourners. Maybe he
cannot cope with the ideas he finds in there? (I'm beginning
to understand what you said about fluent pens; bad pens
actually blunt creative thinking.)*

If Mom's handwriting never recovered from the trauma of
forced change, the barbaric practice failed to even *dent* her
lifelong love of formal learning. Nor did it prevent her from
sewing skilfully and knitting with almost transcendent pleasure. But Mom never wrote with physical dexterity or ease. I
think sometimes of her fervent five-year-old self, scribbling
left-handedly just out of view of her mother's strict schoolteacher friend, and I wonder: how much more naturally might
little Geeske have written her way into the world if no one had
stopped her then? She certainly always had a lot on her mind.

Letter #24 from Mom and Dad   7 March 1987

*For the first time since I don't know when, G.O. Walter
managed to say some significant things.*

perfect correspondence (7)

On 7 March 1987, two days after crafting a long sixth letter to Carla, I frame a twentieth letter to my parents as an ongoing lament for missing mail. Mom writes on 7 March, too, with the unexpected news that Walter is showing signs of growth. Two days later, I use the back of a grocery list to begin an urgent and uncharacteristically unnumbered letter to my parents identifying Nakato Rose for the first time.

Nakato Rose is the daughter of Jonathan Ssendawula, LIC's most senior tutor, the slight but quietly authoritative wise man of the community. Rose inherits her father's palpable intelligence; she is tiny, light on her feet, precise in her movements, razor-sharp, and probably bored with the pace of postwar life—despite her trepidations, she boldly befriends the two strange Canadian women she discovers at LIC when she returns to Ndejje. Over time, I understand better how fearful she was of our first encounters, including of my very light-coloured eyes and sometimes overly intense gaze. When she first begins engaging us in conversation, Rose is teaching at LIC's Demonstration School and living with her parents, a multitude of her sixteen siblings, and a greater multitude of nieces, nephews, and cousins who've been orphaned by the war. Rose initiates the relationship by volunteering to help Frances rehabilitate the library. Soon she's also teaching us Luganda.

crosswords (5) [cont.]

Letter #25 from Mom and Dad   *13 March 1987*

*Before I tell you about Thursday night, I'll go back to what
Walter managed to say on Sunday, which was, "How do we
change people? Not by telling them what they already know
they are, but by telling them what they can become." After
the service I told him I liked what he'd said, and I asked
if he was going to relate his ideas to capital punishment.
He in turn asked if I would come to the Bible study
on the topic later in the week. When Thursday rolled
around I decided to put my money where my mouth is,
and I went.
I think (no, I'm sure) I said some controversial and
theologically unacceptable things. Among others, that the
Bible says at times, contradictory and conflicting things and
that God and or Christ is taking a risk with us, hoping that
we will respond to the challenge of "becoming."*

Mom relished the notion that nothing was static, that everything—including God, as Jung had speculated—was in flux
and therefore in a constant state of emerging possibility. In
Mom's mind, Walter's insight—that people change when they
can imagine themselves as different than they are—could be
applied directly to the death penalty. If you embraced *becoming* as the central dynamic of existence, you believed, as Mom
did, that someone guilty of murder could never be wholly and
permanently defined by that act. In Mom's mind, a church
that sanctioned state-sanctioned killing was a church that

had stopped believing in the possibility of divine love. Mom's visionary passion for the ongoing work of creation's *becoming* was a tacit but deeply felt rejection of Calvinism's authoritarian theologies and was typically met, in the church she attended then, with bafflement, kindly condescension, and simple repetition:

Letter #25 from Mom and Dad [cont.]

Well, Kathleen, "God knows everything" as you "know," so that did not go over very well, but it was an amicable discussion; they didn't boot me out of the door. It was, at points, interesting, but it showed (again) to me that you cannot use "the Bible" as the "authoritative, infallible" guide the way so many people still try to do, including Walter, who still thinks you can make everything in the Bible "fit."

crosswords (6)

Poor Walter. Although he was showing glimmers of improvement, he was clearly never going to make it into the exclusive
category of ministers Mom would have defended to the death.
On the first day of February 2008, ten months before we launch
our inventory of her books, I discover that Mom's loyalty to
clergy she admired began early. On that day, my mother tells
me a secret and a story I've never heard before, about ministers
and newborns and theologies of springtime.

I've intended this conversation as a preview to the visit
we'll make next week to the PostSecret exhibit at the Winnipeg Art Gallery. Frank Warren began the PostSecret project in 2005, inviting people from around the world to submit
postcards that portray a secret they've never before revealed.
Thirteen years on, the project has amassed tens of thousands
of postcards, many of which are reproduced on Warren's web-
site and in the six collections he's published. In early 2008,
the exhibit seems an entirely plausible destination: Mom still
navigates the outside world with relative confidence and she
responds in specific ways to new information . . .

Given what we've talked about over lunch, Mom's secret
seems comically benign. We've secluded ourselves in a quiet
corner of the Millennium Library, and Mom begins by guessing that she was about ten and on her way home from church
when she crossed paths with a little girl from school. She was
a pretty little girl, Mom says, "not particularly smart in class,"
but she had an affluent-farmer father well able to clothe his
pretty little daughter in pretty little dresses. Mom remembers having two: a dress for school and a dress for church,

both hand-me-downs from her older sisters, perfect complements, psychically, to the freckles and straight red hair that engrained in little Geeske the unshakeable conviction that she was, and always would be, "the ugly duckling."

So when little Geeske passed her pretty, curly-haired, blonde nemesis on the steps of the church that *she* attended, and discovered her nemesis wearing not just a pretty little dress but a pretty little *hat*, little Geeske did what any envious ten-year-old might do: she stuck out her tongue. Mom tells the story and we laugh as uproariously as we can and still, technically, be whispering. Uproarious and rueful. Mom's cognitive functions are already significantly compromised, but she can recognize her long-ago gesture for the ineffectual *ressentiment* it was (even if she wouldn't use that word): the cosmic unfairness that a person could be—as little Geeske assuredly was—*particularly* smart at school, and never be as acceptable, as secure, as desired as the pretty little blonde daughter of a successful farmer.

The secret of my mother's tongue unexpectedly prompts another memory, another encounter with the same little girl, but what's crucial to this story is not the gap between a prosperous farmer and a penurious shopkeeper, or the gap between political complacency and radical, unpopular political ideas, or the gap between fine straight red hair and curly blonde hair, or pretty clothes versus hand-me-downs. In this story, all of Protestant theology is on the line, and all because of a baby's birth. In the Netherlands, my mother's family belonged to the *Hervormde Kerk*, the more progressive Protestant denomination in their area of northern Holland. The Hervormde Kerk is roughly equivalent to the Reformed Church of America (RCA), though the RCA is decidedly more socially and politically conservative, closer, ironically, to the Netherlands' other major Protestant denomination, the *Gereformeerde Kerk*.[7]

My mother's second story features the new minister at their church, a relatively young man, relatively fresh from his seminary training, from Amsterdam, and considerably more sophisticated than most of the people of Mom's little town. This, at least, is what I guess, because Mom tells me that when he and his wife announced the birth of their first child, they broke with Nijemardum's conventionally pious invocations of God and instead sent cards with the Dutch words *Een lentekind is ons gegeven in een dochtertje.*

It's almost three years since Mom's Alzheimer's diagnosis, but—prompted by other recollections—she remembers both messages perfectly. The first is the standard announcement of the time: *Met dank aan God en grote blijdschap noemen wij een kennismaking van de geboorte van* [name of child] (literally, with thanks to God and great joy, we publish the news of the birth of [name of child]). The second announcement is the one the new minister and his wife sent, the evocative, poetic claim, "We've been blessed by a spring child in the form of a little daughter."[8]

Poetry, schmoetry. According to Mom, the community's consternation was concentrated in the *other* church, the Gereformeerde congregation, which included the pretty little girl and her family. And it sounds, from Mom's account, that the pretty little girl became a kind of junior spokesperson for the objecting side, sanctimoniously noting the heresies of the Hervormde minister's wording: *because it did not mention God.*

"And that was a significant omission?" I ask. Mom and I are giggling silently. "Oh absolutely," Mom whispers, laughing. "This was not what you *did*. You *did*—" and here Mom uses a light, singsong voice to reiterate the standard, acceptably devout Dutch phrasing, *"Met dank aan God en grote blijdschap noemen wij een kennismaking van de geboorte van . . ."*

"And so I kind of felt I had to defend them," she explains. "I said, 'Well, you know, *gegeven*, that means that *God is in it.*'" She is quietly adamant, remembering the vehemence with which she argued as a child. I ease my way into the implicit theology. "Did you mean," I ask, "that, inherent in the words of the birth announcement is the understanding that what has been given has been given by God?"

"Exactly," Mom agrees in a quick switch to English, "and as I say, I was probably not more than nine or so and I had to defend them." "'That's still good enough,'" she insists in Frisian, quoting her young, remembered self: "'God's *still in there.*'" She sketches the context so that I'll appreciate the breadth of the consternation. "Because they were Gereformeerde"—her voice rises to reflect this elevated status—"and we were just Hervormde . . ."

Mom has been speaking Frisian or Dutch almost exclusively throughout this exchange, and her voice descends here to convey the relative denigration, and then she takes on the persona of a self-satisfied Gereformeerde congregrant, perhaps the pretty curly-haired girl or, more likely, one of her parents: "'What can you expect of those *Hervormde* people? They're not *nearly* as pious as we are.'"

"So you were, in a sense, defending your whole religion," I venture. "*Exactly*," Mom repeats in crisp English, and then she laughs exuberantly. "We'd better stop," she says; "heaven knows what else I'm going to say!"

crosswords (8)

For someone who despised the look of her own handwriting and disliked the physical work of writing, Mom was busy at it an awful lot of the time. By late March 1987, both the Stella group and Winnipeg-based MCC-ers were mobilizing opposition to two proposed government bills, the first to restore the death penalty, the second the harsh Bill C-84, the Refugee Deterrents and Detention Bill.

Letter #26 from Mom and Dad   *21 March 1987*

If you've received my previous letters you will have read that I attended a "Bible study" on capital punishment, which our not-so-beloved Brian Mulroney will be introducing debate on in Parliament soon. I've further involved myself in action because at our latest Stella meeting, we practised letter writing to MPs and MLAs on three topics: the return of the death penalty, Canada's new "unimproved" legislation regarding refugees, and human rights for homosexuals in Manitoba.

It was an interesting and helpful exercise, though I find it very difficult to write with so many people around me, because of course the conversation does not stop and people throw out helpful bits of information as we go along. At the same meeting there was information on another meeting with the purpose of organizing opposition against the death penalty, to be held at the MCC Manitoba Office. Since that is quite easy for me to get to, I went.

There were approximately twenty-five people there including Reverend C. de Haan; he was a minister of the

Canadian Reformed Church, now a prison chaplain for
years already. He was a great friend of Pake de Jong's and he
spoke at Pake's burial service. I didn't recognize him until
we were introducing ourselves and then I looked closer and
said (to myself), Ferrek, dat is Dominy de Haan![9] *(Not very*
ladylike, but you know I'm not ladylike. Sandy laughed
so hard when I told her she insisted that I include it in my
letter to you, which I, obedient mother that I am, am doing
forthwith.) I had a chat with him afterward and he gave me
a ride home; I asked him in for a cuppa tea, but he didn't
have time. Too bad.

Cornelius de Haan had completed his theological studies in
the Netherlands with distinction and was sought after by the
Dutch immigrants who'd established a Canadian congregation
of the Gereformeerde Kerk (Article 31) in rural Manitoba in
the early 1950s. The "Article 31-ers" had broken from the Gereformeerde Kerk in 1943 to form an even more dogmatic version
of Dutch Calvinism, and it didn't take long for the Canadian
congregation to determine that Reverend de Haan wasn't a
good fit. Deemed resistant to authority and too friendly with
the unchurched, the good man was dismissed and spent the
next fifteen years working only sporadically. Neil de Haan
was one of Pake's closest friends and interlocutors, in great
part because he preached a theology of expansive love, centred
on the Beatitudes' radical revision of human priorities. At
the Stony Mountain penitentiary, where he was chaplain for
the last several decades of his career, de Haan inspired enormous affection amongst the men incarcerated. He was, for my
mother, a star in the firmament.

Letter #26 from Mom and Dad [cont.]

The meeting was held to plan strategies for our opposition to
the reintroduction of the death penalty. The focus will be on
1. a letter-writing campaign 2. prayer vigils 3. media coverage.

*I will limit myself to letter writing, which, as I explained,
will be very unsuccessful in my home congregation, but not of
course at Stella, where it is already underway.*

Ultimately, opponents of both the death penalty and the refugee bills claimed measures of victory. The first was defeated in
the House of Commons on 30 June 1987; passage of the second
was delayed for over a year. In the three decades since, there's
been little talk in Canada of bringing back the death penalty,
but in 2015 another Conservative federal government passes
Bill C-51, the Anti-terrorism Act, which dwarfs Bill C-84 by
several orders of draconian magnitude. In the meantime, the
LGBTTQ*[10] community has experienced a slow but steadily
increasing breadth of rights, including, in 2004, in Manitoba,
same-sex couples' right to marry.

Letter #26 from Mom and Dad [cont.]

*Kathleen, I swear I don't know why I got myself so involved
in all this. It all seemed to "just happen." I think I'm pretty
brave to walk into a meeting where I've never been before and
might not have seen one familiar face. I almost feel like Attila
the Hun. (Well not quite, it's meant as a figure of speech,
or, as we university-educated people say, "as a metaphor.")
Actually I don't even know if Attila the Hun was brave or just
cruel, so it might not even be an appropriate metaphor.*

By late March 1987, my mother's Letters #5, 18, 19, 20, 21, and 23
have all been irretrievably lost. Until #40 goes missing, though,
everything she sends arrives, and when I read her letters now,
I'm grateful to remember how articulate and funny she was
in English. Mom would have loved being expert in the literary and cultural references that twinkled through her writing and conversation, fully aware that she might be making
extravagant mistakes, eager—in the safe space of family—for
the ensuing hilarity. Attila the Hun.

crosswords (bonus)

At 7 a.m. on 18 August 1986—a deliciously sunny morning in Nairobi and seven months before Mom walks into a meeting at which she may know no one—I begin my first working day in Africa by fainting twice and breaking my glasses. By 1 p.m. that afternoon, an efficient optometrist in the city's cosmopolitan downtown has repaired the frame and enough time remains to wander through a vast English-language bookstore nearby. A stylish young sales clerk finds me amongst the science textbooks, admires my hair, and asks whether I have to cut it to keep it short like this. When I say that I do, she tells me, "That is *just* like us. I think you must love Africans very much." I like the symbolic heft, beginning by breaking open the frame(work) with which I've arrived.

By mid-October 1987, though, I'll have lived at Ndejje for fourteen months and will still have learned only enough Luganda to know when I'm paying a European premium for milk powder. The reopened college has offered three full terms of instruction and, as more and more students return, sometimes feels like a real school. The country and the region are getting back on their feet, but slowly. Students often arrive late in the term because they've been busy finding money for school fees, or they abandon the program because tuition has suddenly been hiked. Many of them struggle with a range of illnesses almost certainly brought on by trauma from the war. Funding from the Ministry of Education is not always forthcoming and not always forthcoming on time. William Mutema continues to be overworked as deputy principal and is frequently away chasing money through dreary government offices in Kampala. Our dauntingly imperious, shrewdly well-connected principal is rarely present at LIC, busy at international meetings or in Kampala. To diffuse my frustration at her long absences, I dream up irreverent titles and regularly refer to her as "Mrs. *Kabaka*" (Mrs. King), "Mrs. *Katonda*" (Mrs. God), or "Her Eminent Immenseness."

When Daniel Kiggundu arrives, though, freshly graduated from the National Teachers College, I make a new friend and drop East African agriculture from my teaching mandate. I'm still responsible for physics and some chemistry, but can concentrate more time on mathematics, a subject I thoroughly enjoy. Frances and I are increasingly familiar around Ndejje hill, befriended by the community's elders and members of the local church. We juggle scruples against sore muscles and hire a young woman to help us with domestic work. As friendships deepen with our Ugandan colleagues, we are simultaneously more fully at home and more intimately confronted by our privilege in a community and a country and a continent structured by global inequalities. Problems with mail's progress and Walter's theology continue, and then my health slides sideways.

Letter #27 from Mom and Dad   *30 March 1987*

On Saturday we had four of your best buddies over for dinner, to wit, Sharon, Tracey M., and Lil and Roxanne. The purpose was not merely for so mundane a thing as eating (although I made beef bourguignon and it went over very well. Lillian called it "stew" but I know she really liked it), no, the higher reason was the viewing of your pictures. We had a great time. Roxanne and Lillian brought flowers and Sharon and Tracey both came with wine. You'll probably get reports from all of them if and when the post-office people decide to start doing what they're paid for!

Letter #21 to Mom and Dad   *2 April 1987*

You'll be interested to know that we're starting a garden, Dad! Well. Let me not exaggerate. We haven't done much but solicit advice, and Robinah will do most of the actual work (and then we'll loll about in paunchy splendour enjoying the fruits of her labour). Naturally there's more to this old exploitative tale than meets the eye, namely that when we agreed to pay Robinah twice what our Ugandan colleagues said they'd pay for domestic work, we hadn't realized that this apparently generous amount still comes nowhere near what she needs to save for sewing school. But her aunt marched in yesterday to clue us in, the gist being that Robinah will be working for us till she's ninety if she has to buy sewing school supplies out of the money she saves. [. . .] It was Frances who hit on the brilliant idea that we could employ Robinah for extra hours every day if she could work on a garden.

Letter #27 from Mom and Dad [cont.]

These days Walter has at least one hymn with "blood" in it every week. He has another new habit now too; with love, he is always saying, "Jesus, we love you so much," so much that it makes me wonder whether he realizes "love" is the hardest thing in the world, because if you don't do love, then you don't have love.

Letter #21 to Mom and Dad [cont.]

According to our colleagues, though, bush clearing is simply too heavy for a young woman, and so Sekijobba Tomas, one of the college porters, has been breaking his back on our behalf, a sweet and gentle man who insists we can pay him what we think is fair. Arghhhh. What we think is fair!? The Uncle Menno Financial Safety Net is a lovely thing, but entirely obscures how Ugandan money translates into a real human being's time and energy.

Letter #27 from Mom and Dad [cont.]

(Whenever I hear Walter preach, I think how differently I would do it if I had the chance.)

The satisfaction of integrating more and more closely into the community at Ndejje is offset—at first just a bit—by recurring bouts of mysterious pain. In April 1987, Frances and I travel to Nairobi during school holidays, in part to consult with a doctor recommended by our MCC Kenya colleagues, an expedition with mixed medical results.

Letter #23 to Mom and Dad   *2 May 1987*

Safely home at Ndejje, and three of the neighborhood kids, grandchildren of the doughty Mr. Mulenga, local tailor and church pillar, have just left, after formally welcoming us back from Kenya. Cute as buttons they are, but they don't know much English and our Luganda barely extends past the greeting stage. I'm patching together what might be appropriate questions to ask children (and kicking myself for not making copies of my wild animal photographs) when Frances thinks to offer them a back copy of Maclean's. Bull's eye. They're thrilled by everything, especially a photo of a huge Chinese crowd during the Queen's visit, and quickly set to work finding pictures of really important muzungu. "Mistah Fishah!" they whisper excitedly at one of the business pages, flip to sigh "Meessus Reeeed" with heartfelt affection, then turn to a fashion page, which prompts a glance upward and utter delight: "Meeez Francees!" [. . .]

After rereading your #27–29 (waiting together in Kampala when we returned), it seems safe to say that you're getting my mail, I'm getting my mail, we're all getting my mail, hallelujah amen. I'm also feeling much better and the pills (which I keep forgetting to take because I'm feeling much better) are almost gone.

The at-first modest but unpredictably intensifying pain I'm experiencing leaves doctors in Kampala and Nairobi equally stumped. In the meantime, Henry and Dana leave Winnipeg on their way to see me, at a leisurely pace via multiple European countries. It hardly seems possible but it is a fact that we relied almost exclusively on the vagaries of international post to plan this trip and finesse its itinerary, as we would again for my parents' visit in December 1987. I'm eager for every opportunity to get to know my colleagues better, but the more we converse, the more frequently we encounter differences of opinion, experience, and the luxuries of ideological choice. "*Ente yange ezaadde,*" I announce in Luganda to launch my 1987 Father's Day letter, knowing my farmer Dad will enjoy the claim that "my [entirely imaginary] cow has given birth." The letter sobers quickly, though, as I recount an intense discussion with Daniel about nuclear weapons that ended, to my regret, with my friend's confirmed preference for deterrence over disarmament.

It was in conversation with Nakato Rose that I was most frequently buoyed by connection and rattled by difference.

perfect correspondence (8)

I mention Rose for the first time on 9 March 1987 in an unnumbered "bonus" letter to my parents and—until she leaves Ndejje for an upgrading course in June 1988—I mention Rose in almost every subsequent letter I write. I often save extended accounts for Lil and Roxanne, who are keen to know about the friendships I'm forming with other women at Ndejje . . .

Letter #7 to Lil & Roxanne   *4 June 1987*

Hell and damnation womyn, the %!#* toilet is making like it plans to clog up again, not good, since I've recently been promoted to Shit Scooper and frankly, the job stinks. Oh God, oh God, oh God, practically as I write, a live cockroach touched my bare skin. Cockroaches the size of skittering eggs—I almost threw up into the porridge—the wretched, carapacious, disease-transmitting, bloody bastard of a thing crawled over my foot. Over my foot? In broad flippin' daylight? Gad, where is that insect spray?

Eventually I get over myself. I get back to the letter that evening.

Letter #7 to Lil & Roxanne [cont.]

Found Frances quite despondent when I got back from my walk. She'd spent the afternoon working in the library, and Rose had been in, helping, and talking, mostly about the banyanya. The banyanya, loosely translated, are "the bad guys," specifically the UNLA soldiers who wreaked unforgettable horror here, but also, generically, all northerners. Rose is a teacher at the Demonstration School, my age probably, and our language tutor. In a poem I wrote about her, I called her fierce and fragile and she is; also funny, intense, gruff, and loving.

Apparently Rose had talked extensively that afternoon about how there weren't any good *banyanya* and how they should all be killed, ferocious claims I'd heard her make on other occasions, talk that left Frances exhausted and depressed. Frances had travelled around northern Uganda several years earlier and couldn't reconcile Rose's determined animosity with the northerners she herself had met.

Letter #7 to Lil & Roxanne [cont.]

"What got Rose on such a string?" I ask, trying to untangle and release some of Frances's frustration. "Oh," she said, "I think it's seeing all the damage still evident in the library. It reminds her of what it used to look like. She went on and on about how terrible the soldiers were." And then Frances pauses and adds, "Three students were raped along the Bombo road."

Oh God, I think. "College students?" I ask. "Yeah," says Frances and she pauses again. "I just don't know how her aggressive attitude helps anything, though. All that hateful talk about beating northern kids if she ever had any in her classroom? What would that help?"

I understand Frances's frustration. I feel it too when we spend time with Rose, cannot square my vivacious, canny, clever friend with the violent retribution she regularly calls down on her enemies. But I'm a swaddled white Canadian kid who still believes, in some tidily protected pocket of my unblemished and immature soul, that all you need is love.

Letter #7 to Lil & Roxanne [cont.]

So I have to ask myself: how dare you be frustrated that someone who's seen and endured more terror and violence than you likely ever will needs to call down hateful reprisals from a vengeful god? How can you not understand that rape and murder and torture and mindless destruction leave scars that don't disappear because some white kid from the suburbs of North America says, "but we have to forgive them"? [. . .] I wonder if we shouldn't say too much about forgiveness until we've listened and been sickened by the stories, again and again, and cried for our friends and cried with them. Maybe that'll never happen. But if it does, we'll have earned some right to speak, but only a little, and maybe by then we won't need to say anything because we'll have shown the love we thought we had to put into words.

Well. End of diatribe. Let's see how I do with that. [. . .]

P.S. Thanks for asking about my health, Rox. The last few days have been pretty good. With any luck, I've put whatever this was behind me. (Haven't put back much weight yet, but I'm sure that will happen again only too quickly!)

crosswords (9)

Despite my optimism, the illness was socking in, the sporadic, unpredictable, sometimes crumpling pain presenting itself with increasing frequency and intensity, very hard to keep track of, or feel in control of, especially via international post.

Letter #13 to Sharon   *19 June 1987*

Darling pal, please don't tell my Mom, but I'm really worried about my health, mostly the intense and unpredictable big muscle pains. Doc B figures the pain killers will keep them under control until I'm done coughing, but when I ask how leg pain could be related to coughing, he shakes his head and admits he's stumped.

He's ruled out the possibility of psychosomatic pain, which is good but it doesn't make the pains any less scary. [. . .] I noticed the chest ache first about three weeks ago and guessed it was brought on by excessive coughing, but the large-muscle pain appeared not long afterward, the kind of pain you get when you've been exerting yourself in unfamiliar ways, though the only unusual exercise I'd gotten was two weeks earlier than that, when I spent a couple of hours helping the students unload food aid (mackerel from Denmark; curried chicken from Holland; and sugar, cornmeal with weevils, and the most disgusting powdered milk I've ever tasted from the States. And tins of edible fat, origin unknown) (and a double share of everything, because Frances and I are considered individuals for this reckoning). Want a sack of maize meal, maggots no extra charge? [. . .]

The truth is, I'm exhausted, confused, sporadically in intense pain, and afraid (including afraid that I'm a big baby because I really do want my Mom) (but remember my darling: by the time you get this, it will be old news) (oxymoron).

It wasn't an accident that I called Sharon "my other sister." Of all my friends, Sharon was in most frequent contact with Mom, and only my mother wrote me more often. Mom revelled in the qualities that first drew me to Sharon: her focused justice-seeking, her powerful competence, her comedic orientation to the world. I depended on Sharon in a hundred ways, including to swap stories with my mother. Very rarely, I needed Sharon to stay mum.

Letter #38 from Mom and Dad   *20 June 1987*

We are immensely relieved to hear that you're feeling so much better. We've been back from church for a while, but I had to "bekom" before I could write (interesting to note the similarity between "to become" and "bekomme" isn't it?). You could say I had to "become" myself again after the sermon, as there were many things said (by you know who) that I didn't agree with. Without exactly being able to explain, let me say that it's mainly because of the approach to the Bible ("which teaches us clearly, answers all our questions"), the simplistic ideas about "salvation," and, wait for it: the three distinct functions of the Holy Spirit.

There's no precise English equivalent for the Frisian word *bekomme*, which is a shame, because every English-speaking introvert knows the experience it describes, the crucial process by which one calms oneself back into one's recognizable *self*, usually after having been out in the world amongst tasks and places and personalities and demands. Thousands of times during my childhood, after she'd been on short or long stints from home, I heard my mother use the phrase that casually mixes Dutch with Frisian: *Nou moat ik eventjes bekomme* (I just need a minute to become myself again). Mom loved the etymological kinship between *bekomme* and *becoming*, though in one usage, the speaker moves inward, psychically, to reconnect with an interior self, while in the other she embraces ever-emerging possibilities. No matter. Mom loved paradox and contradiction, too, especially once she'd had a moment to *bekom—*

Letter #38 from Mom and Dad [cont.]

Dana's Mom called to let me know that Dana and Henry called as planned but only talked for one minute because apparently it isn't possible to make collect calls from Greece on Sundays? At least now we know where they are. [. . .]

Saturday June 27. The letter carriers have gone on a rotating strike, which means that you don't know until the morning whether your town has been struck (is that the way to put it?). It's a real pain in the neck, not knowing whether to hold onto your letters, or mail them and hope for the best. (I'm usually sympathetic to striking workers anywhere, but in this case I'm not so sure.)

We had a rather unsettled week in another way too. Beppe had quite a few falls and we've had to go over to her place to get her up off the floor. As you know, once she's down she cannot get up again. We began to realize that the reason for all these falls is because she was "in her cups" and Eta, Gerta, and I decided that we better take her home with one of us. [. . .]

Dana's Mom called again last Monday to say the travellers were in a place called Metsovo and Henry called Saturday from Athens, but very briefly, because he couldn't make a collect call. I find that hard to understand. I mean, that a person cannot make a collect call from Athens? I guess it's true: that civilization is really ancient. (This is a very bad joke I know.)

I imagine Mom at an old-fashioned switchboard, plugging us into circuits of connection, Henry and Dana trekking through unexpectedly isolated Greece, Kathleen unpredictably incommunicado at Ndejje, and Beppe lost sometimes to alcohol's fickle friendship. Henry always referred afterward to the African portion of his trip as a life-changing experience, one that directly influenced his career path, including the research he did later in Senegal. Eleven years after his life-altering trip to see me in Uganda, my brother will marry Cynthia, an even more wonderful woman than Dana, but Dana remains fondly vivid in our family's collective memory. "You live in Uganda," we announce from time to time when one of us is facing a challenge, "you can breathe through a hose." And then, on 11 September 2001, fourteen years and three weeks after she helps me breathe under the light-splattered surface of the Indian Ocean, and less than twenty minutes before it collapses, Dana makes it out of the second of Manhattan's towers, covered in debris and alive.

Letter #38 from Mom and Dad [cont.]

Beppe had a lot of bruises from the falls and needed quite a lot of attention especially the first few days, and in the meantime I was busy filling out a scholarship application that had been sent by the University Awards Office. I wasn't going to bother, because I have only one course to finish, but one morning I woke up thinking, if they say I'm eligible, I must be. So I applied. It took considerable time, but Sandy gave me some valuable hints, and now I've finished the "durn thing" up!

My mother rarely imposed her wishes on us, but when, at the end of high school, I contemplated a community college program, she urged me to reconsider. "You can always get practical training later," she reasoned. "Right now you have the marks and the aptitude and a scholarship for university. I didn't ever have this chance. At least try it for a year." She shouldn't have worried. My siblings and I all loved university, accumulating various degrees as we sorted through our interests. My sister graduated with a Gold Medal in honours anthropology before she trained as a lawyer; a few years later, my brother was awarded a Gold Medal in physics before completing one undergraduate and then two graduate degrees in engineering.

Letter #38 from Mom and Dad [cont.]

And on Thursday 25 June, Sandy, along with all the other candidates, was called to the bar. We quite enjoyed it and are very proud that she is now a lawyer. Remember I used to say that Sandy was "cut out" to be a lawyer because she talked so much! If that influenced her choice, I could take at least some credit for her accomplishments couldn't I?

Young Geeske dreamed of becoming a teacher of languages, but immigration to Canada chewed up those ambitions and spit them out, entirely without ceremony. By the mid-1980s and midlife, still intellectually restless, Geeske was doing at least some of her living vicariously through us . . .

Letter #38 from Mom and Dad [cont.]

Yesterday we heard a program on the radio about the problem of AIDS in Uganda. It was interesting and rather frightening. The doctor who was interviewed was certainly very knowledgeable, but I was also interested in his English accent, thinking: this is the accent Kathleen hears all the time. [. . .] Some of the interview was taped outside and you could hear the sounds of Kampala and later a rooster crowing. I felt as though I was right there with you.

crosswords (10)

But in May 1987, propelled by success at university, Grace rekindles her early aspirations and begins volunteering as a literacy tutor. By early July, she's visiting regularly with Khoune M——, a Laotian woman who has, with her husband and three children, spent the previous five years in a refugee camp in Thailand. Mom's letters from this point reflect the active curiosity she brought to her work with Khoune and the insights it prompted, including insights into what we'd now call "white privilege"—

Letter #39 from Mom and Dad   *1 July 1987*

Did I tell you that on my second visit I told Khoune that I'm also an immigrant and speak with an accent myself and that she might end up as the first Laotian in history who speaks English with a Dutch accent?! She has a good sense of humour and laughed at that. Tonight I'm going again. I think what she needs and wants most of all is to hear English spoken, not just the bits and pieces that you get at the supermarket but actual conversation, and also the opportunity to speak and to ask questions. She's been going to evening school but told me that there is not much opportunity to question the teacher because there are so many other people in the class.

At Ndejje, after weeks of increasingly dramatic pain and fatigue, Jake and Amy, William Mutema, Frances, Rose, and I agree that I need more sustained medical care than I can get in Kampala. I reach Nairobi on 28 June and spend the next twelve days visiting a range of doctors, clinics, and labs. Numerous Kenya MCC-ers live in Nairobi, and the Mennonite Guest House sees a regular flow of MCC-ers from across East Africa. My stay in Nairobi bears no relation to Ndejje's "local living conditions," but (despite my conscience) I relish the ready access to engaged, extended, thought-provoking conversations . . .

Letter #29 to Mom and Dad   3 July 1987

It's now been confirmed that I do not have AIDS, I do not have amoebas, I do not have multiple sclerosis, tick fever, tuberculosis, or toe jam; I do not have bilharzia and I do not have lint in the belly button. What I have is a throat infection, a urinary tract infection, and a cough so rasping it turns heads on crowded buses. Dr. D——utterly rejects the stress theory, seems certain the urinary infection alone could be the cause of fever, fatigue, and muscle pain, and strongly recommends lots of liquids, lots of medication, lots of rest, and no unnecessary talking.

Wait, "no unnecessary talking"!? What on earth is "no unnecessary talking" with all these lovely empathic people so close by?

Letter #39 from Mom and Dad [cont.]

On my very first night at Khoune's house, two representatives of the New Apostolic Church came around asking why Khoune hadn't been in church and her children not in Sunday School? She was rather evasive in her answers. I got the impression that these folks work quite a lot with refugees. A few weeks later Khoune and her husband showed pictures of Vientiane, Laos's capital, and of course the Buddhist temple and the yearly celebration there. I questioned them a bit and of course they are Buddhist. I wondered if the New Apostolic guys understand that and how hard they've pushed at converting them.

It reminded me again how much easier it was for us to fit into Canadian society, as immigrants, not being a racial minority and thus more of an oddity and subject to prejudice. There was also the added advantage of a culture based on the Christian religion and our common "source book," so to speak, the Bible, and how hearing it preached about and being able to relate to it helped to improve our language learning.

At more or less the same time, that is, Mom and I are sorting through the differences—and the different differences—between identification and privilege. All my life I've treasured and learned from my mother's curiosity about the world, especially her interest in spiritual questing, religious belief, and the relationships between religious practice and political action. I love that Mom would've been as eager to engage the Kenyan disciples of Holy Shipwreck Wilderness in nuanced theological discussion as she was energized by discovering Khoune's family's Buddhist traditions.

Letter #29 to Mom and Dad [cont.]

In semi-related news, two tremendous books: Obasan, by Joy Kogawa, but don't read the ending before going to bed because you'll never get to sleep, and The Riddle of Violence, by Kenneth Kaunda. Kaunda is the President of Zambia, a Christian, and a one-time pacifist, who writes in part to explain why he has abandoned that position (Kaunda's government actively supported the Zimbabwean Freedom Fighters and continues to aid in the struggle for a just South Africa). A must-read for anyone who claims to be a pacifist and a Christian, especially Westerners who haven't entirely thought through collective resistance to systemic injustice, but who believe, nevertheless, that they've got the right to say and judge what goes on on this continent.

The medical tests are inconclusive, but they rule out many unpleasant conditions. In a number of extended conversations, Nairobi-based friends wonder whether Frances and I might work more fully to our potentials if we lived separately at Nde-jje and could, by doing so, deepen our independent connections to the community. In Canada, Beppe's excessive drinking continues to distress my mother and her sisters. As has become typical, Mom repeats information in case letters go missing.

Letter #43 from Mom and Dad   *18 August 1987*

As you know, Beppe's liked her drink for a long time already, certainly since before Pake died. Over the years as her arthritis and deafness became worse and her isolation increased and her dependence on others, she began to drink more, and more often, and got to the point of putting away at least two 26 oz. bottles of whisky per week. Eta bought one for her every Thursday after they'd been out for brunch, but unbeknownst to Eta, Louie bought her another on Fridays when he did her grocery shopping. And Louie didn't know about "Eta's bottle."

Beppe de Jong wasn't an easy woman to like. Reserved, demanding, and emotionally manipulative, she understood herself to have been a victim of fate. She was, not by her choice, the mother of ten children, and she'd had at least two miscarriages, which means she'd been pregnant a minimum of twelve times. Like many women of her own and previous generations, Beppe de Jong *was* a victim of fate—fate, biology, patriarchy, and economics, and in Beppe's case, medical misinformation as well. She was no one's idea of a doting, cuddly grandma. She was smart as a tack and—despite failing eyesight and hearing—easily as intelligent, if not as intellectual, as my much-vaunted Pake de Jong. Mom's forty-third letter speculates that Beppe's experiences at a granddaughter's wedding in Calgary had catalyzed the drinking bout. My cousin had done a beautiful job of honouring my grandmother's presence, seated her at the head table, introduced her in speeches, and included her in most of the photographs. After royal treatment in Calgary, Beppe's return to ordinary life in Winnipeg had been a shock.

Letter #43 from Mom and Dad [cont.]

We thought things were more or less under control as she went back into her own suite, but on Saturday night at 1:30 a.m. she called me; she'd fallen down again. She called some people in the block to let me in, and when I got there, they said this was the third time they helped Beppe up that day.

She wasn't hurt very much at all except for some bruises, but I was upset and angry I'll admit. Next morning I took her home with me; she was rather shaky, which is hardly a wonder, after drinking two 26 oz. bottles of whisky over two days. She admits that she drinks, and drinks too much, and is in effect alcoholic. It is of course because of loneliness and boredom and partly because it dulls the pain in her knees. She says as long as she's around someone she doesn't feel the need to drink.

But now we have the problem of where she's going to live. None of us has enough room or the proper facilities, she can't go back to her suite because the same thing will happen, and she dreads going into a nursing home and we hate to think of putting her there.

So many versions of what does and doesn't constitute home. While I'm in Nairobi, Claire and Hugh Fisher endure an attempted armed robbery and leave Ndejje for good the next day. Their permanent departure shocks us all and is especially strange to me, this far from home. I never get a chance to bid the Fishers farewell, but their rehabilitated house on the college grounds is suddenly available. If I want to live independently, I can. I'm still being treated for acute bronchitis when I move into the Fishers' smart little cottage on 22 July 1987, eager to re-establish connections with the community.

Letter #33 to Mom and Dad   *28 August 1987*

And that interruption was a visit from the neighbourhood rapscallions! These aren't the Mulengas' well-behaved grandchildren, these are the ragamuffins you've encountered in connection to a request for soap, recorded amidst considerable chagrin and guilt and uncertainty. As far as I can tell, there's no mother in the picture, but their Pop lives up on this side of the hill, and he has almost certainly hocked every single pencil, school book, and bit of soap he managed to finagle from the Fishers. "Soap to wash the children's clothes," the old reprobate says, and they get dirtier every day—

Several months ago, though, after stealing twice and being caught both times, he was officially banished from the village. Unofficially, and beforehand, he was severely beaten, which our friends called common practice when we looked shocked; thieves must be beaten. Ethics, morals, and other common practices aside, it did mean that Claire and Hugh were spared Lassiter's repeatedly devious requests and daily visits from his offspring. I had wondered briefly whether Lassiter might've been part of the attempted robbery, but until I almost tripped over two little bodies reclining against my house, I hadn't given the family much thought. I've made up for it since.

Imagine a stocky little boy, about eight; his fine-boned little sister looks maybe six and feather-light; their older sister, Connie, is probably ten, rib-thin, and always serious, a child's gaze on a world unforgivably old—she has smiled three times in the last two weeks. They're filthy-clothed ragamuffins, but their brains work fine; it hasn't taken more than an hour of careful scrutiny to realize that House 2A is occupied once again.

"There's one born every minute!" I can almost hear them think, and I imagine the conspiratorial nod they

*gave and the scurrying to stretch themselves out, stomachs
on my top porch step, grubby noses on what was the clean
glass (dang kids) of my front door. We exchange as many
pleasantries as our limited languages allow, but they don't
waste a lot of time:*

*"Water." It's stated like a fact. "And bananas."
Oooohooo, we're getting brave. "And nuks," they chirp
hopefully.*

*"You are nuks," I inform them and they smile, a unison,
unanimous yes. "I do not have bananas" (an outright lie,
but I remember Claire telling me that she'd have a banana
with the children every afternoon, and I'd rather not
reconvene that habit), "and I do not have nuts" (which is
true-ish and pronounced with excruciating care, by which
I mean, I haven't yet roasted the groundnuts I have), "but I
do have water for you," I answer, capitulating to something
intangible and almost lost, deep in their dark eyes.*

*For the next few days the children appear regularly,
sometimes in the singular, mostly in combinations of two,
and since I still haven't roasted any nuts, all they get for
their angelic smiles is water. One day when it's just Robbie and
Harriet, I pour it cold, straight from the fridge, and my reward
is their exuberant enjoyment, huge, teeth-clenched grins,
vigorous head shaking, infinitesimal sips, more head shaking,
contagious hilarity. That Saturday the two little girls arrive
just as I'm heading out to dig in my garden. This is something
they clearly haven't counted on, and their faces show their
astonishment: "The white lady knows how to use a hoe?"*

*Harriet wants to do it for me, and is puzzled when I
won't let her take the handle. She stands back and watches
me begin, they both watch, patently unsure about what
they're seeing, and it isn't until I stop and talk again that
their smiles reappear. They might as well work as watch, I
think to myself, and—knowing I've got freshly roasted nuts
in the pantry—I demonstrate how they might help. In no*

time, they're flitting through the yard, pulling at random clumps of grass in a credible burst of wild abandon, but it isn't destructive and it's keeping them busy. Twenty giggling minutes later, we're all slowing down and the suspense, I think, has begun to take its toll. It's certainly about as much weed hacking as my back can stand, and I call a time out while I head into the house—

"Water and groundnuts!! Ooooooooeeeebaby, we've struck paydirt!" their faces say when I come back out, and I laugh. I eat and drink with them first, and they're delightfully, extravagantly polite, nibbling the nuts one by one, or in tiny handfuls of two. When I take up my hoe again though, they eat considerably faster or stick the nuts into pockets I haven't noticed. One way or the other, it's only seconds till the bowl is empty and they're waving the equivalent of kisses as they breeze past me, "Bye-bye mummy," ever so sweet, and they really are incorrigible little beggars, I think, grin-shaking my head.

Letter #43 from Mom and Dad [cont.]

Mostly, it has been very time consuming and a bit embarrassing. I'm sure that at least half the population of Beppe's apartment knows what's going on and they're having a wonderful time gossiping. When Beppe is sober she's very pleasant to have around; she reads the newspaper, is still interested in current affairs, gets annoyed with the Conservatives and loves to talk, especially about the past which can be quite fun. She's also always very interested in what's happening with you.

Letter #33 to Mom and Dad [cont.]

The next afternoon, Connie reappears holding a small papaya. Shy and so terribly serious, self-conscious of the English she hasn't mastered, she doesn't say a word. I'm suspicious that this is Pop's first attempt to eke out a bit of new cash from House 2A, and so, after determining that yes, indeed, the papaya is for me, and although it's a gross cultural faux pas, I ask how many shillings.

Connie shakes her head. I assume she means she doesn't know the number in English, and so I ask again, thinking in child-psych mode that if I'm sufficiently encouraging, she'll tell me in Luganda. "Naut shillings," she says this time. "Naut shillings? Nought shillings? Naught shillings? Nat shillings?" I'm really not sure what she's said; it could be a number I haven't learned yet, I think vaguely. "Wait," I tell her, "I will bring a paper." Thinking she'll at least be able to write the number. What she writes breaks my heart. Reflection first, and then careful childish paper-carving: "Sak you"

Not shillings.

holy shipwreck (1)

My mother worshipped her father and only dutifully loved her mother. I identify deeply with my mother and learn early on the distance between worship and duty, so I'm startled on the afternoon that Mom and I read Beppe's letters to me in Uganda. I hadn't remembered the warmth with which Beppe wrote, the poignant, bilingual urging in her first letter—"Don't cry Kathleen *as't dizze brief krigest.* I cry a little when I am writing this letter"—and the open affection with which she signed off. "Dear girl," Beppe calls me at the end of all three of the letters, and she assures me each time that she is sending me much love. That she does so in Frisian, a language not notable for its endearments, astonishes me.

But I'm also startled by the affection Mom expresses for the mother she remembers as we read. "That's amazing that you still have it!" Mom says when we make it to the end of the first letter, and she repeats her delight fifteen minutes later. "It's kind of neat that you've still got this," she muses, reading Beppe's claim that as long as a person is healthy, they can get used to anything. When we reach the second letter's conclusion—"Kathleen my girl, now I'm going to stop; much love from Beppe"—Mom's voice is bright. "Isn't that sweet," she says, and says again when we finish reading Beppe's third and final letter, "Isn't that sweet." And "*Jah,*" she adds then, answering herself, a rare tenderness in her voice, "that's very nice. That's very nice."

Ten months later, on Friday 12 December 2008, the day we spend upstairs with Mom's books, I will hear the same rare tenderness. After reading from the journal she kept twenty-six years previously, about a memory from seventy years in the past, Mom remembers another story about the strict schoolteacher who forbade her to write with her left hand.

"Did I also tell you about, the same woman," she asks, and explains, "Mom had always a nice Sunday dress on for...for church, and that lady did too, and they were sort of...sort of the same, but different material, and I would feel the different material. I stood behind them, because...because it was quite full in the house when we were all at home; she never noticed; and I would feel the material of their dresses, because...because I wanted to find out that Beppe's was the softest..."

~~~~

At about the same time that Mom and I finished reading Beppe's final letter on Friday 22 February 2008, and just two blocks away, my sister-in-law Cynthia bundled baby Harry into his stroller and hurried ten blocks east to a local medical clinic. The substitute doctor Cynthia had seen a few days earlier was kind, but he'd minimized Harry's symptoms and sent them home with instructions for monitoring a simple flu. Certain that something significantly more serious was wrong, Cynthia booked a second appointment, insisting that this time they see their own GP. Henry left work early to join them at the clinic. Within minutes of beginning his exam, the doctor discovered a tight, hard growth on the right side of Harry's abdomen. "Go home," he told them, "put some things in a bag, then head directly to Children's Hospital. They'll be expecting you," he said, reaching for his phone.

Over the previous several weeks, happy-go-lucky Harry— who'd been pulling himself up on furniture since January in first attempts at walking—had lost his appetite and his infectious joie de vivre. He'd been christened Hendrik after my father's father, though we used "Hendrik" and "Harry" interchangeably, settling most often on "Prince Harry" for this sweet-hearted, smiling boy, a spring child, born with remarkable ease the previous April. Even after Harry's adored father—my "little" six-foot-three brother Henry—returned from a business trip to India, Harry hadn't recovered his easygoing interest in food or play. "It's probably just the flu," my parents and I agreed at the end of that fateful Friday afternoon, not yet aware of the turn our lives had taken. "Little kids get the flu all the time."

Henry phones with updates from the hospital on Friday evening, several times on Saturday, and first thing Sunday morning. When he calls again on Sunday afternoon, I stand in the late-winter sunlight that pours into our porch trying to make sense of his words. Harry's medical team has confirmed stage 4 metastasized liver cancer, with secondary cancers in both of his lungs and in his lymph nodes. "But Harry's a *baby*," I object silently. My parents reach the hospital before Gareth and I do, dowdy in their years-old winter coats, stoic. Dad is recovering from prostate cancer, slowly. Mom's face contorts with the effort of staying connected to our shifting new reality. Henry and Cynthia are meeting with the doctors. Friends arrive with groceries. Sandy reaches us, breathless, lets us know that Harry's four-year-old sister Lydia is still blissfully unaware, deep in "pretend" across the city with her cherished cousin Gwyneth. By the time the meeting ends, we are eight and crammed around a still-sleeping Harry in a room that smells of smoke. It's Sunday 24 February 2008.

For eleven days Harry's doctors work with a preliminary diagnosis of hepatoblastoma, an extremely uncommon childhood liver cancer, but they've sent biopsied tissue to Baylor University in Texas for confirmation. On 3 March 2008, after writing multiple email updates every day to a growing list of addresses, Gareth and I set up a blog that we call "Harry's Journey." On Thursday 6 March 2008, specialists at Baylor send conclusive results: Harry doesn't have a hepatoblastoma, he has a primary rhabdoid tumour, an almost inconceivably rare form of cancer. Privately, at home, Gareth reads out loud from the medical websites that come up when he googles "childhood rhabdoid tumours." When he reaches the word "lethal," I ask him to stop.

Harry's journey (1)

Monday 3 March 2008

Monday morning update

I'm very happy to report that Harry responded well to yesterday's blood transfusion and enjoyed a restful night, something he more than deserved after a busy medical day. Today, a scan of his kidneys will give his medical team an indication of how his body will react to the chemo. The full biopsy report is not yet in, but expected at any moment. At this point, Henry's planning to spend both Monday and Tuesday nights at the hospital so Lydia can have some much-needed time with her Mom. More very soon.

Wednesday 5 March 2008

Reiki for Harry

We got to Harry's peaceful room this evening to find our friend M—— wrapped in a prayer shawl and doing Reiki on the beautiful boy. Harry was calm and utterly engaged in the loving energy flowing through him. He's had a very good day, hasn't needed morphine since the morning, and has remained comfortable throughout. Recent test results indicate that his kidneys and his heart are strong and functioning well. We're still waiting for the biopsy results, hopefully completed soon by top researchers in the field. A friend whose child has undergone many tests wanted us to know that a nurse once told her that sometimes when test results take longer than expected, it's because doctors are checking for the absence of something, not its presence. That offers considerable comfort while we wait.

Thursday 6 March 2008

The pathology report is in

Henry phoned moments ago with the pathology report. Doctors at Baylor U have determined Harry does not have a hepatoblastoma, he has a primary rhabdoid tumour. Apparently rhabdoid tumours are an even rarer form of cancer: there have been just five cases in Winnipeg in the past twenty years, just one of the liver. Cynthia and Henry are relieved to finally know exactly what we and Harry are up against, but the news is surreal and leaves us shocked.

However. As Cynthia says, in broad terms, nothing is really different: Harry is in for a long fight with a pernicious disease and we will be with him for every step of the journey. To the doctors' great credit, chemo is already scheduled, starting first thing tomorrow afternoon.

Friday 7 March 2008

"Where were you guys?"

Dear friends,

Though we don't yet have an update on Harry's treatment plan, we wanted you to know that he came through surgery yesterday with flying colours. Cynthia and Henry were delayed getting back to him by the arrival of the pathology report, and when they reached the recovery room, he was already alert, greeting them with his splendidly articulate eyes and the clear message, "Hey, I'm here! Where have you guys been?"

Cynthia and Henry are checking the blog when they can and will be grateful for all your messages of support. Their world is still too topsy-turvy for now to imagine answering all the emails and phone calls that have come in, and with chemo scheduled to begin this afternoon, visits should continue to be postponed.

holy shipwreck (2)

Harry in the hospital permanently tilts the axis of our lives.
By virtue of proximity and proclivity, Gareth and I become
Harry's information hub. Family and friends from next door
and around the world need updates and want to help. Four-
year-old Lydia needs daycare, playschool, play dates, meals,
and her mother. Henry needs a leave from his demanding
job and regular assurances that this is not his fault. Cynthia
needs a change of clothes, Harry's teddy, Harry's pyjamas,
more details than the doctors can give her, her mother, and
a miracle. Laundry is organized, messages pour in and are
delivered, visitors schedule themselves, meals begin arriving.

I miss two Friday visits but phone my parents every day
that we don't see one another at the hospital. My parents both
tell me, separately, that they wish it could be them. I cannot
bear either possibility and am briefly elated at my powerless-
ness. Thank God I can't trade in this or any other cosmic
balancing act. I falter several times an hour in my attempts
to understand how this can be happening, in the physical
world of biomedical science and in any plausible metaphysical
realm. When either of my parents falters out loud, I repeat a
version of what they've taught me all my life, that our engagement with the power of divine love isn't contingent on *our*
well-being. We can't give up on God because we're the ones
suffering. By the time I've put down the phone, I have no idea
all over again what I believe.

crosswords (11)

When people say, "You are *just* like your mother," they mean that I look like her but they also mean that I sound like her when I talk (minus the Frisian accent), and that I talk about many of the same things that used to interest her. For as long as I can remember, Mom and I have shared a passion for books and reading and language (and the vagaries of language) and biblical texts and their provenances and Christian theologies and Christianity's complicated histories. We've been fascinated, separately and together, with other religious and spiritual traditions, and we've urged progressive political actions on one another, actions we've often taken together.

Letter #48 from Mom and Dad   *18 October 1987*

I am enjoying the course on "Jesus of Nazareth." We have to write a summary of one of the gospels, which is proving to be more difficult than I had anticipated. I find Professor G——not quite as erudite and eloquent as I'd like him to be, and he appears at times either nervous or irritable, or both, but then, he's human after all, just like the rest of us, and I am learning things also from him.

We tackle one another's absence in the letters that make us present even in the midst of disappointment. I'm writing, too, on 18 October, as nervously irritable as Mom's professor. Our principal is briefly on site at LIC and, as has become typical, her visit is marked by a series of arbitrary punishments, most of which involve forms of manual labour. On this particular day, twenty-five outraged students mutter and swing sharp *pangas* as they clear undergrowth from the vast, flower-filled yard in which my cottage sits. Powerless in the face of what is almost certainly unfairness, I periodically bring out cold drinking water and feel complicit in "Mrs. *Kabaka*'s" disciplinary whims—

Letter #37 to Mom and Dad   *18 October 1987*

In happier news, I'd like to report that the Luganda lessons are beginning to "take." Picked up a kilo bag of milk powder in a Kampala shop last week and asked how much. (We frequent this shop because the milk's of such good quality.) "Two hundred and fifty shillings," answered the young man behind the counter. "Whew, it's gone up," I say to Frances, shrug my shoulders, what to do? Two weeks ago it was two hundred shillings, but an increase like this isn't unprecedented. I'm searching for my bag of money when a Luganda-speaker comes in and also asks how much. Not in English.

"Kikkumi," the young man answers. One hundred. I turn only slightly, and though I'm not absolutely certain, I'd be willing to bet my first-born child that the other customer's holding up a half-kilo bag of milk. My suspicions are confirmed when he chooses a kilo bag (this sounds like a story about illegal drugs). "Bibiri," says the young man behind the counter. Two hundred. Wait a second . . .

"Oh," I say ever so coolly, having abruptly ended my search for cash, "two hundred fifty for me, but only two hundred for him." The question is implicit. The young guy is slick, though, and not easily flustered. "He was asking about a half a kilo," he explains smoothly. "Yesssssss," I say, measuring my tones, "and you told him one hundred. Kikkumi. When he asked about a whole kilo you said bibiri. Two hundred."

Silky as melted butter, the young guy says, "There are two different kinds, madam. One is more expensive and you have the last bag." I put down the bag I'm holding. I can't see

my next move clearly but as another microsecond clicks past,
I say, "That's fine. I don't want the most expensive kind. I
want the kind that man is buying."

"What would you like, madam?" This from a tiny,
sharp-eyed older woman who has appeared behind the
counter and has seen the whole thing. "I want," I say,
"exactly the same kind of milk that man is buying for two
hundred shillings." The older shopkeeper should probably
be nominated for a diplomatic post. She transfers from his
hands to mine the very bag the other man has chosen and
says only, "Two hundred shillings, madam."

By October, all our letters reference Mom and Dad's upcoming
trip, planned to coincide with the December school holiday
and my second Christmas in Africa.

Letter #48 from Mom and Dad [cont.]

It's now 7:20 p.m. and I've finished the dishes, while
listening to Jane Siberry (I found it a bit monotonous the
first time, I guess it has to grow on you) and then to my
ever-loving Supertramp (I have a one-track mind when it
comes to music, probably a sign of old age). By the time you
receive this letter, I hope to have talked to you by telephone,
but I feel I must explain on paper also why we're coming
earlier than originally planned. As I was saying (writing),
for a while I was so worried that we wouldn't be able to come
at all in December, I couldn't think of anything else, and
not sleeping very well out of sheer anxiety, so when we were
finally able to get a flight on 4 December we jumped at it.

Letter #37 to Mom and Dad [cont.]

Rose enjoys the story as much as I'd hoped, and when she
tells me that her family ran out of kerosene during a recent
power outage, I see a way to say thank you and pour out half

*my precious store. [. . .] And finally, late-breaking news, all
good: Mr. Muggulu, the angelic electrician, has been by and
I can once again turn off the water heater. I will not die by
drowning!*

I could regret that I didn't also inherit Mom's easy gift for
music, but I treasure her absurd claim of a one-track mind
because she preferred Supertramp to Jane Siberry. Mom had a
lovely alto voice and sang in the church choir for years, despite
never having formally studied music. She had a decided preference for classical, but she loved all kinds of music, including,
when she was introduced to them, the complex rhythms of
music from African cultures—perhaps not surprisingly, since
she was smitten all her life with Elvis Presley. Maybe because
she'd had so few opportunities to be a teenager she took an
active interest in the music that Sandy and I began bringing
home as our adolescent worlds expanded.

Letter #48 from Mom and Dad [cont.]

*I was looking at some atlases in the Reference Room and
found Bombo, which was quite a thrill!*

crosswords (12)

When I consider now how I am and am not "just like my mother," I'm grateful for Mom's many languages and for the languages we share, including on 12 December 2008 when our book sorting reminds us of the poem she memorized and recited for me for the first time a year ago. *"De Goede Dood"* appears almost exactly halfway through *Merijntje Gijzens*, the thick Dutch novel Mom handles with reverent care. "Oh," Mom sighs in English when she finds it, *"Merijntje Gijzens*. Every time I see that book, I think: 'Thank God for *Merijntje Gijzens*.'" And without skipping a beat, she recites the poem again, from memory, in Dutch.

Mom tries on this afternoon, as she has on other visits, to explain her ardent love for the novel, the delight she takes in the eponymous Merijntje as he grows and matures through his adventures with Flierefluiter, a gentle, existentially questing soul, a potent mentor to Merijntje (and the novel's readers) because he's been cast out by their rigid community for his iconoclastic ideas about life and God. Seven years later it occurs to me to ask Omke John, Muoike Bertha's widower, about *Merijntje Gijzens*. John shared with Bertha and my mother a passionate love of literature, including this book, a regional coming-of-age novel. The book's gone out of fashion in the Netherlands, but its appeal, for decades, was its intimate portrait of the predominantly Catholic province of Brabant. The novel's author, A. M. de Jong (no relation) was a prolific writer, explicitly socialist, anti-institutional, anti-militarist, opposed to the entrenched hierarchy of the Catholic Church, and much beloved in his day, especially for the semi-autobiographical *Merijntje Gijzens*.

"The depth and the nuance of human existence that de Jong wove into that novel would astound you," my uncle tells me. "Every page is filled with his love of the people." Omke John pauses a moment to compose himself. "De Jong," he says, "loved the people the way Jesus loves the people."

One year after Mom and I sort through her Dutch and Frisian books, she phones me at my office. "I was thinking about that poem," Mom says as soon as she hears my voice, and I know she means "*De Goede Dood.*" If you translate literally from the Dutch you get "the good death," but it's more accurate to say "beloved death," or, perhaps, "welcome and welcoming death," or "steadfast and reassuring death." The poem's speaker addresses Death as not just an inevitable but a paradoxically enriching, essential element in living, as *the* element—the presence, the fact—without which life would not be worth living. I arrive late for a meeting that day because I cannot bear to cut off my mother's recitation, still, at this point, accurate to the word.

As much she loves *Merijntje Gijzens,* Mom adores "*De Krystreis fen Broder Iwersen,*" the Frisian Christmas story that she returns to again and again in our weekly visits. Mom speaks almost as often about Erich Maria Remarque's *All Quiet on the Western Front,* the Dutch version of which she read surreptitiously when she was just twelve and credits with making her into a lifelong pacifist. Other memorable conversations hinge on Zora Neale Hurston's *Their Eyes Were Watching God;* Golda Meir's autobiography, *My Life; The Deserter's Tale,* Joshua Key's account of abandoning the American army; *Fugitive Pieces,* Anne Michaels's geologic unearthing of Holocaust trauma; Paul Collier's analysis of global poverty, *The Bottom Billion*; and Franz Kafka's *The Trial.* On 8 January 2010, my mother and I have what will be our last coherent discussion of literature, though I don't know it when I craft a long journal entry a few days later.

11 January 2010.

I get to Mom and Dad's on Friday without a clear plan for the afternoon, but the half-finished crossword puzzles on the coffee table offer poignant evidence of Mom's new losses. These days, Mom will fill in a word but not notice that the word needs more letters, or she'll squeeze two letters into one space to make a word fit, or she'll squeeze two letters into one space for no clear reason at all. Sometimes she finds the right word for one of the clues but fills it in "across" instead of "down." Of her new mistakes, the one that makes me inexplicably saddest is when she finds the word for one of the clues and then uses that word repeatedly, filling in blanks all over the puzzle with "crave crave crave" or "indigo indigo indigo." It doesn't seem that long ago that I'd still get annoyed, sitting beside her while she'd do the puzzle, certain she could do more to help herself navigate between the clues and the puzzles. "Mom!" I'd reprimand her, "you're covering the clue with your finger!"

A little more than two years have elapsed since Mom and I worked on the "Senegal" puzzle over the phone.

11 January 2010 [cont.]

Frank's arrival defines the balance of the afternoon. At first I think this will be the usual kind of interruption, "Save-Our-Seine"[11] business that Dad conducts at the door, but Dad invites this visitor in. After a few moments, Frank finds his way into the living room looking slightly confused and mildly arrogant. A clue, but I don't pick it up.

"Hello," I say warmly while Frank makes himself comfortable in Dad's chair. This is curious. No one but Dad sits in Dad's chair. Dad joins us and sits in the untrustworthy rocker but he doesn't introduce me so I introduce myself, which prompts Dad to introduce me

again, though he doesn't tell me who Frank is. "Oh,"
Frank says, "this must be the baby!?" Which prompts
Mom to wonder briefly who the baby actually is. "Who
is the baby?" she asks twice, looking mildly alarmed.
"First Sandy," she muses and then she gets herself on
track. "First Sandy, then Kathleen, you're Kathleen, then
Henry. Henry is the baby."

And then she asks me about Kafka, specifically, have
I ever read it and what did I think about it. She says "it"
and indicates a copy of The Trial that's lying on the coffee
table. The word "Kafka" is by far the largest word on the
cover of this edition. I decide not to make the distinction:
as far as Mom's concerned, she's been reading Kafka.

"I've wondered if it would be a good thing to read,"
Mom says. We siblings concluded months ago that Mom
no longer comprehends significant amounts of what she
reads, but Mom is always looking for new books. "I have
nothing new to read," she complains mildly, "I've read all
the books in the house."

Over the next half year, Mom gradually but completely loses
the ability to read books, though for a long time she will still
read aloud any text that appears as simultaneously coherent
to both her compromised vision and her cognitive processing.
Sandy and I share a bittersweet gratitude that Mom has lost
the ability to read without registering the loss, something we
had dreaded.

11 January 2010 [cont.]

We guess that her rereading goes as fast as it does because
she understands so little by now. "It's a little strange,"
Mom says now, meaning Kafka. I flip through The Trial
as I think how to answer her. "Kafka is hard going, Mom,"
I say. "Kafka's not easy to read at the best of times." I
realize I'm skimming excerpts from Kafka's journals that

have been appended to the novel; this really is strange. "Do you know what it is, Mom," I ask rhetorically, "it's absurdist. Kafka's writing could be called absurdist, and absurdist writing is never easily accessible."

Mom's response is instantaneous, intense, and glorious. "Absurdist!" she repeats turning to me with a look of translucent recognition. "Absurdist." She says it several more times. "Jah," she says, "that helps me understand. That's exactly what I needed. 'Absurdist.'"

"That's it!" says Frank, who's been listening to our exchange. He hits his forehead several times. "Drum it into her!" I frown at him. Who are you and why are you here? I think. And why would you imply that my mother needs anything "drummed into her"?

Frank offers a glimpse into a stage Mom might have passed through some time back, though Frank is clearly experiencing his failing cognition differently than Mom is hers. On two separate occasions, he searches around Dad's armchair for a piece of paper to write on. Both times he assures Dad that he won't actually write on anything. Both times, he uses his finger in lieu of a pencil to demonstrate the mistake he's sure his doctor made. "So he's just going down the list," Frank explains, "ticking boxes and—"

Frank's finger makes a series of rapid, vertical ticks, "—and then he's not paying attention, he ticks the one for 're-test.'" Frank gives a first impression of thoughtful intelligence and something I'd call, archaically, "good breeding." Even in old age, he's an almost distinguished-looking man. In the space of just a few minutes, though, he refers to three different women as "bitches." Each time he does, Mom flinches and glances over at me. I carefully do not return her look but think sternly at our visitor, "Well, Frank, we've certainly established that you're no gentleman."

> *Frank toggles between repeated claims that "that's life" and a firmly held, unselfpitying conviction that a simple series of mistakes have been made. First his doctor, in an inattentive moment, checked off "driver's retest." Then Frank failed the re-test—with only seven errors—because they weren't asking him the questions in a way he could understand. "I couldn't understand a word he said!" Frank tells us several times. Frank is so convinced of his interpretation I'm almost ready to take his side. I gather from Dad, who's in the kitchen making tea and rolling his eyes, that he's heard this story before.*
>
> *According to Frank, he failed the section on signs because they didn't show him the signs "in the same way." "I coulda got that if they'd showed me that," he insists, referring to a copy of the driver's test guide that Dad has handed him. "I coulda known those signs if they'd told me what they were." "You have to look at this computer screen," he tells us too, aghast at this newfangled technology, "but then they have these lights comin' in from all over. I told 'em, I wanna take that one verbally. If they just ask me, I'll know the answer."*
>
> *It is, according to Frank, in the same moment of inattention that his doctor ticked the box for "dementia." Just a series of small, understandable, correctible mistakes. Reversible mistakes.*
>
> *"Absurdist!" Mom has exclaimed. "That helps me understand."*

A week later, Mom is still keen to talk about *Kafka*. She seems to have forgotten our earlier conversation, but she remembers that she's discussed it in the meantime with her friend Margaret, a former teacher whom she knows through the still-vital, increasingly elderly R.A.R. group. "Margaret said it was a parody," Mom tells me, "but I think it's more sinister than that." I tell her she's hit on the perfect word to describe Kafka's writing and she repeats "sinister" at least ten times over the course of the afternoon, sometimes pronouncing it correctly, sometimes not.

Mom herself is *sinister* in the original Latin meaning of the word, "left" as distinct from "right" (*dexter* in Latin). Still a passionate "leftist," Mom is also still—in her heart and in her body—a "leftie." On this afternoon, contrary to reason and every existing biomedical image of the disease, I let myself ponder the absurd notion that my mother has Alzheimer's because sinister pedagogical forces obliged her to write and sew and draw and think with her wrong right hand and permanently ruptured crucial connections in her brain.

When the intake worker for a new respite organization concludes her visit, Mom can finally tell me more about what she's been thinking about *Kafka*. She wants to read to me from notes she's written on the inside of the back cover, but finds them baffling. "This doesn't make any sense," she says, stumbling over her disjointed phrasing, "but what I'm meaning to say is this: it seems like a kind of experiment, to see how much a person can take. Like a test. Like something they might do in a war."

post secret

post secret (1)

Geeske de Jong is born on Friday 24 January 1936 in Nijemardum, Fryslân, the Netherlands. On Friday 10 May 1940, eight months after declaring war on Poland, France, and the United Kingdom, and despite having issued the Netherlands a guarantee of neutrality six months earlier, Germany invades Holland. Hopelessly unprepared, the Dutch army surrenders five days later. Geeske is four and a half years old. This means that the sexual assaults she experienced were occurring simultaneously with the buildup to, and the declaration of, war. Almost exactly five years after the war begins, the Canadian Army liberates the areas of western Holland still under German control, and World War II—for the Dutch—is finally over. It's 5 May 1945. Geeske is nine and a half and about to stick her tongue out at the pretty little blonde-haired girl.

post secret (2)

By October 1987, Mom's letters have filled with plans for their trip to Africa. Details change frequently because it turns out to be more difficult than Mom had bargained on, getting flights to Nairobi in December. In case any of the letters go missing, Mom regularly repeats the (changing) information, but we rely for the last of the planning on Cindy, Cindy's phone, and Cindy's good nature, all in Kampala. My letters from the time document harrowing events, but they also record funny encounters, thought-provoking exchanges, deepening friendships, and a discernibly new level of integration into my home at Ndejje. By late October, I feel impressively professional, hiking the district to evaluate my students' teaching practice at distant schools, but I'm still only beginning to understand the complex lives of others.

Letter #39 to Mom and Dad   *31 October 1987*

*Halfway up the hill out of the first swamp I'm accosted
by a screaming adolescent. A shrieking adolescent. Now I
know how rock stars feel. I hear her coming for what seems
like minutes from a house set well back from the track, but
the maize is thick and high and hides her till she's almost
jumped me, grinning madly and shrieking "muzungu"
over and over, as if I'd arranged my skin colour just for her.
She's more than a bit beside herself (it's not hot enough
yet for me to be seeing double), and I stop to offer a formal
greeting, thinking it will calm her. When I do, the gestures
that seemed threatening become self-directed, her piercing
screams give way to incomprehensible babble, and she grabs*

*clumsily at her raggedy clothes. She's clearly struggling
with some sort of mental delay, but her gestures are easy to
decipher: "See how poor I am?" she asks. "Give me clothes,
give me money, give me food, give me something out of the
riches I know you have because I see so clearly that you are
muzungu."*

*I open my arms wide, palms turned upward, my personal
sign language for, "I'm sorry, I have nothing for you." "Sorry,
kid," I mutter as I walk off, irritated: "I'm not Santa Claus."*

*Not more than ten minutes later I encounter an ancient
woman who's just reaching the track from a bush trail I
wouldn't otherwise have known was there. I greet her in
Luganda and she's delighted and returns the greeting, but
as soon as my response is out, she's gesturing too, one hand
clutching the top of her grey-faded busuti, the other reaching
out in an instantly recognizable attitude of humiliation.*

*Inside I groan. "Lady," I think, "Mama, Nyaabo.[1] I've
got a sweatshirt, a rain cape, a pen, a scribbler, and a sheet of
carbon paper in my backpack. Which of those would you like?"
I repeat my lying gesture and walk off hurriedly, annoyed, first
at her for asking, annoyed all over again at the squealing teen,
annoyed at the old woman who chased me yesterday, begging
too, and finally I'm most annoyed at myself.*

*"You hate it," I think, "because it doesn't ever let you
forget how much more you have than almost anyone here.
As long as no one's begging from you, you can maintain the
illusion that you're doing without. You have five sweatshirts.
One would be lots. Chew and chew, but you can't swallow.
You have no idea what it's like to be poor."*

*I reach Nandire school without having resolved the
burden of four extra sweatshirts and promptly forget it with
less soul-searching work to tackle. First stop, the latrine,
and then off to the classrooms. By break, I've seen two very
decent lessons but it's still scary to think that in half a year
these young women will be fully-fledged members of the*

profession. At break I run face first into a stick brandished by a short hellion who has not seen me coming.

"Lousy timing, little buddy," I think, as I collar him for a succinct lecture in English (which he almost certainly can't understand) on the dangers of brandishing sticks. I'm reminded, when I release him to a wildcat dash anywhere-as-long-as-it's-away-from-the-white-lady, of Rose's fears as a little girl that she'd be eaten by a muzungu. And she likely saw many more of us Europeans than the short hellion has.

The LIC students gather around during what remains of break, and their pupils collect around them, unabashedly curious about my every move. "The children would like to play with you," says Solomey, one of our sweetest students, and I can't help grinning. I ask her if she was curious about bazungu² as a little girl, and she says she was, all my students say they were, and as a few more wander up to join us, I think they're enjoying showing their pupils how well they know me. [. . .]

I miss these girls at the college, the first group to have arrived after Frances and I did, a good-natured bunch, with a healthy sprinkling of characters among them. Betty's one of the characters, but she's gone home with malaria, so I only have one lesson after break to observe. It's a Primary One class, and two things strike me: Mary has her six-year-olds (most of them boys) immersed in their work, and she has spent what must be weeks making a fantastic collection of teaching aids. I'm blown away. No Canadian teacher working with only the resources our students have could have done better. [. . .]

I'm able to leave a little earlier than I'd expected, but the sun at noon isn't a whole lot less hot than the sun at one, so I wind my double-purpose bandana around my head, aerobics-style. By the time I reach Ndejje, my hair (recently cut back into something vaguely chic by a canny stylist in Kampala) is standing on end all around it. "Nice," I think sarcastically when I catch a glimpse of my reflection.

I devote the afternoon to making up my part of the math exams and when that's done, I need to start thinking about supper. I'm halfway through some pre-supper fumigation (having spotted cockroach relics in one of the cupboards) when Joseph the Papaya Seller hallooes from the front porch, and it seems, when I investigate, that J the PS wants more kerosene. Arghhh. I point out that I've given him rather a lot of kerosene in the last two weeks, and surely if it's not available through the Resistance Council, he must have other friends he could borrow from. J the PS insists it isn't and he hasn't and he can't and that he's walked a long way today in search of kerosene. This is unassailably true: I caught up with him at Nandire and he was going still further. He also promises that the next papayas will be free of charge.

I'm not sure why I bother to say I have very little left when I know I'll give him some till I'm down to my last refill. While he's pouring he has the nerve to tell me that the beans I gave him yesterday were the wrong kind. They were beans for eating. He wanted beans for planting. "Well, buster," I tell him in more or less these words, "you might have mentioned that before. How the heck am I supposed to know you wanted beans for planting?!" The point is taken with considerable aplomb, and he agrees that next time he asks, he'll tell me the kind of beans he wants!

It's an hour later and I'm up to my elbows in lemon juice when Daniel bicycles up with what looks like mail (hurray), but turns out to be the magazines he's returning. He hasn't got time for tea, he tells me, though he stays quite a while for a man in a hurry. We banter as we always do, and he notes that my recent walks to Nandire are turning me red.

"But it looks very nice," he adds quickly, "when you are a bit red," and glances at his own brown-black arm as if for verification. Certainly better than slug-white, I retort (not in exactly those words), and we both laugh. Unfortunately, he has some less than lighthearted news: there's an as-yet-

*undiagnosed problem with the water pump, and our roof
tanks won't be filled again for some time. [. . .]*

*One hour later yet, I'm maneuvering around the jerry
cans (hastily filled with water after Daniel's warning) and
the contents of the (fumigated-for-cockroaches) cupboard,
and almost ready to eat, except there's another knock at
the door. I'm teetering on the brink of irritation when I
recognize Rose in the dusk. I can't imagine not having time
for Rose. She's returning a magazine, too, and a shawl, and
says she thinks I'm busy and so won't stay, but I talk her into
a cup of tea, and she tells me about her harrowing journey
yesterday, how she was sitting in the passenger seat of a lorry
when a rock shattered the windscreen.*

*From the way she tells it, she must have panicked, but
the driver, whom she describes as "a courageous man," must
also be a gentle man, able to calm her into completing the trip
home, dark night of rapid sunset, wretched roads, and shattered
windshield notwithstanding. It's far too soon after the war for
people to manage even minor explosions. Rose is tough and
funny, electrically alive, but she is also slight and fragile-boned
and suffers headaches that are easily as bad as mine. For the
178th time since we've met, my heart goes out to her.*

After writing Letter #48 on 18 October (reporting the final,
unavoidable rescheduling of their East African holiday and celebrating having found Bombo on a map), Mom takes a break
from our correspondence in order to plan their trip's myriad
details. She doesn't write again until after she and Dad return
to Canada at the end of December.

Letter #40 to Mom and Dad   *7 November 1987*

*After the fact, you say to yourself, I knew it, I felt it,
some second-sight sense that something about today was
different. But that's after the fact. Before the fact, it's been
a good day so far. I've had enough energy for both of the*

evaluations I scheduled, and completed both by noon. [. . .]
After writing after lunch, the weather clears enough for a
walk, so I tramp off [. . .]. Not far from the college I catch
up with Alice, our new typist, who tells me she's away to
Kampala for the weekend, and she expects the bus in, oh,
not too long—

This is good to know. Our bus, an extraordinary boon
to the community and only two weeks old, already has a
reputation as a pretty damn reckless old thing. Knowing it's
imminent heightens my senses and I walk with an eye out
for spots to duck into. I'm almost at the halfway point when
an enormous army lorry speeding toward Ndejje forces me
into thick grass far taller than I am. I'm well off the track as
it passes, but it's so wide I could've reached out and touched
it. "Holy crap," I think, "that is damn dangerous now that
we've got our bus."

I've reached the turnaround and am heading back
when a second speeding vehicle overtakes me. This one's
also army-lorry green but it's a van, no windows except the
heavy-grilled front one, and looks as if it serves some grim
official purpose, serves it so hastily it reminds me that my
first-aid training confers responsibility. "They can't possibly
know our bus is on its way or they'd never drive that fast," I
think, shaking my head, and then the world gasps.

One short, sucking gasp and then silence and then the
birds sing again. I feel chilly, suddenly imagining that the
van and the bus did meet, but I know I'd have heard it, the
unmistakable sound of high-speed metal meeting metal. I
walk on, surer-footed because headed this way I can see the
bus if it comes. But I hear the bus before I see it, then round
a corner at the top of a small hill to find it just beginning
its crawl past a Red Cross lorry stopped half on, half off the
wrong side of the track.

When the bus stops level with the lorry, there's no room
for anything to squeeze by, so I duck into a bare patch about

fifty yards from the two vehicles. Ten yards from me, a young boy's done the same. The waiting stretches into minutes, and I think, from its laborious sounds, that the bus is stuck, half off the road. The boy moves back to join me. By now the shivered sense of unease has returned—the two drivers are not just passing the time of day and if the bus were stuck, the passengers would've been out by now pushing.

Taking a chance that my bare-patch friend knows a little English, I ask him what the matter is. I decide that my friend understands but he's limited by a small vocabulary, because he replies, "There is a boy dying there," and gestures to the place beyond the bus.

No, I'm telling myself, that has to be wrong, there's someone sick and that's the reason the Red Cross is here in the first place, and they're just delayed getting the patient loaded onto the lorry, and the bus driver is just checking to see if there's any way he can help, but I'm already walking again, faster now because a hollow sound inside me says there really is a boy dying . . .

The bus inches back into motion as I do and the passengers and I peer at one another, searching for some sort of explanation, because surely dear Jesus that is a small body prone beyond the bus, and an agitated crowd all around. I'm almost running now, but not too fast to notice that no one is actually near the boy. What does that mean, I wonder, in the midst of incoherent mental shrieking—they don't know first aid, or is he already dead? I reach them scouring their faces, battle down the conditioned pulse-taking response because I feel my strangeness here so strongly—

"Who can tell me what has happened?" I implore, "Who can explain in English?" and an older man with an aura of responsibility approaches and explains that the boy was travelling on the top of the lorry, the lorry hit a bump, and the boy was thrown off.

"Is he dead?" I ask, praying that he isn't dying, and my right leg shakes so uncontrollably I will myself not to

collapse. I've seen the boy, and he's crumpled with his face
mercifully turned toward the bushes, but I know you don't
lose that much blood from minor head injuries. Dear God,
I think, so self-centred I want to weep, let him be dead,
because otherwise I'll have to give him first aid.

He is dead, they tell me conclusively.

A young man is hacking off branches and placing them
at metre intervals behind and ahead of the boy, the road sign
that something is amiss. The responsible man and another
man pilot the Red Cross lorry, and after a few more minutes
of consultation, they drive off, for Bombo and the police, the
two phrases in their rapid Luganda I understand. I stand
and watch with the others, because... because you can't just
leave the presence of the dead. I stand and watch and listen,
and an elderly woman with whom I regularly exchange
traditional greetings surprises me in English:

"He was a very naughty boy," her eyes flash on him, and
then back to me, and she adds, "to be so high on the lorry
and then the bump, and then"—she snaps her hands in an
infinitesimally short clap, then spreads them, palms down—
"dead. This one," she indicates another young boy of maybe
nine at her side, "had just climbed down. Lucky. Maybe he
would be dead too."

Just one of myriad existential imbalances. Death
here is as riveting as death at home, and accidental death
more so, augmented by the compulsion to live and relive
our experience of it. I can't understand the words, but the
gestures and the tones of voice are like their own language,
as first one and then another person in the crowd recounts
what they saw, what they heard, who's to blame, who's
responsible. I stand in the elephant grass and hug myself and
discover that a man on a bicycle beside me speaks enough
English to explain the boy died when he hit the ground.
I desperately want him to be right or I'll flog myself with
the possibility that if I'd hurried when the world gasped,
I could've been here to help. The man on the bicycle also

tells me that the boy is from Sambwe. We were in Sambwe once, for Liberation Day celebrations, a village about five kilometres into the bush southwards. Someone has gone there to inform them, he adds.

I'm alienated in and by my wonder. What does this event mean here, where so much violent death has come and gone in waves of incomprehensibility? What is young death here, where children younger still die of diarrhea and whooping cough and typhoid, and children not much older carry machine guns? How is the loss of a child measured here, where so many children die young, where children are rarely, past infancy, accorded anything we would recognize as physical manifestations of affection? The dead boy is about the size of one of Rose's younger brothers, and he'd be one to perch precariously on the rungs of a speeding lorry. What would I say to her if he were the one dead? What would she say to me?

The crowd ebbs and flows. New spectators appear, shake their heads, ask their questions, offer their opinions, and others disperse, to spread the news or get on with the day. It's okay, I sense, after what must be almost thirty minutes, to leave now, and I do, alone and cold, with the eloquent gesture held in my mind: hands brought together in one sharp clap, arms flung apart, palms down, paused for the briefest of moments. A life over.

[. . .] Frances drops by late in the afternoon with the kind invitation to come down any time I want to talk. "Just a few days ago," she says wonderingly, "I started a journal entry with the sentence, 'Children die here.' At home you always think of children as having their whole lives ahead of them, but here that just isn't always the case." We'd learned earlier in the week that a pupil of one of our students had died, completely unexpectedly, from typhoid. No one—school, parents, medical personnel—had thought the little girl's illness was that serious.

*[. . .] I can't stop thinking about the boy on the lorry and
I can't stop thinking about all my students over the years.[3]
It's true, children die here, but children die at home too, of
neglect and malnutrition and drowning and cancer and
suicide attempts, too many die, on reserves and in inner
cities, to imagine that the two-thirds world has a monopoly
on unspent lives. If we think of this place as distinct from
home because it's where children die young, I'm afraid we'll
stay blind to all the injustices of "home."*

In just four more weeks, Mom and Dad will reach Uganda. "We
live so long with the incredible," I tell them, "it's not hard at all
for me to believe you're here." Twenty years and three months
later, I reassess what is and is not credible.

Harry's journey (2)

Saturday 8 March 2008

Chemo has begun

Dear friends:

As of 4 p.m. yesterday, Cynthia and Henry have a detailed treatment plan for the first chemo cycle and a working plan for the second cycle. Harry had enjoyed a calm day yesterday at the point that cycle #1 began. At latest word, all is well. [. . .] In logistical news, I invite anyone interested in providing food-support to leave their contact information in a comment to this entry.

Tuesday 11 March 2008

Harry's Room of Healing

Harry has come through the first round of chemo in good shape, thanks to the excellent care he's receiving and all the loving prayers and healing thoughts you send. J—— and Auntie C—— gave Harry's spirits and ours a very big boost when they secretly transformed his room on Sunday evening. "Harry's Room of Healing" is bathed in sunlight, organized for efficiency and comfort, and decorated in early modern cheeriness and delight. Your cards and notes are up on the walls, stuffed animals vie for the pleasure of cuddling with Harry, and bright colours everywhere light up the room.

Thursday 13 March 2008

Post-chemo update for Harry

Thank you all for keeping us in your thoughts and prayers [. . .]. Harry finished his first round of chemo on Tuesday and his oncology team is pleased with the way he's managing the effects. Cynthia and Henry confirm that he's suffering minimal nausea and has lost a considerable amount of the weight associated with fluid retention, which means he can be off oxygen for the first time in more than a week!

Saturday 15 March 2008

Please, no visitors for the time being

Dear friends,

As we expected, Harry's resistance to infection has been seriously compromised by the chemo. As a result, Cynthia and Henry are requesting that, for the time being, no one visit the hospital. We'll keep you posted as Harry's strength returns. Many thanks for all your care . . .

post secret (3)

Two days after the specialists at Baylor send Harry's biopsy results, Mom and I have tea downtown before attending a play. Two and a half years earlier, after spending the summer reeling in the wake of Mom's diagnosis, I decide that season's tickets to the theatre will offer us multiple opportunities to keep our minds sharp together, especially if we debrief afterward.

On 8 March 2008, we share a dessert before the play while I try, unsuccessfully, to get Mom to talk about Harry's illness. Mom feels acutely self-conscious as her formerly lucid self steals off, and she abandons several attempts to put words to her intense anxieties about Harry. So I tell her about a theory Gareth and I have heard from a friend who's a nurse. According to our friend, infants don't experience nearly the range of negative effects from chemotherapy that children and adults do because infants don't yet have a cognitive framework for anticipating consequences. Mom listens closely and tells me, "I *think* I understand what you're saying," and then grows animated when I tell her about the drumming we've been doing in healing circles for Harry.

Over the past decade, Mom has become quietly interested in North American Indigenous spirituality. "Isn't that what the original...the Aboriginal people also do," she asks intently, "drum?" I answer yes, and we talk about drumming in musical cultures around the world. "And it's also for, to con...con...com...communi...communitate," Mom struggles to say and corrects herself impatiently. "It's *not* 'communitate.' *Communicate* with other tribes or other people," she clarifies and adds, "and by the drum they know what the urgency is..."

Facing her beloved grandchild facing chemo, my once jaun-tily articulate mother struggles for the first time ever to say *communicate*. Stitches in my heart snap, threaten to unravel.

I resume my regular visits the next Friday, 14 March 2008. Mom is furious with Dad and storming out of the house as I arrive. She pauses long enough to tell me that Dad has criti-cized the (dishevelled) sandwiches she made for their lunch and that she cannot fathom how he can focus on such a minor detail while, as she says, "Our grandson is fighting for his life." It's a distressing interlude that confirms for me that Mom is never *not* worried about Harry. It also gives Dad and me some rare privacy. By early 2008, Dad is handling more and more of the telephone contact with us "kids," especially when logistics need arranging, but Mom regularly listens in, ready to take offense at our questions or Dad's responses. When Dad's sis-ter Griet calls from the Netherlands for an update on Harry, Dad's careful, heart-wrung side of the conversation lets me in on how he's managing these layers of crisis.

Thirty minutes later, Mom returns. She's no longer urgently angry and asks me to tell her again the latest news from the hospital, so I repeat what I said earlier: we need to discourage visitors for now, but Harry continues to recover well from his first round of chemo. Mom processes the information this time and agrees with my assessment. "That's good," she says, "that's very good." I don't want to trouble her yet with more details, so we sit quietly till I remind her that we need to finish the application for a MedicAlert bracelet. We started the application on 22 February, the afternoon we read Beppe's letters.

"Oh yes," Mom says then with conviction, "*that* I remember, I remember that quite well," and I'm surprised when she also remembers her affectionate response. "Those letters were—" Mom adds and pauses. "I was actually quite touched," she says quietly. When I reiterate the letters' value to me, Mom agrees. "Beppe was a pretty smart woman, you know," she notes emphatically. "I was explaining that to Vivian, that...that my mother had worked in an, ah...a hospital, for people with dementia."[4]

I struggle to keep up with this mother of mine. Until now, it was always clear. My mother did her duty by her mother and adored her father, understood the two of them to have enjoyed a unique bond, always believed that she, of the ten children, was most like him: bookish, scholarly, and ready, in an instant, for a debate, ideally a fiery one, ideally about the nuanced imperatives of progressive Christianity. As the months of our conversations unfold, I come to suspect that my mother also experienced intense and intensely repressed resentment about two of her parents' most significant decisions: the decision to immigrate to Canada just at the point when she would otherwise have gone on to higher-level studies, and, earlier, their rackingly wrong allegiances during the Second World War. Well, Pake's.

I don't think my mother could bear to imagine her beloved father as responsible for such vast errors. She was, after all, "just like" Pake, and of course, Pake was the one who discovered that she was being abused. If Beppe hadn't pulled Pake away from the boy, Pake might've beaten him to death, but that is never the point of the story. What I suspect is that my mother focused her anger on her mother's shortcomings and actively suppressed her rage at her father's contradictions. In a funny way, it makes perfect sense; she'd inherited the rage from her father too.

In the middle of March 2008, Mom remembers clearly that her grandmother encouraged her mother and her aunts to go into nursing, but what she really wants to tell me about is how much she and her siblings disliked their maternal grandparents. "We didn't like them!" Mom says emphatically and repeats herself in case I haven't understood. "We *didn't* like them." And a story that is not exactly a secret emerges again, a story I've known for as long as I can remember, though I don't yet understand its potent, contorting effect on my mother's life.

My mother's grandparents were, by all accounts, unpleasant people: rigid and narrow in their thinking, crass in their dealings with their grandchildren, exacting, critical, spiteful, mean in at least two senses of the word, and pro-German, including, unabashedly, for the whole of the Second World War. My great-grandparents were so pro-German that they joined the NSB, the *Nationaal-Socialistische Beweging*, a fact that acquires increasing horror the more I learn. The National Socialist Movement in the Netherlands was founded in 1931 on a program based on Italian fascism and German national socialism. In 1941, after outlawing all socialist and communist parties the year before, the German regime declared the NSB the Netherlands' only legal political party. Under Anton Mussert's leadership, the NSB actively collaborated with the occupying forces and the consequences were catastrophic. Despite a nationwide strike in February 1941 to protest the first deportation of Dutch Jews, and the Catholic Church's public condemnation of the collaborationist government, the Netherlands, by the end of the war, had the highest per capita Jewish death toll of any Western European country.

Dutch resistance to the Nazi occupation was effective over the long term, taken up at first by small, decentralized cells. Members sabotaged phone lines and railways, forged ration cards, counterfeited money, distributed food, prepared maps, and collected intelligence. Resistance-authored assassinations of collaborators and attacks on German troops prompted harsh reprisals against civilian populations. A. M. de Jong, for instance, who'd written *Merijntje Gijzens*, my mother's favourite novel, was arrested by the Germans in 1942 because of his openly socialist convictions and released shortly afterward because of his poor health. One year later, Dutch SS-ers shot and killed him in his home in retaliation for murders, by the Dutch Resistance, of several prominent NSB-ers.

All my life, my mother underscored the fact that her parents never joined the NSB, but Pake was pro-German until very near the war's end, until long after anyone who wanted to could know what was happening in the camps to which over a hundred thousand Dutch Jews had been deported. Pake read German literature with deep pleasure, spoke German fluently, including with the German soldiers who came into his store, but—my mother repeats it for years, long before we begin recording our conversations—Pake *d-i-d-n-o-t-e-v-e-r* join the NSB.

Later I understand more clearly: it was Beppe who made sure that never happened.

post secret (4)

Letter #40 to Mom and Dad [cont.]

This is likely the last you'll hear from me before we meet at Entebbe![5] Have just received your #46 and 47, Sandy's #7 and 8, and Henry's latest unnumbered wonder, an unprecedented haul. Have also just purchased three Kenya Airways tickets, Entebbe–Nairobi for 9 December. This is going to happen!

Before it happens, I begin dreaming. LIC's teaching schedule frees up significant stretches of time, and Jake and Amy encourage Frances and me to develop locally focused projects during school breaks. They've wondered if I might direct my interest in women's lives (and my perpetual writing) to collecting women's stories of conflict. What I'd like most is a project Rose and I could work on together.

Letter #11 to Lil & Roxanne   *28 November 1987*

Everything about these three years will have been worth it because I got to know Rose. [. . .] Her name, "Nakato," signifies how special she is, as a twin in this culture, which reveres twins. [. . .] At twenty-nine she has two children and doesn't live with either father. She's so tiny that both girls had to be delivered by C-section, but she says still the doctors in Kampala pressure her to have another baby because she has no boys.

* "Here it's better to have boys," she answers my skeptical eyebrows. "There were too many killed in the war." We leave*

*the topic and return to it, and I refuse to be convinced, can't
hide my pleasure when she announces that one of her sisters
has had another baby, a girl this time.*

*"Why is that good?" she interrogates, and I grin and
tell her, "If I ever have children, I'll want girls." Her stern
features crinkle into a reflective smile. "Father is the same,"
she says. "He has always wanted to have girls most."*

*Rose takes after her father, is similarly, quietly, defiant
of rigid social structures. Here, children belong to their
fathers. That translates as: if the father chooses to accept
responsibility, he has 100 percent final say in the details of
his child's life and can, without censure or legal obligation,
take the child away from her mother. [. . .] And if he chooses
not to acknowledge responsibility, there's no one to chase
him down for support.*

*These days, with more than five women for every man,
many men are reverting to traditional polygamy. Church
weddings, by contrast, define clear societal parameters and
work, for a change, to the woman's advantage, because they
bind husbands legally to support their children. But they're
astonishingly expensive propositions, and so most men
establish "wives" in various places and father numerous
offspring.*

*Rose's second baby stays with the baby's father in
Masaka, three or four hours from here and the AIDS capital
of Uganda. Rose can't afford the special food the baby
needs, but the father can, and he's pressured Rose to move to
Masaka too. But she's afraid of AIDS, has to let her daughter
go, and worries now for the child she can't watch out for.*

*"Would you ever marry the father?" I ask, feeling almost
weightless it's so nice to be this straightforward. "Hah," Rose
practically snorts. "No." She could not be more definite.*

*"He wanted me to come that way," she adds, "but I
fear AIDS too much. So he got angry with me. He has
other worries there too. Co-wives." Her upper lip draws up*

in derision. She shakes her head, with the one, two, three distinct movements I've become accustomed to. "No," she says, "I won't go there, I can't compete."

I think what my independent friend means is that she won't compete. She pauses and gives her head one more reflective half-shake. "Hah!" she says, "men these days!? They don't have to have any good qualities. They think they can have as many wives as they want just because they are men," and she wrinkles her nose again in disgust.

She's amazed to hear that my mother always encouraged me not to get married [. . .] and we talk about women's lives in North America, the problems, the struggles, the violence. For her birthday I give her my "Take Back the Night" sweatshirt and a card that explains why a courageous, intelligent, independent woman here might want to wear it, and she does, almost constantly between washings. Just last week we spent the evening hooting with laughter at how the world would be different if it were men who had the babies. She tells me how badly she wanted to have an abortion when she got pregnant the second time.

I need a day to let the words sink in.

Letter #11 to Lil & Roxanne [cont.]

I thought my heart would stop when Rose said that about abortions. It hadn't occurred to me that abortion would be an option, though I realize now how naive that was. Apparently the father told Rose that he wasn't accepting responsibility or offering support and I guess she figured, fine, then I'll take matters into my own hands. She'd been engaged to the father of her first child, but the war separated them; later, when communication was easier, he found out about the second baby and he got angry. By now, he's got another wife, though he isn't church-married. [. . .]

She says she'd have had the abortion if she'd been living closer to Kampala. She'd found a doctor who would do it, she'd have found the money, but then her grandmother, the one who only ever had three children herself, encouraged Rose to continue the pregnancy, and that settled it. But at five months pregnant, Rose was getting up at two in the morning to walk three kilometres to fetch water, carry it back on her head, and teach the rest of the day. "I did it alone," she remembers in a tight voice, "and I went to the hospital alone, and I had my Caesarian alone, and I brought my baby back. Alone."

And not a whole lot later, the barbarians who were the army then overran the school where she was teaching and she had to escape on foot. Walked ten kilometres in the heat with the tiny daughter she was certain would die. "I was lucky," she says, "that both of my babies resemble their fathers. No one doubts who they belong to."

I quickly forget life before Rose. We see one another almost every day, certainly after early January 1988, when we hit on the idea of moving one of the unused student beds to my house. Knowing she can sleep at my place gives her a reprieve from the constant busyness at her home, filled as it is with siblings, cousins, nieces, nephews, and more distantly related kin. Rose and I visit as often as our various duties allow. It feels as if we talk constantly, but we also often knit and weave in comfortable silence . . .

~~~

On 29 November 1987, after months of planning, Mom and Dad leave Winnipeg and reach Uganda on 2 December. They stay a week with me at Ndejje and we leave together for Kenya on 9 December. For seven days Mom and Dad and I spend hours catching up, hours being hosted in my friends' and colleagues' homes, hours meeting and hosting my friends and colleagues and students and acquaintances, hours walking the neighbourhood. Dad is enamoured with this lush and fertile land and hatches elaborate plans to move to Uganda and farm. Among other possible crops, he dreams about tea, maize, turkeys, and tobacco. Mom, who has never liked the cold, is shocked by the winter that waits for them when they return to Winnipeg. She includes weather reports in every letter she sends until April. From this point onwards, Mom and Dad's letters regularly reflect their first-hand experiences in Kenya and Uganda and specifically at Ndejje. Unexpectedly, their visit also prompts Mom to much more explicit expressions of homesickness for me—

Letter #49 from Mom and Dad   *4 January 1988*

My dear daughter:
It's hard to decide where to begin, so I'll pick up where we left off, which was at the airport in Nairobi. I know how hard it was for you and right now I wish we had taken you with us; I am so homesick for you, but I know I mustn't go on like this, it'll only make both of us feel worse. [. . .] It is very cold here, −29°C overnight and some snow, rather hard to adjust to after the balmy weather in Africa.

[. . .] Of all the places we visited I liked being in Ndejje with you best of all; wouldn't mind being there now. I've noticed in my journal that I sent my last letter on 28 October 1987, so it's high time I resume my weekly letter-writing schedule. [. . .] I miss you terribly, but soon you'll be at the halfway point and the countdown begins.

—though I am integrating more and more deeply into life at Ndejje . . .

Letter #42 to Mom and Dad   *8 January 1988*

*Today, even without power, is a gift of a day after yesterday's
adventures. [. . .] I knew the adventure was starting when I
found William propped up on my porch. (I'd just been down
to offer Frances supper and a hot bath after Robinah had
reported that Miss Frances was "suffering" and I'd guessed,
correctly, "period.") William has also been suffering, but I
don't think it's his period. Weak and aching joints, dizziness,
no strength, declining appetite; when I saw him Sunday he
could barely shuffle one foot ahead of the other.*

*I've been keeping loose tabs on his trips to various clinics
and hospitals and knew he'd seen more doctors the day
before. Which was what we talked about for twenty minutes,
that and minor college news, though we both knew there
were more serious matters afoot. Eventually it transpired
that William's latest doctor believes that part of his problem
is the psychological stress his sister's illness is causing.
(William recently learned that his sister, who has a history of
mental illness, is once again quite sick, often unmanageable
at his father's home in the village.)*

*The sister begs to see William, begs either that he come
home to look after her or that she be brought to Ndejje
to stay with him. She's far too weak to be transported by
bicycle, but she must be transported. William himself is far
too weak to travel to the village by foot or bicycle, and who
has a car?*

*Well, we do of course. ('Course, so does the principal,
to whom William devotes the 97 percent of his energy he
doesn't spend on his family, but that would violate the
cardinal rule that the LIC vehicle not make anyone's life
easier except that of Her Eminent Immenseness.) Our
conversation ends at about noon. Forty minutes later, Rose,
Nathan Muggulu (William's best friend, the cherub-faced
man I call our "angelic electrician"), and I pile into the
Suzuki and head for Bombo, where, rumours suggest, there's*

petrol to be had (we're still feeling the effects of Kenya's childish Christmastime embargo). [...]

I rediscover that I hate driving the Suzuki, and it does not help knowing we're driving on the spare, and it does not help not knowing what kind of terrain we'll have to cross to get to the village. I'll have to cross. (Rose offers to come, but she'd have to sit in the back and that's about as much fun as an outdoor shower in January in Winnipeg.) It doesn't help either that rain clouds are gathering. [...]

Back at Ndejje, Rose and I drink tea until 3 p.m., when Nathan reports his certainty that the rain has ended for the day, but it's after four by the time we reach William's village, having driven half the journey in second gear. I'm glad, as it turns out, that I don't have the station wagon. In some places the track is nothing more than a bicycle path, and for all its limitations, the Suzuki is perfect for this kind of bush travel. Racketing down one particularly bumpy hill, all dark and damp and overhung with trees, I can't imagine, between involuntary lunges, that this doesn't qualify as assault and battery, but a calm little corner of my mind remembers to be thankful it's not raining; we haven't had a flat tire; it's not so relentlessly sunny I'm cursing myself for forgetting my sunglasses.

We find the sister tied to stakes. Wrists and ankles, so she won't run away. Nathan's eyes are a study in pain. He carries a chair outside and I understand I'm to sit quietly while they complete the necessary preparations. Five women, a few young girls, and an unhealthily light-brown baby with rickets sit some distance from the house. I manage an appropriate greeting before the chair arrives and what to do then but sit. And smile. (It's a very low point for "presence.")

The sister can hardly stand she's so dizzy. With coaxing and time though, she makes it into the back of the Suzuki, and I wait with her while the others collect her bags. She's much thinner than I remember, there are deep indentations

on her arms where they tightened the ropes, and her hands
are swollen. There are gouges too on her arms, as if she's
tried to rip the ropes off, and small red recent ones as if
she tried just today with her teeth. She doesn't appear
particularly mad, mostly very, very weak, and she thinks to
greet me in English.

"Zis is my children," William's father explains painfully,
waiting too at the truck. "She is very ill." I tell him how sorry
I am that his daughter is so sick, and I know I can't cry. A
crowd has gathered to wave us off and we're a memorable
sextet: a mad woman, an old woman (in the passenger seat),
a baby and a teenager, able-bodied Nathan in the back in
case the sister is taken with a spell, and the female muzungu
is driving. [...]

I drive back more quickly than I did coming out—I know
what to expect road-wise and I'm powerfully possessed to
get these people home. Still, it's after 5:30 p.m. by the time
we reach Ndejje. William is shocked by his sister's condition.
He'd hoped she could be taken directly to the psychiatric
hospital. Now he thinks she'll need to see a regular doctor
first. He turns sad eyes on me and says: "That is the trouble
with our lives."

I feel, more than I know, what he means. We confer
another few minutes and since it's clear the sister can't travel
tomorrow by public transport we agree that I will drive. If we
leave at eight, we'll have time to get more (rationed) petrol
in Bombo and do a day's work in Kampala. Frances has
been enjoying a long soak in the tub and is just packing up
when I reach my place; she readily engages in quick plans to
use the day in town tomorrow as efficiently as possible.

Beginning with the alarm set for 6:30 a.m. What I
don't account for is the raging rainstorm that wakes me
in the night, batters the hill for hours, and blasts out the
power. When I sleep again, it's so deeply I completely miss
the alarm. Yikes. Breakfast is tetracycline, vitamin B, clear

tea, and five sweet bananas. The power's still out and since
I don't have time to cook, there's no point in opening the
fridge. Frances arrives a little after eight, and we shuffle
across to William's place, where we discover that there's been
a change in plans. Because the sister is still so weak; because
it's Friday (and we all know how poorly the city functions on
a Friday); because, like most other hospitals, the Mad House
doesn't provide meals for its patients; because William
would like to fatten her up for a few days and watch her
behaviour; because . . . because . . . maybe it would be best if
we waited till Monday? Sounds fine to me, but then, I'm still
half-asleep. I feel bad for Frances, though, who heard her
alarm and crawled out of bed at 6:15. [. . .]

Sunday morning. On a happier note, Rose was over last
evening with the mat she's weaving. While getting tea, I told
her I was glad she'd come, that I'd been meaning to remind
her that she was welcome to drop by any time. She smiled
and said she knew that, but added, "But sometimes, those
people . . . talk—"

I'd wondered about that. So we talk about what people
say when Africans are friends with bazungu and about what
Rose calls Africans' prejudice against the bazungu, and she
slides me one of her wise, sidewise looks and says, "They are
thinking about the British. Most of the bazungu our people
knew were the British. And they were not like you and
Frances. But Mr. Fisher—"

She pauses, shakes her head. "You could never visit Mr.
Fisher," she says emphatically. "He had a seat"—she twists
her body so that she's facing the porch, and her voice gathers
momentum—"there, outside, and that was where he said
visitors would sit. And he would stand in the doorway and
say, 'What do you want? What do you want?!'"

"Ahhhhh," she breathes out, exasperated. "I cannot come
back to visit a man like that."

Letter #50 from Mom and Dad   *9 January 1988*

My dear daughter:

Doesn't it seem hard to believe that a few years ago we thought Lynn Lake was far away? I'm at my usual letter-writing spot trying to write down what I've been thinking and one thing is that if we'd arranged our trip as originally planned we'd still be in Ndejje with you and would have had more time to talk to you. Another is that visiting you was wonderful but knowing that we had to leave again made it hard. I don't know why I'm writing this; I'm not being very eloquent and it won't make you feel much better I'm sure. I guess what I mean is that I still feel, at times, guilty for having encouraged you to go to Africa. Once you're back home I don't want you to go so far away again, or at least I hope you won't want to go so far away again. [. . .]

Carla and Joe came over on Tuesday to pick up the gifts and letter you sent along for them; we talked about their trip and looked at the map of Kenya, Uganda, and Tanzania that I'd bought in Nairobi; Carla said it made her feel that now they were really going. [. . .]

I didn't continue this letter yesterday because my last half-course has started. It's the History of Biblical Interpretation. So far I've not found it terribly interesting. Our professor is a "rookie" and a bit dull and too soft-spoken. I'm probably a bit hard on him. If I revise my opinion I'll let you know. [. . .]

On Sunday we went to church, the first time since getting back. I had dreaded listening to Walter again, but was rather surprised at what he said in his sermon. He's not an eloquent speaker, but the content was quite good, about the powerful and the powerless.

post secret (5)

Typically, though, Walter's insights were fleeting.

Letter #51 from Mom and Dad   *16 January 1988*

Today it was our turn to clean the church, and from the questions Walter asked it was obvious that he knows very little about Africa. Which is not too surprising I suppose, but it meant he did not ask the right questions. He is, in his heart, such a conservative evangelical that politics and social concerns play a very minor role in his world view. [. . .]

Every time I go to the supermarket I think of Africa, and of Rose, and I wonder, if I could pluck her from Ndejje and transplant her (I hope you or she won't mind the garden analogy) here in Canada, what her reaction would be to the overabundance of things, and also (since it is winter) to the climate. Every black person that I see on the street reminds me of Africa and I look at their faces to see if they don't remind me of someone I met down there and I wonder where they've come from, which is very silly, I know. It's quite likely that some of them were born in Canada or at least in North America.

Mom had been sending greetings to Rose for months by the time they met in person in December. After their trip, Mom regularly included letters just for Rose.

Letter #51 from Mom and Dad [cont.]

After grocery shopping we picked up the rest of our pictures
and then we had to explain to Henry where and who
everything and everybody was. I wish we had taken more
pictures in Ndejje, especially the night we had the dinner at
your place, and of the archdeacon and his singing children.
Also the dinner at your principal's house. And I wish I had
remembered to write something on the back of the pictures
we sent of Rose's parents and us. [. . .]
Many people at church have asked about you and our
trip and want an "official report." Dad and I had better
start organizing our thoughts and writing some things down;
at least I kept a journal and Dad has a very good memory.
[. . .] I'm wondering all the time what is happening at Lady
Irene right now.

Letter #6 to Henry   *16 January 1988*

So I'm sitting around minding my own business, little
brother, and what happens? I get elected to the local
Resistance Council![6] (Well, the first part of that is not quite
true: Rose and I have deliberately taken seats near the door
at the back so we can mind each other's business; she skims
a recent Manchester Guardian and I try to rest, using her
kikoy[7] as a pillow. It's a public, participatory-democracy
meeting, though, and minding one's business isn't exactly
encouraged, so we comply with a modicum of attention,
whispering just to one another our witty observations about
the people being nominated.)

So far, we've elected a chairman—someone, I note to
Rose, inclined to be childishly petulant when he doesn't get
his own way, but she whispers back that he is a very hard
worker, so we both vote for him. We vote alike for the vice-
chair too, the only woman in the running, the deputy head
at the secondary school, someone I know only by sight.

"We are all equal here," Rose asserts fiercely, and I
concur with the logic that a council chaired by a man should
have a woman as its vice-chair. "That way," I add, "we
can be sure of having two women on the council, since it's
unlikely a man will be elected for Women's Concerns. One
woman alone on a council of men? Ahhhh, that is too hard."
I punctuate with a short defiant shake of my head, a gesture
I've learned from Rose.

The meeting is conducted in English[8] amidst considerable
chuckling, procedural questions bantered back and forth,
teasing camaraderie. It's nice, for a change, to be "inside" of
this. Nice, when I look around the room, to feel at home, to
catch the eyes of friends with whom I share conspiratorial,
condescending grins. "Really," we say to one another
inaudibly, "must we prolong this nonsense? We're busy
people—could we get on with things?!"

An amused dignity prevails, and proper procedure
unfolds at its own pace while the sun eases toward the
horizon. Chair and vice-chair take their chairs and
nominations are declared open for the position of secretary.
Expecting it exactly not at all, my brain skips a breath when
the first name called from even further back in the room is
mine: "Katherine Venema!"

"Noooooooo," I mouth at Daniel whose eye I catch,
thinking surely this is a joke and I only have to decline
and it will be over. Daniel just grins. "I really don't think
so!" I retort with what I hope is firmly casual indifference.
"Second?" asks the presiding officer, paying me precisely no
attention at all.

"No," I insist this time. "Yes!" contradict at least
three other voices. The presiding officer smiles. "Other
nominations?"

Kiggundu Daniel and Nakazibwe Cate are also
nominated. Beautiful Cate is beside herself. Nalinya Girls'
Primary, where she's now senior teacher, has been deluged

with new pupils since the beginning of term—they're
already well past capacity and the children keep coming.
"Where are we going to find time to do this?" she demands
of Daniel and me when we leave the room to let the others
vote. Her complexion argues with her answer to my "How
are you?" She is thinner than usual and pale. For her sake, I
hope the people inside realize how sincerely she intended her
own attempt to decline.

"Isn't this a democracy?" she demands again,
rhetorically. "In a democracy we should have the right to
say 'No.' That is why," she addresses this last remark to me,
"people are not working; they are being forced to do jobs they
haven't volunteered for."

Daniel smiles. "You should win," he encourages me; "you
have beautiful handwriting." "Ooooooooooooooooooeeeeeeeeee
my brother," I think, "now there's solid political reasoning,"
but I'm suspicious that this is precisely why my name came
up. Daniel can afford to be encouraging (or discouraging,
depending on your perspective): there's an undercurrent of
common-sense agreement in the room about who should make
up this council, and my sense of the common sense says that
Daniel will be on this council, but he won't be on as secretary.

According to the Handbook, anyone present can present
reasons that one or more of the nominees should not stand,
so I stand close to the door with my ears perked for murmurs
of dissent. Perked, they think they catch the word "visitor,"
and I breathe a half-sigh of relief: someone has realized that
a non-Ugandan temporary resident isn't the right person for
the job—

And a minute later we're called back into the room to
hear the results. Daniel and Cate split sixteen votes between
them and I win with fourteen. "Come take your seat," urges
the presiding officer, and I do amidst the rhythmic clapping
that's greeted the two winners before me. "What a hilarious
thing," I think from the front of the room, surveying the

*crowd of familiar faces, "and what, exactly, is MCC going to
say about this?!"*

*The six remaining members are elected, the sun sets
inexorably, and we finish after dark. If I thought I was tired
and hungry when we arrived, I'm exhausted and famished
by now, but also curiously elated at this turn of events. At
the very least, I'll get to know eight more of my neighbours
well, and I'll always know exactly what's going on! [. . .]*

*P.S. Nathaniel has lost all my letters. There's a piece of
my life gone.*

As it turned out, Nathaniel hadn't lost my letters, he'd misplaced them briefly, but Mom's next two letters go permanently AWOL. Everything since Mom's missing Letter #40 has
reached me, but over the next eight months, her Letters #52,
54, 62, 64, and 73 fail to arrive. This series of losses happens at a time when my anxiety about letters' safe arrival
heightens, which hardly seems possible but is. Since October
1987, I've been in frequent enough contact with Luke—the
young Canadian stranded in southern Uganda when Frances
and I arrived—that we've begun numbering our letters. By
February 1988, the correspondence has taken on increasingly
affectionate tones.

Letter #44 to Mom and Dad   *24 January 1988*

*Sunday Frances acquires local homebrew with which to
season the beef stroganoff she prepares for supper to celebrate
Jake's arrival for mid-term evaluations. Bowing to the
extreme social pressure they exert on one another,[9] the three
otherwise staid development workers consume most of what
remains in the bottle after the meal. Kathleen is rendered
incapable of pronouncing clearly any words that contain the
letter s, which is unfortunate because conversation revolves
on the theme of the morning's sermon. "Seriously, was that
'Godly pleasures' or 'bodily pleasures'?!" [. . .]*

Monday evaluations proceed. Jake, in utter seriousness, proposes to Kathleen the possibility of extending her term with MCC. (Kathleen assumes he's had leftover homebrew for breakfast.) [. . .]

Tuesday the college continues on hiatus. Weekend rumours suggest the Ministry may come through with funding by the end of next week. The situation is particularly bad for our second-year students who should be completing their course work this term. Closer to home, unmistakable scrabbling from inside one of the speakers reveals the presence of a rock-till-you-drop cockroach. I detach the speaker and shake out more than a hundred pellets of cockroach poop and one dried leg ("I could have danced all night!"). [. . .] Tuesday is otherwise a rare day because it's a day without visitors. I decide it means no one likes me anymore and wonder what the point is of living if you don't have friends. Late in the day I see a gazelle at the bottom of the garden, which partially restores my faith in the universe. [. . .]

Wednesday my pity party ends abruptly when Rose arrives for mid-morning tea and dazzling conversation. I've already spent three hours on a letter to Tracey and feel vaguely guilty that so much of my time goes to "just" writing, but I'm mostly elated the rest of the day. "Is my bed still there?" Rose has asked, "Am I welcome?" and when I tell her of course, she says she'll probably sleep, "this way" tonight. [. . .]

Thursday is another day of writing. I finish letters to Sharon and Paul and wonder how much better my accounts are than sensationalist photojournalism, exploiting other people's tragedies. My afternoon walk provides an entertaining interlude and possible example when a hopelessly drunk young man implores me to give him a shirt. I ask in disbelief where he thinks I have an extra shirt on my person. He is stumped and quickly shifts to a more general

*request for aid in rearing his daughter. She is clean, neatly
dressed, and obviously well fed. I tell him I think he's doing
a fine job without me. I also impress on him the fact that I
haven't so much as a shilling to spare. (For a change, this is
the truth. Joseph has eked out every cent of my remaining
cash with various solicited and unsolicited pawpaw and
pumpkins.) I amuse the young man's companions by
matching him, dramatic gesture for dramatic gesture,
pathetic supplication for pathetic supplication. [. . .]*

*Roasting groundnuts late into the evening, I make two
mistakes. 1. To the sound of the roof tank filling, I marvel
at the fact that though there've been enormous storms this
week, we haven't lost power once. Heart-of-the-mistake: I
imagine that no more natural disasters will touch Ndejje
until the end of my term. 2. Almost perfectly content (minus
my nagging conscience) to lavish my days on writing, it
occurs to me that I haven't had an adventure for almost a
week and may soon run out of letter fodder. Heart-of-the-
mistake: I wish for a break in the routine . . .*

Friday lightning strikes my house.

*7:15 a.m. Lightning strikes my house. 7:16 a.m. I shut off
the main electrical switch and begin searching for whatever
it is that I smell burning. 7:16:20 a.m. I discover a smoke-
filled bedroom. My torch and bedside lamp have exploded.
Bits of burned cord, plastic shards, chunks of insulation, and
plug wreckage are strewn across the room. The wall socket
is burned black, as is the wall behind my bed, a direct line
from socket to lamp stand. The storm continues. We still
have power but I feel queasy. I leave the lights off and begin
cleaning up in pre-dawn greyness.*

*[. . .] 8:15 a.m. With the storm passed, I finish making
breakfast, amazed and grateful that none of the electrical
appliances or sockets has been affected by the hit. I extend
the letter to Tracey, exacting from the situation every
possible ounce of humour. 10:00 a.m. Robinah arrives and*

inquires about the large chunk of cement missing from the bottom corner of the house just outside my bedroom. Quick investigation of the rubble scattered across the front porch suggests that the lightning struck and shattered that corner, then passed through the wall in a direct line into the house, past the torch—Kaboom—and the bedside lamp—Zap—

It occurs to me to be thankful that I wasn't in bed when it happened. At about this point I discover that the fridge is not, contra my earlier jubilation, working, so I send Robinah to request William to find Nathan the Electrician. Best, I figger, if I don't do any more unsupervised poking about. I'm not sure how Robinah tells the story, but in eleven minutes the house is full of people surveying the damage, checking the fuses, testing the sockets, and theorizing.

The general consensus is shock at the fire marks, relief that I wasn't in bed, and bewilderment that the fridge isn't working. Everything else is functioning perfectly, including the bedroom socket, which Daniel and I test with the toaster. 11:30 a.m. The crowd is finally gone. I finish the letter to Tracey but my hands are still shaking. 12:15 p.m. I empty the fridge, toss it onto its head, and consume everything that will spoil quickly. The rest of the day is blessedly quiet and Frances has invited me for supper. [. . .]

Over pizza, Frances and I work on shows for the TV she made out of a cardboard box a few weeks ago, and, since she's spending the night at my place, Rose joins me on my walk home. (When I ask if she's afraid of more lightning, Rose assures me that the lightning's done its damage, it won't be back.) We're almost at the top of the hill when one of the porters meets us with a lengthy story in Luganda that Rose doesn't translate until we reach the house. "Do you see it?" she asks then, and I have no idea what she means.

"The snake," she clarifies. "They killed a snake at your front door this evening and his body is still there in the bushes." Well I'll be, I think, so it is. Holy smoke, I add silently, no pun intended, I thought I was running out of material.

Letter #53 from Mom and Dad   *30 January 1988*

Remember Dad's idea about starting a coffee plantation in Uganda? In this cold weather, getting up in the dark and icy cold and having to start a cold car and shovel the cold snow, the Ugandan climate seems like a beautiful dream. Although of course we haven't experienced the whole spectrum. That one shower we had was nothing like the thunder, lightning, and the downpours you've written about. [. . .]

Next time I hope to write a more profound and introspective letter.

post secret (7)

Until the summer of 2014, when she got up abruptly and walked away from the piano where Sandy and I had been singing with her, we could still communicate with Mom through music.

Five and a half years earlier, on Friday 14 March 2008, my first visit to my parents after Harry's diagnosis, I arrived as Mom stormed out of the house, infuriated at Dad and her inability to articulate her constant concern for her grandson. I recorded more than three hours of conversation that afternoon, including Mom's story about the grandparents she so disliked, and the fact that they spent time in a prison camp after the war, punishment for their membership in the NSB and their explicit support of the German cause. Mom reminds me again that afternoon that neither of her parents ever belonged to the NSB, though she recalls fragments of a memory of an older child in the village, who, after the war, forbade Mom and her siblings from playing in their yard, because they were *"Harmen Ynzes' ben"*—

They were, that is, their father's children. "And I connected that," Mom says, "with the Germans and that Dad had maybe not been as anti-German as he should have been." I've heard all my life about the soldiers with whom Pake would speak German in the store, but on this afternoon I try to get clearer about how frequently that would have happened. Every day? Every week? Were they stationed in Nijemardum? No, no, much less frequently than that, and they always came from other locations. What Mom remembers vividly is an occasion on which several German soldiers were in the village and had leaned their bicycles against a fence near the store, and a friend of Beppe's who was also visiting—maybe a friend from Beppe's nursing days—flattened the German soldiers' bike tires with a pin. Or perhaps just one of the tires. And maybe not a pin, but certainly something sharp.

What Mom *wants* to tell me about is how beautifully those soldiers sang. "*Man*," she repeats fervently, "could they *sing*. And they were taught to sing from an early age, from high school and even earlier!" And so we talk about music and its political uses, and when I suggest that music can be exploited for nationalistic purposes, Mom could not agree more. "So how is it," I ask her, "that patriotic songs function so effectively, how is it that music can be used for propaganda?" "Whoa," I add jokingly, "this is hard, this is a *test* question!"

"This *is* a test question!" Mom responds enthusiastically. "This is a very good question. I commend you for this question; just for the question you get an A-plus!" And she jumps up to answer the question, and as she answers, she conducts an imaginary choir, and for the next several minutes, Mom tells me about music with her words and with her body. "If you have enough people," she says, "like, a big choir, a *big* choir, and they sing their hearts out all together for the Fatherland"—she waves her arms—"well, *man*, that has a big effect, it makes you feel wonderful, it makes you feel great! Because you belong to this group, and hey, we can sing these beautiful songs, and we sing them together, and if we can do that?!" She pauses. "If we can do that, what else can we maybe do together?!"

"Music is a very...a very...it can be very thrilling," Mom adds, "it can be *very* thrilling. They say in Holland, '*It sweeps you up*'—you become in a sort of ecstatic state, certainly to a degree. In that ecstasy, you think: 'This is wonderful, the singing is beautiful!' To incorporate that into the war—? It makes some sense that that's how it works: you lose your sense of self, because if you're standing outside yourself, you're beside yourself. If you lose your sense of self, you're not *in* yourself anymore, you're beside yourself!"

Mom swing her arms, exuberant at the thought of music's potential, and deflates when we recall the context of our conversation, the ways in which musically inspired ecstasy can be harnessed to deadly militaristic purposes. So for the next half hour we talk about other things: the jobs Mom held when she was first in Canada; the bosses she remembers; the kind of work she would like to have done; and then I ask, "Mom, if there was one story from your life, anything that you've thought, or something you've read, that you would want to make sure would get into a book about you, what would that be?" And once again we talk about music, because the story Mom remembers is *"De Krystreis fen Broder Iwersen,"*[10] the Frisian children's story that Pake read every Christmas Eve. "I always found that such an ... such a ... what's the word," Mom says, "not 'interesting,' but 'spellbinding' story, *jah*, because that man, Broder, was right away willing to do that job and walk all the way into town. Only he looked for the wind: where the wind was coming from, and whether it was safe for him to walk through those islands."

"But then on the way back," she continues, "there was that mist, and he knew all the places where it was safe to walk, and not safe to walk, but when you're in the ... that mist ... when it is foggy, there's nothing for you to orientate ... *That* I found always so spellbinding." Mom pauses and starts again. "And of course, that his wife and their kids started singing and that, in a sense, saved him. Because he had lost his way. But then he had stood for a while, and then he heard singing, and then it became louder and louder, and he walked toward that singing, and then they ... matched up together."

"*Jah*," she adds thoughtfully, "it makes a big imprint. It was pretty damn dangerous. You could drown in that sea. It was the *sea*, not just a pool, and he could have drowned—but the singing brought him home."

~~~

By the time we admit Mom into full-time care, she no longer knows what a "daughter" is, but, especially at first, she still smiles beatifically when I tell her I'm "Kathleen," and sometimes she finds "I'm" and "happy" and "see" and "you" in response. For the first year and a half, when I ask if she'd like to sing, her face still radiates joy. "Oh yes," she answers clearly, "I'd like that."

If we're lucky, the piano in the multi-purpose room is free, and then I play as many hymns as the afternoon will hold. "How was that, Mom," I ask after every few verses, "should I continue?" "Oh yes," Mom whispers in reply, "it's so beautiful." I play some more and Mom responds to them all, the simplistic, sentimental hymns whose theology she scorned in her prime, and the thought-provoking hymns we've learned more recently.

"How was that Mom?" I ask, noticing again that her face is alight and her eyes have filled with tears. "It's so beautiful," she says each time and sometimes she ventures complete and otherwise elusive sentences. "Music does something to you here," she murmurs one memorable afternoon, her right hand touching her chest near her heart, then gracefully wafting skyward: "It lifts you up."

post secret (8)

Determinedly blind to his limitations, my mother adored her father all her life. Because I adored my mother, a logical progression offered itself to my child's mind: if my mother was her father's intellectual and spiritual comrade and heir, then clearly I was hers. I wasn't troubled as a child by the now readily discernible contradictions and my retrospective awareness of gender entitlement. I could completely trust my loving mother and stand in terrified awe of my fiercely unpredictable grandfather.

I vividly recall the handful of moments when Pake's too-easily-blazing anger targeted me directly. It's a bright early morning in the summer of '69, Dad and Pake busy building an addition to our house, when four-year-old Henry and eight-and-a-half-year-old Kathleen leap into action, chasing one another across the not-yet-completed foundation, jumping over batts of insulation in a spontaneous game of tag, which is fun until somebody gets hurt—not so much by missing a beam and sinking into fibreglass up to my knee and itching for hours afterward as by the ego-shrivelling blast of Pake's fury, teeth grinding, veins in his neck engorged.

"*Potferdomme!*" "*Hoe kreis't 'it ein 'e kop!*" "Jesus Christ!" he might've said, if he spoke English in moments of passion, if we were a family in which names of the Divine were used profanely: the materials damaged, the time wasted, the fun had. I'd like to believe it was because he was worried about me. Because it wasn't that Pake was opposed to fun on principle, not at all. His children remember with great fondness his love of silly jokes and wordplay, the words and rhymes and whimsical songs he made up, sometimes spontaneously, and the deliciously wacky nicknames he had for each one of them. Pake loved to tell his children stories and he loved to read his children stories, and they remember the rapt attention they paid when it was Christmas Eve again at last and time again, at last, for "*De Krystreis fen Broder Iwersen*," the old Frisian story about Broder Iwersen and his fraught and dangerous Christmas journey home.

But Pake had a wicked temper and he grew into parenthood and grandparenthood long before common knowledge caught up with corporal punishment. Pake's anger is a central element in the story about how he rescued Mom from the abuse she'd been suffering. Over the months and years that Mom and I talk, the subject comes up several times, usually when I'm not recording. As soon as I can afterward, I turn on the iPod and cautiously remind Mom what we've been talking about, but she typically skirts details the second time around, offers truncated versions, changes the subject. This happens on 1 February 2008, the day Mom tells me about sticking her tongue out at the pretty little blonde-haired girl, and it happens again on 1 May 2009.

On 1 May 2009 the subject comes up because, just two days earlier, Pope Benedict XVI has addressed a delegation from Canada's Assembly of First Nations specifically to express his sorrow over the abuse that Indigenous students experienced at Catholic-run residential schools. When Mom and I discuss the mixed reaction that the pope's statement has generated, Mom says, thoughtfully, "*Jah*." "*Jah*," she repeats and adds, "I wonder how the people that were on the receiving end, what *they* thought about it, because—it's them that, you know, that had to go through it."

I hear the most extended version of the story in the last ten minutes of one of the long walks that Mom and I are still taking in the dreadful winter after Harry dies. I listen intently, anxious to get home, to have Mom revisit the story as soon as we're inside, but as we approach the house—which, in early 2009, Mom still recognizes—she says, "Let's talk about something else. Dad doesn't like it when I talk about this."

There are details I never get clear on. How old was little Geeske? "I was yay high," Mom gestures on 1 May 2009, "four or five. I wasn't going to school yet. If I'd been going to school," she adds, "it would never have happened." In other versions, she might only have been three. How old was he? Fourteen. Thirteen. Fifteen. He worked for Pake in the store, doing what, unloading boxes, stocking shelves, running errands. He ate with them at mealtimes. How long had it been going on? Blank. Weeks? Blank. Months? Blank. Blank blank blank blank blank. And then little Geeske was rescued, on a day when Pake returned home early on his bicycle from one of his many grocery deliveries, opened the door to the shed, and—Mom whispers on 1 February 2008 in the Millennium Library—"caught him in the act."

Letter #45 to Mom and Dad   *31 January 1988*

I started cutting down on sugar and groundnuts when I couldn't swing my skirts around my body anymore and after two people told me, separately, that they thought I was growing "bigger" (they both meant it as a compliment). I've also increased my raw vegetable consumption by about 300 percent but that's because I hardly ever cook anymore and that is because I have nowhere to store leftovers and that is because, when we went into Kampala on Monday and Nathan (the Angelic Electrician) Muggulu did my running around for me, we learned that fridge heaters like the one the lightning fried might be available in town, and that for just 15,000 shillings, a mere $250 US dollars, oh yeah, oh yeah.

In the face of this untenable option, Nathan converts my fridge to gas and we experiment to determine how much fuel it will take to run this temperamental appliance. The results are economic disaster, light years from anything resembling local living conditions.

Letter #45 to Mom and Dad [cont.]

As I say, highs and lows, and the week's unassailable highlight came Sunday evening when Rose appeared at the door out of breath, eyes bright with the news that Moses had arrived.

We'd been waiting for Moses all day. He'd been scheduled to arrive sometime between ten and noon, and after lunch Rose was going to bring him up for tea and photographs. I suppose we shouldn't have been surprised. We've been expecting Moses for the last six months: after pinning him down to an exact day, it really wasn't bad to be off by only eight hours. Moses is the first-born son, the army captain, and he's spent most of the last year fighting various rebels in the north, and then Alice Lakwena's forces in the east.[11] He hasn't made it home for at least two years, and the last time he was home, Rose couldn't be. She hadn't seen him since '82 when he went into the bush with Museveni.

When Museveni called all the high-ranking officers in for a special meeting, Moses decided to take the opportunity to make a trip home. A real-life hero, and for all my anti-militarism, my imagination is captured. "Oh Rose," I say instantly, "will we have a chance to meet him? Will you bring him for tea?" She grins back shyly and says, of course, and maybe we could take a photograph? You betcha honey!

By midday, the Ssendawulas are all best-dressed and busy waiting. No Moses. I've baked pumpkin bread and it's even edible and boy oh baby, am I set for this tea. No Moses. Frances shows up mid-afternoon for the festivities, and still no Moses. Frances and I both do every possible bit of paperwork in advance of tomorrow's Kampala foray, I finally start and then finish cooking supper, and we're sitting down to eat when the knock comes, but it's not Rose and it's not Moses, it's her Eminent Immenseness, Mrs. God herself.

Mrs. G was away (again) during the direct-hit lightning bolt and she's come now, she says, to commiserate and count my toes! [. . .]

Frances and I are finishing up the dishes when Rose's deep "hallo" finally sounds outside the door. Moses has arrived, he's just taking his supper, he must leave again very soon, and should she bring him up to say hello? "Mother said," she says, "'Hurry to Katherine's and say Moses is here!'"

Rose is agitated: I can tell she'd like to get back quickly, she doesn't want to miss a minute of this visit, but she did promise to bring him, so, even though it's a bit forward, culturally, I say, would it be alright if we came down instead, we shouldn't take him away from the family, and it's that easy, decided, and off we dash, down through the dark for what is only my second time inside at the Ssendawulas', my first time at night, and this is a party atmosphere. Every one of the family members is here, sitting or standing; Daniel Kiggundu and Mrs. Nsubuga and a few other familiar faces I can't immediately put names to are on a bench against the far wall, and, along the side wall, six young uniforms who look, to my inexperienced eyes, as if they range in age from nine to about twenty-one.

"The driver is a baby," Rose had giggled on our way down the hill, "I think he needs a cushion to see where he is going!" There are also at least two AK-47s. I am almost immune, I don't even shudder. Moses sits at one corner of the table. His full beard helps him look the mid-thirties he must be; slim, uniformed but not ostentatiously—you'd never know his rank looking at him. Rose tells me later that Museveni doesn't believe in military decoration. Moses is definitely a Ssendawula and certainly the most handsome of the brothers I've met. He also, to my surprise, speaks very good English. Rose had warned me earlier that although Moses is an accomplished linguist—he speaks at least two tribal languages besides Luganda and Swahili—he hasn't *had much chance to learn English. She tells me later he surprised the entire family with his ability to converse with us.*

And couldn't he converse! I discover to my chagrin that I'm still a sucker for handsome, fast-talking men in uniforms and glorious wholehearted smiles. Some people can excite an entire room with electric tension and Moses is definitely one of them. He jokes with everyone there, flashes out questions, teases the little sisters, launches into dramatic stories, and finally, with all of our attention, addresses an impassioned apology to his mother that he must leave so soon. Just before he does, though, Jonathan asks if we could pray. And we do, Mother and the multi-sized children, the other visitors, Frances and Rose and I, the bench of baby soldiers, Moses and his fine-boned driver and his lovely sullen wife who doesn't speak English or Luganda.

We say the Lord's Prayer first, bilingual, like a warm-up, and then, warmed up, Jonathan talks to God on our behalf. I've never heard Jonathan pray in Luganda before, and it strikes me, as the cadences rise and fall, as the well-worn phrases slip like poetry off his lips, wisps of something divine and present there with us, that it could be Pake praying for himself and all of us, the melody and the passion riding over each other like waves, it could be Sunday dinners and cigar smoke, our family hushed while Pake talks to God in Frisian . . .

We hurry out after "amen" to wave goodbye, and I think now of cold late childhood nights and Stony Mountain departures,[12] shouts and laughter, excited still, despite the hour. Half the moon lights the way and the trees rustle ominously as a storm approaches. Whine, squeal, rev, and reverse, Moses's childlike driver points the jeep toward Kampala and they're gone, a last bright flash of headlights, shouted instructions, high spirits. We finally disperse, reluctant; it's been such fun for so few minutes. Rose shakes her head, says it's just as well Moses came at night or the

*crowd would've been unmanageable, everyone would've
come, all the school children because—shake of head, palms
brought together—"ahhh, Moses, he is so social, he never
forgets anyone, he knows them all; he asks how is this one,
how is that one . . ."*

Pake returned from a grocery delivery, opened the door to
the shed, caught the boy abusing little Geeske, and vengeance
rained down from the sky. "I'm reporting this!" Pake raged,
"I'm bringing him to the authorities," he shrieked, meanwhile
delivering the boy massive blows, *skoppling him op*,[13] as the Frisian expression goes, which I imagine Pake doing—or wanting
to do—with vicious, nail-studded boots, lifting the boy into
the air with each tremendous kick, ready to punt him all the
way to the police if necessary, eager for carnage, so loudly and
wrathfully out of his mind with retribution that Beppe rushed
from the house to discover the matter.

If Beppe had not physically restrained Pake, he might have
killed the boy, little Geeske looking on. Later that day, Beppe
persuaded Pake not to go to the police. The shame. The boy
never appeared after that, in the shop or their home or around
the kitchen table, but in 2000, Mom refused to travel back to
Nijemardum for a worldwide Frisian homecoming for fear
she'd see him again.

perfect correspondence (9)

I've discovered an expansive freedom in writing to Luke. Luke had lived in Uganda for more than two years at the point that he returned to Canada, and he understood, in ways my other correspondents didn't entirely, the intensity of the days of our lives. On 1 February, I haven't yet received his imminent and lively response to my Letter #4, but I've been reading the latest *Guardian* and am distraught at conflicts around the world and conflicts closer to home. In my distress, I believe that only Luke will really understand the wracking complexities of *sides* in a war...

Bonus letter to Luke   *1 February 1988*

Is it that halfway through your term something snaps and you realize that the friendships you've worked so hard to form leave you more vulnerable than you've ever been? [. . .] Why, I ask Rose, when we go walking yesterday, have they cleaned up the skulls? They'd almost been lost in the grass; they tumbled off their trestle tables months ago, and with them hidden, it was easy to forget they were there, easy to imagine it was time to start healing. And then, almost two and a half weeks ago, the grass has been slashed and the skulls neatly arranged again, miscellaneous bones stacked tidily alongside. Frances and I can only speculate, and Rose isn't sure either, but she wonders if maybe someone came in a dream from the dead to say where they were. And though no one can be certain whose those bones are, the dreamer has cleaned them—in honour and just in case.

*We walk on and Rose says something I've thought a
kazillion times, but never with the chilly clarity it has when
she says it: "They were people once." Yes, dear God, they
were, just like Rose and me, though more like Rose than me
in this unfair and pain-wracked world . . .*

"That is why I can never forgive those northerners," Rose
*adds after a second or so of silence. "How can I forgive the
people who tortured us like this? No, I never can."*

"I ask Mother," Rose says, after another silence, "how
Moses can do that, how he can have that Acholi wife, when
it is her people who have done this to us?"

*It all gets so complicated. Moses is the first-born son, the
hero, the captain in the NRA. Moses is the handsome, fast-
talking favourite, home for the first time in years just for a
day, just last Sunday, and we met him then, briefly, when
he squeezed in a visit between meetings with Museveni.
Moses smiles and laughs and jokes with everyone, and it
is unfathomable that he could have killed enough people
to become a captain. Moses brings home his Acholi wife
who speaks no Luganda and no English, and Moses says he
knows now he'll live to be an old man because he survived
the fighting in Gulu.*

"They earned high ranks there," Rose says as we walk,
"the officers who fought in Gulu, who won those battles in
the north. Moses says that when they moved back from the
airstrip everyone said, 'Oh, the NRA has lost Gulu,' but no,
they just waited till the rebels had come back and then they
brought their planes and their bombs . . ."

*Of all your friends in the north, I think I only ever met
Nicholas. I will probably never see Gulu or Kitgum, but
when my friends talk about the fighting there, I think of your
friends and thrash in the soul-chilling waters where nothing
is clearly right or wrong, good or bad. [. . .] You were no
more in enemy territory then than I am now, and I love my
friend Rose, but my sympathy's uncomfortable, double-
edged, disturbed. [. . .]*

"Moses says," says Rose, "that when they fought the rebels in Gulu, they did many tricks. They would even put grenades in the water pumps so that when the rebels would come for water—there would be nothing: no water, no pumps, no rebels." I feel repeatedly ill as the image of that destruction plays in my mind. Under the hurrah-for-our-side bravado with which Rose tells the story, there's a sense of lurking horror. "Moses says, if they hadn't used those tricks they could never have won. He says he has never seen fighting like that fighting in Gulu, and he knows now he will live a long life . . ."

When we get back, she gathers up the mat she was weaving earlier in the afternoon, and I say, let me accompany you, since I must go to Frances's to find some food for supper. Rose asks then about the fridge, and I shake my head; we had it hooked up to gas after lightning fried the heating element, but it sucked a quarter tank in four days. No way can I justify that kind of expenditure to keep my food luke-cool (haha). No, I say, I will manage without, and Frances has very kindly offered to keep things that will spoil. Rose continues concerned and I laugh; to live without a fridge is a small, small thing. To live without friends, though?

"That is why we say, ah, those bazungu must love us very much, to risk so much to come so far and live with us here, when life is so difficult and so expensive," Rose repeats from our conversation earlier in the afternoon. She'd talked about the college before the war, and the shops all around and all the things they'd sell, soap and sweets and eggs, lovely milk and Blue Band margarine and bread. "Bazungu food," she adds with the sloe-eyed, half-turned grin I know so well.

I grin too and ask her, did she ever imagine that she would have a muzungu friend, and she laughs, eyes bright, says no, she always feared the bazungu, she still fears bazungu.

That brings me up short. Even me, Rose? You fear me?

Sometimes. The grin is shyer now. "Not always, but sometimes funny thoughts come into my head, and I *wonder, now what does the muzungu think of me, does she think, 'Oh, there is that Rose coming to bother me again,' or when I come and you make me tea, I think, 'Now here is this muzungu making me tea, I am making her my servant, when I should be making tea for her,' and sometimes when these thoughts come into my head and I am almost here, I turn and I go back home."*

A sharp pain tears through my chest. "Sometimes," I tell her, "funny thoughts come into my head, and I wonder what you think of me, coming all this way to live here with so many things when people here have so little, and I wonder whether you don't think, 'Ah, those bazungu, to come here to do what for us? Why don't they stay in their own place?'"

"No, no," she says then, and she is insistent, defiant as only Rose can be. "No," she repeats, "when we think of the risks you take to leave your homes and come all this way when we would leave Uganda if we had the chance, we say, 'Ah, those bazungu must love us very much.'"

One of Cindy's colleagues at Makerere University helps define my story-collecting project. "What if you ask about women's visions of peace," Maxine Ankrah suggests. "You'll hear more than you want to about conflict, but you won't hear it in a context of accusation and recrimination." I'm eager to learn from Dr. Ankrah, a feminist social scientist at work on multiple projects focused on women's empowerment and women's health. At best, though, Frances and I are in Kampala twice a month and Dr. Ankrah is so busy she frequently needs to reschedule. Our collaboration proceeds, but slowly. And then my illness returns and the stories we've dreamed of remain permanently uncollected. Throughout it all, Rose and I continue to talk as constantly as is possible, but—though we return to the topic many times—we never resolve the question of which one of us loves the other one more.

post secret (9)

The first meeting of our newly elected Resistance Council is a mitigated disaster. Unclear on the rules, the chairman has failed to put the secretary (me) in charge of communication. Communication is, as a result (and as I put it in my next letter) "&!@#%-ed up." I spend several paragraphs describing ensuing events, including the chairman's blatant attempts to blame the debacle on me, and the vociferous and successful defence that Nathan Muggulu (angelic electrician, RC Secretary for Defence, and the man who nominated me in the first place) launches . . .

Letter #47 to Mom and Dad   *15 February 1988*

That all said, I learned something last night that shot my respect for our chairman sky-high. Both yesterday and Monday I encountered Lassiter (father to the incorrigibly sweet children who paste their grubby noses to my glass front door) while I was out walking, and both times he tried to get the child who was with him—Harriet on Monday and Robbie yesterday—to tell me something. You can imagine how well we did. About all I could figure out was that Connie, the older sister, was gone somewhere. I couldn't get clear on where, couldn't get clear on whether Lassiter himself was clear on where, and couldn't figure for the world what it was he wanted me to do, though it was clear that he was hoping I'd do something.

Last night I remembered to ask Rose, and of course Rose knows, and what Rose knows is that one of the Nalinya teachers was recently transferred to Nandire, and when he left, he took Connie with him and put her in school there. Rumour has it that this teacher and the headmaster (our RC chairman) had planned the move and that they're sponsoring Connie's school fees.

"I wish," adds Rose, "that they would also take the little girl. Lassiter is a wicked, wicked man. A wicked man." She shakes her head and rasps out one short breath between her teeth and her tongue. "They say he was trying to marry Connie to someone in Kisoba. Marry?" She spits out the word. "What can a little girl like that do? I only wish they would take the other one too. That man is very, very, very, very wicked."

The next letter of Mom's I receive after her promise to write a "more profound" letter is #55, a letter Mom begins on 20 February, a day after she's been out with Sharon and Nathaniel and other Lynn Lake friends. Mom notes that she and Dad have been to see the Steve Biko movie, *Cry Freedom*; claims Pastor Walter's been speaking "unspiritually about spiritual gifts"; and reports the arrival of my Letters #45 and 46 in the record time of just nine days.

I've mentioned my temperamental fridge so often by this point that Dad wants to know the brand. He thinks he can find the heating coil I need in Winnipeg and send it along with Carla and Joe, who are scheduled to arrive at Ndejje on *their* East African adventure on 24 April. Mom laments the gap she thinks exists between her interest in philosophy and theology and her scholarly abilities in those areas; muses about the ethics of sending a "care package" for the LIC students; and notes that Henry has commented on how much more settled I sound at Ndejje. To that she adds, "As long as you don't feel so at home that you want to stay longer. We all want to see you here at home, too."

According to Mom's next letter, the Gods of International Post continue to smile. My Letter #47 spends just eleven days in transit and Mom worries that I'm catching up. "I'm less than ten letters ahead of you, and last week I slipped," she writes. "I got bogged down in Barth's theological ponderings and consequently a little frantic." She's been working on the Karl Barth essay for weeks, but is otherwise comfortable in her small class, intimidated by neither the "meek and mild" instructor nor the other students. Because all of them are young, she says, "I basically treat them and talk to them as though they're my kids." The next time Mom writes, on 12 March, she apologizes for having been unprepared for my telephone call the day before, during which I'd clearly hoped to talk about the state of my correspondence with Luke.

About two months earlier, I'd begun a series of private letters to Mom that track both my feelings for Luke and the tempo and rhythm of our developing friendship. Even these secret posts reflect life as it unfolds around me, though: in the first one, I note in comically taciturn passing that I've been elected to our area's new Resistance Council and add, "Because of intense quarrelling at home generated by her sister's pregnancy and consequent intentions to marry a man the family doesn't know, Rose spent last night here. Like teen sleepovers!" The truth—which I'm more likely to admit to Luke than I am to Mom—is that while Rose is certainly glad to escape busyness at her home, she's also keen to be nearby because I'm once again so frequently in pain.

post secret (10)

Over the next several months, crucial changes occur. Cindy's three-year MCC term comes to an end in May and I'm loath to see her leave Uganda. When I'm ill, I often rest at Cindy's apartment between doctors' appointments. Dingy, musty, badly neglected during the worst years of the fighting, the apartment shouldn't feel comfortable but does because Cindy and I have our best talks there. Cindy is remarkably quiet, intense, wise and wryly insightful, powerfully simple in her wants and needs and possessions, and more successful at "presence theology" than anyone I've met, before or since.

My letters, by contrast, continue to feature Ndejje's access to electricity and running water. In late May, I joke that I'm going to write a book and everyone will know it's a parody of *Out of Africa* because I'll call it *Right Inside Africa* and begin with the line—imagined in a ponderous, cinematic voice-over—"*I had a fridge in Africa.*" My humour's a cover for desolation, having brought Cindy to Entebbe days before for the first leg of her journey back to America. Intense desolation, because I've just learned that Beautiful Cate is leaving for a year-long upgrading course at a college in Ggaba, Kampala's most distant southern district. What I can barely bring myself to acknowledge is that Rose is leaving, too, also for Ggaba, also for a year.

"Lord," I write, "I knew this was coming, but it's a bit much. Rose says she'll come back every weekend she can find free transport, but still." As if this is not enough, Mom is suddenly mourning one of her dearest friends and juggling best ways to respond to the illness I've recently begun to admit . . .

Letter #65 from Mom and Dad   *23 May 1988*

Sunday 29 May. I've been trying to avoid this but can't escape the fact that I have some sad news, namely that Tante Ans[14] died this past Friday 27 May. This was not as sudden and unexpected as it will appear to you. While we were visiting you it was discovered that she had lung cancer. We found out a few weeks after our return but I could not bring myself to write to you about it. After thinking it over for a long time, I decided to wait until the end, since there was nothing you nor anyone else could do to help and knowing it would only add to your other anxieties. [. . .]

It's hard to believe, and it'll take me quite a while to get used to the idea that Ans is gone. She was one of my oldest friends. It's kind of strange, there were some things which are important to me that I never talked about with her, but I did feel close to her. She knew Dad and I since before we were married, and knew the three of you since you were born. We shared a lot of memories. Such things create a bond between people. I am mourning her considerably and have been pretty despondent this week.

We received your #56, which was none too cheerful either, which increased my anxiety over you and your well-being. Gerta told me yesterday that Muoike Line had said to her that I should put my foot down and tell you to come home.[15] But even though there is a part of me that would like to do that, there is another part that tells me I cannot do that to you. I have to trust your good judgment to decide for yourself when the time has come to leave. Perhaps this is a good place to repeat what I wrote in #64: "If you don't notice considerable improvement, wouldn't you then consider coming home?"

By the time she writes again, Mom has recovered some of her equilibrium. She addresses many of her regular topics, but most of her long 66th letter describes the process that ensues

when one of her fellow students lodges a sexual harassment
complaint against their professor.

Letter #66 from Mom and Dad   5 June 1988

*Beppe and I have been reminiscing about the time she
was working as a psychiatric nurse and about the war but
now we've exhausted pretty well both topics, so I decided
to continue this epistle and I've brought Beppe the latest
Sojourners to read. [. . .]
I had lunch this past week with Trudy T, a woman I met
in last year's course. She is around my age and came from
England as a young woman and I find her quite a likeable
person, but the reason for getting in touch with each
other is a somewhat unusual story which I will now relate
to you:
As you may or may not remember, in the aforementioned
course our professor was Dr. J, a rather jolly, friendly man,
sixtyish, I would say, with an easygoing manner. This is the
same man who asked me to translate a Dutch Christmas
song because he liked the music so much. At the same time,
he also told me, to my immense astonishment, that one of
his students (in the same course) had charged him with
sexual harassment. I could not believe my ears. Professor J
was quite upset about it and asked, if it came to a formal
hearing, if I would give (be?) a character reference for him.
This harassment had supposedly taken place during class
hours with all other students present and consisted of two
or three remarks made by him directed to a young girl
(woman?) in class. The whole thing sounded so absurd that
I agreed to support Dr. J, but I was sure at the time that the
person in question would come to her senses and drop the
matter. [. . .]
By the middle of May, when I'd almost forgotten about
the whole thing, I got a phone call from Dr. J thanking me
for the translation of the song and asking if I could come to*

*a hearing related to the charges against him. Besides myself,
he had asked four other people, all from the same class,
including Trudy. The next evening Trudy called me and
we talked the whole thing over. By this time we knew the
identity of the person making the charges and a few more
details; we both agreed that the charges were unfounded
and that we would speak on behalf of Dr. J. During that
week we received a five-page statement by Dr. J, which was
a response to the allegations made against him. The hearing
was held in the evening at the university. We met in
Dr. J's office, we being Trudy, myself, one other young
woman, and two men, all of us classmates, and then
another of his supporters, someone I know from the
United Church. So he had actually six supporters, five of
them students.*

    *At the hearing Trudy read a statement which she had
prepared beforehand which responded to all the specific
allegations and her conclusion was that any allegations
of sexual harassment against[16] the woman (by this time
I remembered her quite well) were totally unfounded. I
spoke briefly as did the others, and so did Dr. J. Then the
committee members (three young women and one man)
asked him and us some questions. The whole thing took
longer than I had expected, about one and a half hours.
Nothing was concluded at the hearing, of course. As we left
and said our goodbyes, Trudy and I decided we'd stay in
touch and meet for lunch some time and that is what we did
last week.*

    *Before we met Trudy had called Dr. J, who still had not
heard anything from the committee. He's quite worried
because the "complainant" had threatened that if she did
not get satisfaction from the university she would take it
to the Human Rights Commission. We both think that
there's little chance it'll come to that. Trudy spoke to her
lawyer-boss and he told her that, judging from the available*

information [the complainant] "does not have a leg to stand on." So we'll just have to wait and see. Trudy and I were trying to analyze [the complainant]'s possible motives and the most plausible ones are that either she was sexually abused as a child and mistakes harmless friendly remarks for sexual overtures, or, she is a radical feminist, possibly lesbian and has man-hating tendencies. I also suggested that somebody has put her up to making the allegations; she seemed like such a nice, friendly girl.

As it happens, mail is moving efficiently from Winnipeg to Kampala, too, and on 22 June 1988 I pick up a mittful of letters, including both Mom's #65 and 66. I'm surprised, all these years after the fact, to discover that the long response I begin four days later engages directly with various of Mom's observations and questions in #65 but says nothing at all about her participation in her professor's defence.

It's impossible to know what happened in that classroom in 1987, but when I reread Mom's letter, I'm staggered by the witnesses ranged against the young woman in question, the relative ease with which an established older male professional amasses multiple, credible, legitimate forms of support. I believe that if my mother were in her right mind now, and given all the ways our collective understandings of sexual harassment have changed in the past thirty years, she'd consider the situation differently.[17] But, "she seemed like such a nice, friendly girl," Mom writes in 1988, having aired a series of hoary theories—childhood sexual abuse, radical feminist, man-hating lesbian—as if there might not also be more to jolly, friendly, easygoing, sixtyish men than meets the proverbial eye ...

Twenty-two years later, Pope Benedict XVI publically expresses his sorrow over the abuse inflicted on Indigenous children at residential schools run by the Catholic Church. In the midst of myriad cognitive losses, Mom still tracks revelations of systemic child abuse, and when I visit her two days later, on Friday 1 May 2009, I ask her what she thinks of the pope's statement. "It was high time," she tells me vigorously. "The highest person in that church should be the one to apologize certainly, and he did, at least." We discuss the mixed reaction that the pope's statement has generated, and when I suggest that it just barely scrapes the surface of what history requires, Mom agrees. "*Jah*," she says with chillingly clear emphasis, "and if I go by myself—you'll never forget it."

Alzheimer's and Mom's multiple languages muddle her meaning slightly here. When she says, "if I go by myself," she means, "if I judge by my own experience." In case I do not understand, she repeats the second part of her statement with dramatic emphasis: "*You—will—never—forget—it*," she says. "*Unless you are so old or whatever that you can't think anymore.*"

holy shipwreck (3)

The first time Pake's too-easily-blazing anger targeted me directly, Sandy and I were just three and four, or four and five, and we'd spent an intensely satisfying summer afternoon at our neighbours'. This was wrong because it was without permission.

In June 1960, when my parents pay eighty-five hundred dollars for their first and only home, the Red River Floodway is just a dream; Winnipeg is prone to frequent, widespread flooding; and the house on St. Anne's Road has water to the top of the basement stairs. But the property includes three-quarters of an acre of land and a tiny island in the Seine River, irresistible for my father the farmer. Eleven years later, developers began constructing the swathes of suburbia that now throttle my parents' property, but until then and for a long time afterward, my sister and I inhabited a blissful child-space midway between "city" and "country." There weren't many other youngsters close by, but we had one another and our two shared, imaginary friends, and, just across the street, the three utterly real Appelmans boys in whose company we played raucous games of tag, hide-and-seek, cars, race cars, cowboys and Indians, explorers, and war. The Appelmans boys spoke French as a first language and Sandy and I spoke Frisian, so we learned English together. We built tree forts and snow forts in season, obstacle courses, racing courses, and a variety of lumbering vehicles, sometimes in the service of "race cars" but usually in the service of "war."

A sixth child made up the complement of neighbourhood kids, a reclusive little boy who lived next door, which is to say, about seventy metres north of our house. Sandy and I were cheerfully jealous of Andreas L, having quickly fathomed that being "an only child" meant that Andreas didn't have to share even one of his impeccably constructed trucks, cars, robots, puppets, building sets, machines, guns, or games. Andreas wasn't exuberant like the Appelmans boys and couldn't match any of us for imagination, but Sandy and I coveted his toys and often begged for permission to visit. On this particular day, Mom had taken a nap after lunch, and Sandy and I decided against rousing her, having convinced ourselves that she would've said yes if she'd been awake.

By late afternoon, temporarily sated after a fine go at Andreas's grand toys, we loped home to find my mother, her parents, her two youngest sisters, and a neighbour frantically planning emergency measures in the kitchen. Dad and another neighbour were at the river searching for our bodies. Mom, having woken to find us gone, called, in quick succession, Dad home from work; her parents, who lived about one and a half kilometres north of us; the Appelmans across the street ("no, the girls aren't here"). Years later, my Mom's youngest sister, Gerta, who'd been with Beppe when Beppe picked up the phone, told me she could hear Mom's bloodcurdling scream across the room: *"De famkes bin wie!"* "The little girls have vanished!"

The mental progression follows its own logic: since we were missing, we must have disobeyed the cardinal prohibition of childhood and run away to the river, and if we'd run away to the river, then we'd also drowned, since every child who runs away to the river drowns. The logic of gratitude is similarly skewed. Massively relieved to see us come through the door alive, they meted out the severest penalty they could think of: Dad spanked us, one of only three such occasions in our memory of a shared childhood. It could've been much worse; it could've been Pake who spanked us. His fury that day was colossal, towering, terrifying, and it's only now—with the decades in between having piled their accumulated detritus between me and that afternoon—that I choose to interpret his outrageous behaviour as an expression of the fear he must have felt for my mother.

~~~

For weeks in the spring and summer of the first year that she lives in personal care, Mom and I walk along the same Seine River and I hear her interminably cycling and inconsolable anxiety about "*de lytse famkes*, the little girls, where are the little girls," and I speculate about Pake's tendon-ripping fury at the careless wandering that caused his beloved daughter such fear and anxiety.

Some of the happiest memories of my happy childhood are of Sunday afternoons at Beppe and Pake's, where Pake and Dad and the uncles filled the homely front room with cigar smoke while Pake (who did not attend church anymore, having been invited out of several) held forth with a week's worth of animated theological reflections. If the weather allowed, we cousins raced the deep backyard, skirting Beppe's gardens in hectic games we wouldn't dream up again together for seven days. Neither bouts with asthma nor knowing the danger of second-hand smoke entirely diminishes the pleasure I still take in the aroma of a cigar or the sight of a comfortingly smoke-filled room.

But little girls in peril—sometimes because of rivers and drowning, sometimes because there are fates worse than drowning—come up repeatedly in the family stories I've been piecing together. "Honestly, Kath," Gerta will tell me about that long-ago afternoon, "Beppe was holding the phone but it was like I was in the room with your Mom, I could hear her so clearly. It sounded like she'd been stabbed: '*de famkes bin wie!*' And Beppe ordered me, 'Get on your bike and ride like thunder!'" Rivers are dangerous places. More than a decade earlier, Beppe had threatened to use one for her own grim purposes, but that time, sixteen-year-old Geeske stayed home to keep the little girls—about the same age she was when she was sexually abused—safe.

When I watch my mother in the bathroom of her comfortably sterile new home, in the first weeks and months after we've admitted her into the kind care of strangers, in other worlds where she tries to pee and tries to remember that she is peeing and is, instead, ambushed by memories of pain and horror and cries out to a person I cannot see not to hurt her, I wonder, anguished, whether it's possible that minds can fold around experiences and encase them permanently, render them impervious to Alzheimer's erosions. "*Wer is Pake?*" Mom whimpers in the midst of other desperate hallucinations, "*Wer is Pake dan?*" Where is Pake, why has Pake not yet come, if only Pake would come, Pake would rescue me from this.

new meadow

new meadow (1)

Pake Harmen Ynzes de Jong was a giant in my mother's eyes, and for a very long time, he was a giant in mine. Born in 1900 in Sondel, a village in the south of Fryslân, he didn't ever amount to much in any public world where status and wealth are monitored and measured. For all his stellar qualities and because of them, he was not an industrious man, inclined exclusively to intellectual initiative. Post-secondary education hadn't been an option, though, and so his family thought of him as having missed out on the one vocation that would've suited him perfectly. "That man should have had a chance to study," my Beppe would lament in frustrated Frisian, "he should've been a *professor*," sufficiently often that it became a truth that attached to my grandfather, whom almost all his children and all his grandchildren, including those who didn't know any other Frisian, called Pake.

Fryslân is the only Dutch province in which a majority of the population speaks an official language other than Dutch.[1] Contrary to popular inclination to call it a dialect, Frisian is its own language, distinct from both Dutch and German and strongly linked to Old English. Never mind that Fryslân is the Newfoundland of the Netherlands, nor that my sister and I understand more Frisian, having learned it as a first language in Canada, than do the children of aunts and uncles who stayed in the Netherlands. My paternal cousins unlearned as much Frisian as they could as quickly as possible in order to accommodate the larger culture's scorn,[2] while I imbibed my mother's and her father's possibly perverse pride in a language almost no one except my blood relations speaks.

By the time my siblings and I were in school, my parents spoke English confidently, and we used it as our primary language at home. As my mother's Alzheimer's "progresses," though, she reverts more and more often to Frisian and, more frequently than I would have guessed, to Dutch. For about a year and to my dismay, my mother also resorts to German phrases to make or emphasize her points. During that year, I waste time and emotional energy insisting that Mom explain what she means in a language I can understand. I've inherited her powerful aversion to "the occupiers' language" and feel, perversely, as if *she's* betraying *my* loyalty by speaking German now. But my discomfort with German is a historical distraction: Mom's decline has almost certainly been slowed by her love of languages and her multilingual skills—I learn to be grateful that my mother can still speak and be understood.

I'm grateful too, on every one of our visits, for the ease I retain with spoken Frisian. When I turn to the work of transcribing, though, I discover that conversations I experienced as linguistically whole (however fractured by Alzheimer's obstacles) are messy patchworks of intermingled languages and voices. I begin boldly, thinking it will be easy to indicate which of Mom's words were in English and which in Frisian (or Dutch or German),[3] but the effect on paper is almost incomprehensible, especially when Mom struggles repeatedly to pronounce, find, or translate a word and switches languages between attempts. Mom and I are so accustomed, moreover, to thinking together that we regularly anticipate how the other's sentences will end—and we so typically endorse one another's opinions and jokes that, if talking at the same time weren't confusing enough, our frequent laughter obscures another whole portion of what we have to say.

My visits focus on my mother (and offer my father some respite), but my father often takes a part in our conversations. Dad's contributions, not all of which are in English, need to be recorded too. So I struggle on, creating a paper version I can live with, of the lilting, lifting, drifting, often hilarious, often frustrating, multilingual, multi-temporal, multi-discursive weekly weave of our lives.

I still haven't found a way, though, to convey the deeply comforting sound of my mother's voice or my mother tongue.

new meadow (2)

Letter #69 from Mom and Dad   *26 June 1988*

*Back from church, and now to the weekly letter writing.
[. . .] Your #58 and 59 arrived on Friday, and it's nice to
have some new input, but a disappointment that you are
not feeling any better, and had the flu besides. So I'm sitting
here debating with myself and this is how it goes: Should
I now, as Muoike Line suggested, "put my foot down and
tell Kathleen to come home"? Or should I just urge her a
bit more strongly than before to come home? Or should I
continue doing as I have up until now and say, "Kathleen,
I trust your own good judgment to know when the time has
come to come home"?*

*Should I "read between the lines" that you want me
to tell you to come home, or am I then reading something
that isn't there? Or is it both there and not there? Which,
considering the sometimes ambivalent (or should that be
"ambiguous"? No, I think it is "ambivalent"; I looked it
up) nature of human emotions, is also a possibility. Added
to that is the frustration of knowing that it is already three
weeks ago that you wrote, and I don't know whether by now
you're feeling better or worse, and by the time this letter
reaches you it'll be at least three more weeks. In your own
words: "arghhhh."*

My ongoing illness through much of 1988 exacerbates our collective frustrations with international post. On 26 March, three months before Mom articulates her insights into the undecidability of both language and emotion, I've written a sixth letter to Luke, vexed that I'm in Kenya for the second time in less than a year for medical reasons, waiting this time to be admitted into Nairobi Hospital. "The good news," I write, "is that the list of ruled-out-ugly-diseases gets longer every day. What I do have remains sufficiently mysterious, though, that the Jessups and the specialist at Rubaga threw up all their hands in dismay and cried, 'Take this woman to Nairobi, she's getting worse not better!'" Luke writes right back; his response reaches me at the Mennonite Guest House just before I fly home to Uganda.

Letter #7 to Luke   *18 April 1988*

The Ruled-out List is, by now, at least twice as long. Among other things, I learn that my heart is "perfect" (probably from all these years of wearing it out on my sleeve). The first diagnosis, by The Consultant (a man described as the "second-best doctor in Nairobi" and, as far as I'm concerned, about to win Dork of the Year), is stress. This is difficult to accept, partly because I'm certain The Consultant decided on his diagnosis before he'd even met me, partly because I know my stresses well enough to know that this is not how my body should be reacting.

I spend a long dark-night-of-the-soul deciding not to insist on further testing. I've been promised an Easter Sunday discharge if I comply, and in the meantime, our friends have arranged to have me see a Jungian psychologist here whom they're certain will be better able than these Exclusively-Medical-Type-Guys to assess the whole of my situation. [. . .]

I hate to write people off categorically so I give The Consultant one more chance. "Since we've decided this is stress," I ask politely while we're signing the discharge papers, "what can I do about it?" "Ignore the pain," he says without looking up. Ignore the pain? What kind of doctor is this clown? I decide to start with him. "Have a good day, Doc," I say only slightly sarcastically; I am out of here. [. . .]

By now there's a second tentative diagnosis (tentative because it's only recently been recognized as a medical condition and researchers are still developing laboratory tests): "neuromyasthenia." Isn't that a word to take to the bank? The good news is that it isn't contagious, congenital, or degenerative. The bad news is that back in North America it's being called "yuppie flu."

"Doc," I say (I've gone back to my Kampala GP), "I'm no yuppie." He grins and says, "No, but maybe you would be in Canada." Eeeeeyow, too true, don't remind me. There's a third name and it's probably the most informative for us non-medical, non-yuppie types, and that's "post-viral fatigue syndrome." The bad news is that it can last for years. The good news is that I've probably already had it for a while. The bad news is that Dr. B is pretty sure it will reoccur. The good news is that resting seems to be the best treatment, so I won't need to rush off to Nairobi if it does; resting I can do at Ndejje as well as anywhere.

One of Dr. B's other Canadian patients returned to Toronto in January after several months in a situation much like mine, and she's since sent him literature on the subject. It's almost eerie how closely my symptoms match the descriptions, and the patient profile lists "young, well-educated, independent, creative women," but listen, people: I am not a yuppie!

By 26 June, on the same day Mom begins her Letter #69, I have—with the support of the LIC staff and administration and my MCC colleagues—been resting seriously for more than two months.

Letter #61 to Mom and Dad   *26 June 1988*

Pillow-propped on the front porch. Morning is cool, still, bird-sung. Lizard antics begin when the stones have absorbed half a day of sun's warmth. For now, nearer

*rows of trees are dew-dripped dark, farther ones are hazy,
mysterious, indistinct, and in between, one ragged band
glitters in the jewel-green of first light. Moon Joyce has just
crooned her haunting, anti-nuke "Infinite Edge," and I'll
soon be treated to "The World of Christmas," courtesy of
my erratic taping habits several years back. From this edge,
nuclear destruction seems a whole infinity away, and yet I
keep reading in the news about "Toxic Waste Dumping in
the Developing World."*

*Countries so debt-ridden (and that, thanks to whose
global economic system?) they welcome our garbage;
figurative eyes light up at the fantastic sums we First-World-
ers will pay to get those poisons off our hands. Scrub, scrub,
scrub, a whole civilization of ineffectual Lady Macbeths,
bent on one kind of destruction or another, as long as it's
categorical, definitive, irreversible. [. . .]*

*And boom, the power's out again. It's been a bad week
for erratic electricity. Well, not that bad, we've had much
worse, but the last year or so has spoiled us. Just as well I'm
still not used to the marvels of refrigeration, or there'd be
much more than me spoiled. The Makerere students next
door (five young men finishing their Education degrees and
sent here for teaching practice at Senior Boys' Secondary
across the valley) are less than impressed. They were
promised non-stop power and enjoy their music at least as
much as I like mine. Luckily, I don't mind theirs, so when
we're all home together, mine is turned off. A change is as
good as a rest, right (unless you're a yuppie with the flu, and
then apparently you need the rest).*

*It's nice, actually, to have neighbours, not that I see or
hear that much of them. I think they were sternly warned
that I'm not to be disturbed, but their presence means
there's life around the place, a change of scenery, and
occasionally—when we catch glimpses of one another—
intelligent conversations. Otherwise, I sometimes feel*

isolated, our students under far-stricter orders than the
neighbours not to visit—

I can't know, of course, that Mom is writing that day too. I'm
still answering her melancholy Letter #65, in which she'd written about her friend Ans's passing, her anxiety about my continued ill health, her sisters' advice regarding my continued
ill health . . .

Letter #61 to Mom and Dad [cont.]

Seriously, Mom, when was the last time Muoike Line got
any of her kids to do anything by putting her foot down? I'm
touched by the lateral maternal anxiety, but we all know
that it's been decades since you "made" me do anything. But
it is absolutely true that one of the worst things about being
sick this far away is that there's very little I can do to calm
your worries. Rest assured that I know with utter certainty
that I can always come home, I always have a home to come
back to, and that no one could look after me better than you.

The letter I begin on 26 June gets longer and longer. Mom's is
relatively brief. Having expressed the dilemma she's in regarding my illness, she notes that Letter #58 arrived with perfect
timing. I'd added travel notes on the envelope, for Mom to
relay to Tracey (who's just begun planning *her* trip to see me),
and by a lucky coincidence, Tracey phoned Mom the day the
letter arrived. Just before she signs off, Mom adds:

Letter #69 from Mom and Dad [cont.]

I am writing this letter with short intervals spent on the
swing. The view is not quite like it was before but at least the
swinging feels the same and if I close my eyes I can imagine
the scenery as it used to be.

My siblings and I enjoyed the swing set my parents set up in the summer of 1967, but Mom depended on it, spent at least some time swinging every day the weather allowed, swinging to *bekom*. If my parents' forty-sixth letter hadn't arrived, I wouldn't understand her lament here for a lost view, but Letter #46 was one of the rare letters that included a note from my father.

My dad isn't a lot like my mother's father, though my father is quick to identify Pake as one of the great influences on his life, especially in relation to his socialist politics. My father reads constantly, mostly history and biography, but he isn't tormented by existential questions, nor does he love literature in the passionate, sometimes reckless ways that Pake did. A bittersweet effect of Mom's retreat from the wider world is that my siblings and I begin to understand more clearly who our father is. Without our eager, articulate, opinionated (paradoxically introverted) mother to dominate our family's interactions, we discover dimensions to our solid, stoic, frugal father that we hadn't imagined.

He is, for one thing, startlingly sociable. He has accumulated a wide circle of friends—at their church, in the Save-Our-Seine group, amongst neighbours along the riverbank, in the NDP, at R.A.R.—and we are, frankly, surprised by the warmth of their affection. But it's clear: Dad has many friends who value his loyal care for Mom, the hard physical work he's willing to put into causes he believes in, his ability to jury-rig solutions to all kinds of small and large engineering problems, his aversion to waste, his quietly generous kindness, his powerfully felt capacity to nurture land and animals. In the fall of 2005, when my cherished cat of fourteen years became fatally ill and I'd made the difficult decision to euthanize her, it was Dad who drove us to the vet. Dad and I agreed on the drive home that we'd bury Oscar that evening in a sheltered spot in their garden, but he worried out loud several times that I wouldn't find an appropriate box. Though I assured him I had at least one large shoebox in the basement, he phoned shortly after he got home to let me know that I could stop looking: he'd unearthed several scraps of good-quality wood and would build Oscar a proper little coffin that afternoon.

During the three years I lived at Ndejje, Dad added notes to at least a dozen of Mom's letters, but several of the first went permanently missing, and for a while, Dad thought he might be jinxed. The notes that arrived cover some or all of my father's main topics: my financial solvency (something he worked hard behind the scenes to ensure, perpetually anxious about my decision to give up a professional salary for volunteer work); the state of his prized gardens; politics, especially related to the nefarious work of capitalist and neo-liberal (though he wouldn't have used the word) forces; and our quirky little homestead, flowering amongst the encroaching development.

Dad's relatively long addition to Letter #46 includes chagrin that unionized jobs are being lost at Canada Post; disbelief at the house prices people are willing to pay; and regret to see construction begin on a condominium development next door. "When you come back," he writes, "you may find it a real shocker to live again in a so-called affluent society. I guess we have been spoiled by years of living as nonconformists, or at least slow ones." So I understand that by late June 1988 Mom is mourning the view of our former neighbour's little meadow, obstructed now by an apartment block and multiple condos.

Back at Ndejje, I'm emulating my father's slow nonconformity and grateful to understand "yuppie flu" as something I might have developed in Canada. Abhorrent as I find the name, it means I can resist the attempts some of my correspondents make to blame my illness on living in "dark and dangerous Africa."

Letter #61 to Mom and Dad [cont.]

*Lil sent an article on "yuppie flu," which is depressing but
makes me dig in my figurative heels. If that's what this
is, we're in for the long haul, and location won't change
much. Whether I'm in Ndejje, Winnipeg, Boston, Belleville,
Brampton, or Mozambique,[4] what matters is that I'm able
to rest when I need to, and to feel, even resting, that there's
some point to being where I am. [. . .]*

*I'm not staying for Frances (although she says she'd leave
if I did), and I'm not staying for Jake and Amy (although
they couldn't be clearer about valuing my presence, sick or
well), and I'm not going home for Luke, because I know
he's joking when he says I should join him this summer at
a friend's wedding, and the Uganda alumni retreat, and in
Mozambique whenever he gets there! If there were any good
reason to believe I'd be better in Canada than I am here, I'd
consider coming home, but at home, I'd be an "in-valid."
Here, even sick and a little lonely, I'm in the middle of life.
It's hard to explain. I'm staying because it feels enormously
hopeful to stay. Ndejje is just getting on its feet. What will I
miss if I leave now?*

Mom and I begin writing one another on 26 June 1988 and we
end on strikingly telepathic notes:

Letter #61 to Mom and Dad [cont.]

*Tante Ans's dying didn't come as that much of a shock (the
quantities she smoked; her frenetic work habits), but how
much you miss her and will miss her? That's what's terribly
hard and makes me wish I could come home, if only for a
few weeks, all of them to spend with you. [. . .]*

*P.S. Thank you for making me strong enough to trust my
own judgment; thank you for trusting my judgment.*

Letter #69 from Mom and Dad [cont.]

If you feel you can still stay, then we'll trust you. Whatever
decision you make, I know it has to be the right one for
you. We are always thinking of you and send all
our love.
P.S. Beppe also told me to say hello, she thinks often
about you.

new meadow (3)

Pake and Beppe de Jong belonged to the *Fryske Beweeging* (Frisian Movement), a society committed to the preservation of the Frisian language and its centuries-old literature, and to (eventually successfully) establishing Frisian as the official language of the province's schools and courts. Pake was ecumenical, though, even promiscuous in his love for reading. Like my mother until the fall of 2010, after which she no longer absorbed anything she found in the books she'd still page through for hours, Pake enjoyed reading more than any other activity, and he held reading material of almost any kind in higher regard than anything (and often *anyone*) else around him.[5]

A coffee-table book titled *Nijemardum sa't it wie*[5] was produced by a citizens' group in my mother's home village in 1985 to commemorate the hundredth anniversary of the community's founding. Nijemardum—or "new meadow"—was an offshoot of Oudemardum—"old meadow"—my Beppe's home village. The de Jongs are referenced at various points throughout the book, usually as a family, though a telling anecdote about my grandfather appears alongside a photograph of his grocery store.

"*Links*" that caption reads, "*de winkel dêr't Yke Foekjes, Harmen Ykes de Jong en Harmen Ynzes de Jong winkelman wiene. De earste en in skoft de ienichste tillefoan fan't doarp hong by him yn 'e winkel. As Harmen Ynzes kaam te boadship-opfreegjen en der lei in boek op 'e tafel, koene de froulju earst it wruk wol dwaan. Harmen Ynzes siet te lêzen en fergeat syn hiele hannel.*"[6] I learn from this anecdote that the first—and for a long time, the only—telephone in the village was located in

Pake's grocery store, and I learn a story that will delight my mother repeatedly, though in increasingly truncated form, until the point that we admit her into care. According to Nijemardum lore, if a book should be in view in the homes Harmen Ynzes visited to collect grocery orders, the women of the house could go about their work undisturbed: Pake wouldn't ask again about their kitchen needs until he emerged from whatever irresistible textual world it was that had come to hand.

Long after Mom stopped comprehending writing of any kind, she'd still regularly begin conversations by asking, in a tone of high amusement, "I've probably told you that funny story about my Dad, haven't I? How he'd read *anything*?" Followed, typically, by gales of laughter. I often played along but I didn't always play along. Sometimes I didn't play along because I wanted to talk about other things. Sometimes I didn't play along because I wanted Mom to acknowledge the ambivalence many of her siblings feel about the ways their charismatic, domineering father too often added to Beppe's work instead of helping to reduce it.

Several years after World War I ended and long before he became my Pake, Harmen Ynzes courted Gepke Visser of Oudemardum with a focused determination he usually reserved for intellectual pursuits. Gepke's parents believed she—and they—could do better than Harmen de Jong, who, in his mid-twenties, hadn't yet demonstrated a knack for any kind of sustained work. Gepke herself preferred another young man entirely. Sadly for her, *his* relatively well-to-do parents considered the match below them and quickly ended that barely kindled romance. In the absence of financial independence and despite having trained and worked as a psychiatric nurse, Gepke did not have a plausible alternative to marriage and so, on 13 November 1928, after her parents had determined that Harmen should be set up as the proprietor of a dry goods grocery in neighbouring Nijemardum, she acquiesced to the life he was eager to offer.

Harmen looks serious but pleased in their wedding portrait. At twenty-eight, he's a weedy, cerebral young man with an impressively large nose and an oversized, already-balding head. Gepke's jaw is square and accurately forecasts jowls in later life, but her deep-set dark eyes dominate her lovely, carefully serene face. It's a photograph of its era and so its ethereal twenty-four-year-old bride betrays no discernible emotion. "She should never have married," my mother told me about her mother from time to time over our many years of talk at the kitchen table, a sentiment various of my aunts have repeated since I began trolling for the stories behind the stories. The pronouncement was typically, and still typically is, followed by a hasty amendment. "At least," the speaker corrects herself, "she shouldn't have had so many children." "But really," they'll sometimes backtrack, "Beppe would probably have been much happier if she'd stayed single like her friends from nursing." "She wasn't really cut out to be a mother," someone might add, which another sister might qualify, after the briefest pause, "Certainly not of so many kids."

The truth is that, more than twenty years before effective birth control was legalized and widely available, Harmen and Gepke were far more fertile than they could afford, economically or emotionally, to be. My oldest uncle, Ynse, was born just before my grandparents' first wedding anniversary, and my three oldest aunts followed in quick succession: Line fifteen months after Ynse, Hinke less than a year after Line, and Bertha fourteen months later. With little Bertha's arrival my Beppe had, as she liked to say in Frisian, one child walking, one in the playpen, one in the high chair, and one in the cradle. Two young women were hired to help Beppe with the store and the house, but these first four children were already a strain on her physical and emotional health. Beppe may have had a miscarriage between Bertha's birth and my mother's in January of 1936, because the almost-three-year interval was unprecedented. During that time, Beppe's clandestine search

for information about birth control discovered a description
of "calendar-based contraception" in a book on homeopathic
medicine.

Dominy van der Marel appears regularly in my mother's
stories about her father's love of intense, intellectual discussion and his disdain for the theologically rigid, socially tepid
ideas he encountered in the churches he'd stopped attending.
Pake considered Reverend van der Marel—a relatively young
but learned man from Amsterdam—a welcome exception
to the mediocre clergymen typically sent to provincial villages like Nijemardum. It was likely Reverend van der Marel
and his wife whom ten-year-old Geeske was defending when
they made the unconventional decision to announce their
daughter's birth as a gift of spring. According to the stories,
the discerning young pastor enjoyed his lively, undoubtedly
smoke-laced conversations with my grandfather as much as
my grandfather did.

But they disagreed on birth control. Reverend van der
Marel was staunchly in favour—I don't know on what theological grounds—while Pake was vehemently opposed on
a predictably patriarchal set of reasonings. At least once in
anticipation of van der Marel's arrival, my grandmother—
who took an active part in the visits when she had time—
suggested to my grandfather that they raise the question of
"family planning," a suggestion Pake vetoed furiously. Beppe
was out of patience, though, with the veto and alluded to the
subject sufficiently clearly that van der Marel's assurance has
become a part of family lore.

In the middle of rural, conservative 1940s Netherlands,
that is, van der Marel was prepared to assert that it was not
God's will that children should be born, one after the other,
year after year, without taking considerations of health—the
mother's, the child's, the other children's—and financial
welfare into account. My mother used to remember that on

one occasion at least, the topic prompted such fiery disagreement that van der Marel either left of his own, perhaps angry, accord, or Pake tossed him out on his metaphorical ear. If my mother were in her right mind now, I'd ask much more about these stories and the relative time frames. How old was Mom when these conversations took place? Did Pake and the good pastor patch up their disagreement, and how? At what point, if ever, did Pake acquiesce to the prohibitions on sexual activity that the homeopathic manual described?

My mother's two younger brothers were born in quick succession, sixteen and thirty months after her, Lieuwe (Louie) in May 1937, with World War II still a somber impossibility, and Hendrik (Henry) in June 1938, amid rising international tensions. During the almost four-and-a-half-year reprieve before the three youngest daughters arrived, Beppe suffered a miscarriage, possibly her second. This is the time frame within which my mother was being abused, so it's possible that, though I'll never know whether, Beppe was pregnant when she wrestled Pake away from the boy who'd been abusing little Geeske. My youngest aunt Gerta remembers Beppe describing the pleasure she felt at finally being slim again and engaging easily with the physical work of mothering seven children (ages four to thirteen, Geeske in the corner scribbling in her siblings' notebooks), keeping house, and running the store (since it never did well under Pake's management).

"Be careful," Mark Twain allegedly once quipped, "about reading health books. You may die of a misprint." Funny enough, till somebody loses an "I"—till somebody loses her self. It's not at all clear, you see, at what point my grandmother discovered that misprints in the homeopathic manual had been advocating a precisely incorrect understanding of the fertile and non-fertile days of a woman's menstrual cycle. My Aunt Jessie (Jikke) was born prematurely in November 1942, two and a half years into the German occupation of the

Netherlands; Eta (Itte) was born in June 1946, a year after the end of World War II; and little Gerta (Gepharda) arrived halfway through 1949 and would celebrate her third birthday on a sticky July day, two months after immigrating to Winnipeg, Canada.

new meadow (4)

When I arrive on 11 January 2008, eager to record my first official conversation with Mom, she wants to tell me what she remembers about her father's death thirty-six years earlier, having been reminded of it by something on the radio. Mom's account emphasizes the peacefulness of Pake's passing and I can't resist asking if she's afraid of dying. Mom can learn and forget a name between breaths by now, but she is more than capable of sustained engagement with subtle ideas: for the next twenty minutes we meander pleasurably across a range of existential issues: our fear, or not, of dying, which leads us to the perplexing Christian theology of resurrection, which prompts my mother to ponder the purpose of our life on earth, given her relative certainty that if we *are* resurrected, we'll be resurrected without a memory of this existence. "What's the point of the whole thing, if we can't remember anyway?" she muses and adds, "Since most of it is eating!" and the recording crackles with our laughter.

We reflect on the forms that consciousness and memory might take after death, and when Mom repeats her wish to "just melt away," she immediately wonders, "If you have a spirit, maybe that spirit stays?" In the discussion of spirits and souls that follows, I ask Mom to point to the place in her body where she locates her essential self. "I think here," she answers promptly, with a lovely but inadvertent double entendre, touching the middle of her forehead: "In my mind; I live in my mind. [. . .] I live in my *body*, but I also live in my mind. [. . .] That's a simultaneous process: while I'm in my body my mind is—"

And then she pauses and asks, "Is it *in* my body or is it just around me. . .?" "How do you experience it?" I ask, and her response is instantaneous: "I experience my self as being in my body." "And if it's not in my body," she quips, "then it has maybe taken off for a little jaunt!" Mom is quiet then for just a moment before she observes thoughtfully: "There is so immensely much that we don't know really, isn't there?"

Dad interrupts to ask if we smell an intense smokiness (something may be wrong with the wood stove), and our conversation veers abruptly. When we refocus, it's to consider the Andy Warhol exhibit we visited the previous week and to speculate on art's capacity to critique commodification. Characteristically, Mom both doubts her ability to say anything meaningful about art and declares that it's everyone's human right to have an opinion: "Because the painter himself throws it out to the public and says, 'What do you think of that?'!" Our conversation shifts then to Barack Obama's successful bid for the Democratic leadership, and when we survey the racist and misogynist attacks that Obama and Hillary Clinton have weathered, Mom is eager to condemn entrenched American racism. Wait, though, I caution, Canada is a racist society too. Canadians, I propose, have only *barely* begun to understand systemic racism here against Indigenous people.

Mom could not agree more. "*Jah, jah,*" she emphasizes, "I told you, eh, when we came to Canada? I said to Pake, 'Yeah, but Dad, there are also other people there, you know, who already live there; what do *they* think of it that we're going there?' But then Pake said, '*Jah,* but you know, the government, the Canadian government? *They* are letting us in.'" Mom pauses. "Well," she says next, more hesitantly, "we certainly didn't, you know, peruse and see what all had happened before—and after. We knew very little about that. But, *jah.* They let us in."

Ironically, I learn far more about my mother *because* she has Alzheimer's than I would if the disease had never encroached on our lives. Never mind that what I learn is often telegraphic, truncated, partial, fragmented, and possibly untrue. My sister doubts Mom's story about the schoolmaster who made a special trip on his bicycle all the way to Nijemardum from the M.U.L.O. in Balk to urge Beppe and Pake to find the money to send gifted young Geeske for further education. I, for my part, am skeptical about young Geeske's intuition of the fraught imbalances that have characterized Canada's Indigenous–settler history. But my skepticism is moot. This is one of several stories that Mom will return to again and again. "I told you, didn't I," she begins innumerable times, "how when I heard we were moving to Canada, I said to my Dad, 'But what about the people who are already living there; do *they* want us to come?'"

On 11 January 2008, I ask Mom if she has any memories of encountering Indigenous people when she was first in Canada. "No, no," she insists, agitated—talk about the immigration years typically prompts more than usual anxiety—"all I can remember from those first early years, is, that, [. . .] how terribly sea, uh, sea, uh, uh, *homesick* Mom was, and that I had to stay with her for crying out loud, and [. . .] of course I didn't go to school, I didn't go to school, at all in this country you know." We explore the dramatic shifts taking place these days, as Indigenous Canadians are increasingly politically active, increasingly shifting our collective sense of who we are together—and then I maneuver the conversation back to Mom's first experiences here. "When you're in the middle of, you know," she explains, "your mother is so ill that she's going to drown—, after the dr . . . dr . . . jump in the river and then when she's over that, then you'd just better get a job [. . .] and what kinds of jobs they are, and you have to figure out where to go and what to do, and—ah, I remember how *nervous* I was. *Fanke*"—girl—"*you can't believe it . . .*"

There wasn't much about Canada that young Geeske liked. She remembers the cold, and she remembers the barren look of the place, the desperate lack of trees, the dearth of walking paths (so different from Nijemardum, or glorious biking with Bertha through woods and villages to the M.U.L.O.), the worry at home, first about Beppe and constantly about finances, because some things didn't change. Details of her various factory and clerical jobs are obliterated by anxious memories of constant distress. "Especially then when I, I went into that place where you had to [. . .] they had a machine where you posted all the incomes and, you know, what people had bought, because it was a wholesale, and then you had to, at the end of the month, I guess, you had to make sure that the money was, you know, correct. *Och ben*," Mom says. Oh kid. "*I was so nervous.*"

"I hated Canada," Mom declares. "I thought, 'Why would anyone live in this godforsaken place where there is *nothing* beautiful.'" Until my Aunt Jessie came home from Grade 3 having learned a song about a linnet and her secret. That, Mom remembers repeatedly, is when she began to believe that if she could find this beautiful song in Canada, other beauty might also emerge.[7]

~~~

By June 1988, Mom's letters frequently reflect the loose ends she's at now, having finished the final courses for her university degree in April. In July, however, there's excitement when my father's sister Griet visits Canada with her husband and their three children.

Letter #71 from Mom and Dad   *18 July 1988*

A cool morning, with the promise of a sunny, but not too hot day. We arrived home from our camping trip yesterday with the Holland relatives [. . .]. Considering the fact that they are not very used to our distances and our heat, I feel justified in calling it a considerable success. [. . .]

We took the Yellowhead up to Edmonton, camping twice along the way. [. . .] By the time we got there, the kids were

ready for a break so we visited the notorious, gloriously
gaudy, glitzy West Edmonton Mall. Can you believe Dad at
the West Edmonton Mall? Well, I must say he took it with
good grace [. . .]. Then we went to Red Deer and visited
Dad's cousin, with kids approximately the same age as our
visitors, another piece of luck, all the more because they had
a computer.

Mom is hurrying because she wants to send this letter with
Frances's parents, who are about to leave for their second trip
to Uganda.

Letter #71 from Mom and Dad [cont.]

I will just tell you about one of the campsites on our way
home and that we spent an evening with Henry in Calgary,
who took us to the Stampede [. . .]. We took the No. 1, which
leads through the most barren and bleak areas of Alberta
and Saskatchewan. But there is one area, the Cypress Hills,
a provincial park that is totally unlike its bleak and dry
surroundings. It is quite a bit higher than the surrounding
land, covered with fine trees mostly and a few lakes like an
oasis but larger than I've imagined an African oasis. There
is of course a scientific explanation for this phenomenon,
but I was convinced there must be also an Indian legend
connected with it, which has a more mystic and symbolic
meaning. It's a beautiful area, now, of course, occupied with
several campsites although a protected area, and I couldn't
help wondering if we were not perhaps insulting the Great
Spirit by desecrating the spot, with our cars, tents, noise,
and everything that goes with the conveniences of modern
civilization.

I should never doubt my mother's intuition, though "mysti-
cal legend" isn't quite right: archaeological evidence makes it
clear that for over seven thousand years, Indigenous people

of the northwest plains of North America have wintered on what are now called the Cypress Hills. The peculiar geography of the place offers a range of resources, abundant game animals, protection from the prairie winds, and a powerful site for spiritual ceremonies.

~~~

The day before Mom begins her Letter #71, thieves break into the Reads' former house and make off with all manner of resaleable goods: door locks, door bolts, light sockets, electrical outlets, and both the bathroom and the kitchen sinks. The day *after* Mom begins her letter, Frances lets one of our passengers off in the middle of a quiet intersection on the outskirts of Kampala and a passing police officer charges her with "Being Discourteous to Other Drivers." We attend at the courthouse that afternoon. As I write later to Cindy, "I went into Central Police Station with Frances, thinking to play Dying Missionary in aid of my pal The Criminal, but none of the uniformed who's-ems looked remotely interested in staying the charges. Realizing the jig was up, we agreed I'd wait in the car. Court is several hundred yards down a rutted alley, and while there isn't much point in driving, the walk, for me, would be equivalent to two weeks' worth of very painful exercise."

Twenty minutes into my wait, gunfire erupts around the corner and chaos ensues. A man emerges from the far side of the police station running headlong past our car where I'm crouched below the windshield gauging the distance I'll have to run to rescue Frances. Onlookers scatter, then regather to join police officers, their guns drawn, in a foot chase. Just minutes after the street quiets, Frances returns, entirely unscathed by gunfire and almost unscathed by the judicial process. Comparing notes with the people remaining on the street, we determine that the running man, arrested for possession of a stolen pistol, had broken free of his police escorts, who'd responded by opening fire.

On an unarmed man in a street filled with civilians. When the adrenalin shooting through my body recedes, I'm left with staggering pain in each one of my joints and all the large muscles of my arms and legs. "Honey," a voice sounds in my mind, "you couldn't rescue a fly."

Letter #71 from Mom and Dad [cont.]

We were very pleased to find both #61 and #62 waiting for us. Many thanks for all the information and the wonderfully introspective and reflective musings. We are of course also very happy to hear you're beginning to feel quite a bit better.

Two days after our escapades in Kampala, thieves—likely the same ones who looted the Reads' house so thoroughly the previous Sunday—attempt to break into Frances's home. I muse extendedly on adventure and helplessness in letters to Cindy, Sharon, and Luke before rallying the courage to let my parents know the news.

Letter #3 to Cindy   *24 July 1988*

That takes us to Thursday night, followed by Friday morning, very early, when an indeterminate number of someones attempt to break into Frances's place. Shattering back-door glass wakes her up and she does exactly the right thing—starts a pot-banging, lung-bursting alarm that scares off the would-be villains and brings her neighbours to the rescue. (Daniel said he couldn't tell where the alarm was coming from until he realized it was in English!) So that's bad news followed by good news followed by a bit more bad news: the thieves do get away with a few things, namely, both Frances's front- and back-door keys, and my back-door key.

I spend Friday night at Frances's place (William doesn't want my house empty, though, so he sends two students

*to sleep chez moi) where we both don't sleep through five
hours of the worst thunderstorm in the history of the world.
We lose power after the first hour and agree that end times
would be fine with us; I'm certainly ready for either heaven
or Canada. Having made a pact not to tell the scariest
stories we know, I entertain Frances with readings from an
old flame's recent letter, a marvel of innuendo; he might as
well have put a fluorescent sticker on the envelope: "Eat your
heart out, I've found somebody else!" [. . .]*

*We do, eventually, sleep. There's much more, of course,
to the story and by now, lots of good news, starting with
the UEB[8] guys who arrived yesterday to begin hermetically
sealing us into our respective hovels. (They're welding the
locks so it's impossible to remove them from the door frames,
which is what happened down at Reads'.) Just in case we
can't get out of the hermetic seal, I'm counting on you to hop
the next flight in, secure transport from Entebbe, and spring
me before I die, starved of human company and overdosed
on relief aid chicken curry. [. . .]*

*The good news gets so much better it's practically
miraculous: after I use up most of Sunday morning crying,
the front door opens and an angel or Rose walks in. Holy
moley, Ggaba let out early! The last time friends looked this
good, it was December 1987 during the petrol shortage, and
there you were at the arrivals gate with just enough fuel to
get us back to your place.*

*Later in the afternoon, Rose helps me carry pillows
back from the drama festival I've had to leave early and
announces that if it's alright with me, she'll be bringing her
mattress up to keep me company for the next little while?!
"Honey," I tell her, "I just wish I had a chauffeur, I'd send
him down that fast to get your things."*

*(I'm amazed at how afraid I can admit I was, now that
Rose is back.)*

In the comic version I send my parents, I focus on the UEB man who surprises me a week later with a social call that is also—I don't realize until I'm pouring tea—a courtship call. I'm so far out of my cultural depth I might as well be on the moon. My yuppie-addled brain struggles to derail this conversation politely—Rose is away for the day working in one of her family's distant fields, and all my usual visitors are still careful of my need to rest—when cherubic, telepathic Nathan Muggulu, recently church-married to Kiyingi Caroline (the "bright zing" of Letter #18, one of LIC's most promising graduates), appears at the door. Nathan claims the sweet bananas he's brought are a gift from his grandmother in the village, greets my guest in Luganda, accepts my offer of tea, and chats with apparently endless stores of gracious ease. It isn't until the UEB man finally leaves that Nathan leaves too. More than an hour has passed. I'm not sure what Nathan says besides the English I can understand, but the UEB man doesn't come calling again.

new meadow (5)

Pake Harmen died on Christmas Eve, 1972, having been in and out of the hospital throughout December with increasingly severe health problems, complications of the emphysema he'd developed after years of heavy smoking—endless cigarettes, most of which he rolled himself; a range of cozy-smelling pipes; and, best of all in his estimation, good Dutch cigars when he could afford them. He was 72. Pake's passing left Beppe, whom he'd frustrated most of her life, bereft. Beppe outlived the man she hadn't wanted to marry by twenty-five years, dying in February 1998 after a long decline, a little less than a month before her ninety-fourth birthday. It isn't clear whether Beppe ever forgave Pake for abandoning her to the life he had promised to share. Sometime after his death, she began to drink, to ease the pain of arthritis exacerbated by loneliness.

crosswords (13)

Harry sleeps through much of his hard first round of chemo, then rallies to laugh through a second round. By late March he has so entirely exceeded his doctors' expectations, they discharge him early. This is a carefully calibrated break before the third round of chemo and will be monitored closely. Harry wafts home 31 March 2008 on an ocean of our collective relief and the timing feels auspicious. Because I'm on sabbatical, Gareth and I have planned a first-ever winter holiday. The flights we booked months ago are for 31 March, and now, Harry coming home makes it feel safe enough to leave. I let blog readers know we're taking a short break and that the news is as good as we could possibly hope.

Three days earlier, my parents and I are already cautiously over the moon: Harry's coming *home*. We celebrate over lunch on Friday 28 March, and Mom asks if we'll be reading letters today. I've got #42 and 43 with me, with some of Mom's responses to my first bout of pain and exhaustion, and details of Beppe's drinking. Mom and I begin, though, by completing several of the week's crossword puzzles.

As Mom's abilities shift, I adjust the level of our collaboration. These days I take charge of the newspaper and frame elaborated verbal clues so that Mom can concentrate on the words forming in her mind. We're almost done when a three-letter synonym for "tipsy" trips us up. Bereft of further clues, I simply say, "This one's 'lit,' Mom," and she agrees cheerily. "I'm sure I've seen that somewhere," she imagines and explains, "I guess I see so few people that are actually lit, I'd forgotten," and we both laugh. She gets "caller's need" without hesitation ("telephone"), and when I read the final clue, "clock unit," I also ask, "What are clocks divided into?" "Hours," Mom replies instantly and repeats it, carefully pronouncing the *H* both times, so I'll know to spell it correctly. Buoyed by crossword success and (more) celebratory chocolate, Mom is eager to resume letter reading.

I'm curious to know what Mom remembers about my illness, but far more curious to know how she'll respond to her twenty-year-old description of Beppe's drinking. Until I'd unearthed the letters, I'd forgotten completely. When we read them, Mom and I are aghast at the quantities: two twenty-six-ounce bottles in a week? "Whisky?" Mom asks, deciphering her own handwriting; "Did Beppe drink *whisky*?!" And she chuckles as Beppe's scheme reveals itself, the bottle Eta bought for her on Thursdays after brunch; the bottle Louie brought over with the groceries on Saturday.

"Beppe had quite a scam going, didn't she?" I say, and we explode with laughter. "Holy Dinah," Mom muses, subdued by the time she's read to the end of the section. "Now that I read it of course I remember. And I remember that I found her fallen off her bed, you know. I remember that and of course, I was, basically, the nearest daughter. Holy Dinah," Mom repeats, and then she switches to Frisian. "*Achhhh*," she says, an untranslatable expression of compassion from a class of sounds I jokingly refer to as "guttural-noises-of-northern-Europe." "I feel so sorry for her even now. Poor soul. She was so homesick."

I press on this for the next twenty minutes. When I listen to the recording, I discover my father on the phone in the background, talking with his eldest sister, Tjitske, in the Netherlands. Our Dutch relations faithfully follow the blog, but it's clear they want to get the news directly from Dad: *How is baby Harry doing?* At the time, I hear only what I think of as Mom's inadequate answers to my questions. I'm relentless, driven by an unarticulated conviction that if Mom can identify what Beppe might have done to combat loneliness, Mom might still be able to take action in her own life. "But Mom," I object, "Beppe had been in Canada for *thirty-five* years by then. Surely after thirty-five years you're done with being home-sick?" "Weren't there organizations she could have joined," I ask, "other Dutch people she could have stayed in touch with?" and in case my mother has missed this, I elaborate on the iro-nies of Beppe missing Pake to the point of alcoholism, when they'd hardly had what could be called a happy marriage.

I pull my cruelty up short, though, when I hear my mother say—for what the recording reveals as the third time—"I can explain nothing to you." Mom isn't interested any more in psychologizing her mother or blaming her. She has only empathy left. "I'm getting older now too," she reminds me, and I slowly grasp, in the "excuses" she makes for her mother, how alone my own mother feels. So I ask her instead about the friends she's had over the years and what she values in friends, and she tells me about Ans, who died while I was struggling with "yuppie flu" in Uganda, with whom, Mom says in Frisian, "you didn't maybe have earth-shaking con-versations, but you came from the same country." She names each of her sisters, especially Bertha, who died a year ago and whom she misses intensely. She pauses briefly to remember again *how* much she and Bertha enjoyed biking together to the M.U.L.O., one hour in each direction every day to fill with talk and laughter and singing—

She laments the fact that her two good friends from uni-versity both live far away now, one in Victoria, one in New Brunswick. And she speaks with great fondness about her best friend, Rimi, from the M.U.L.O., who lived in Balk but would sometimes bike to Nijemardum to spend Saturdays with young Geeske, Rimi, whose father—Mom remembers with more than a frisson of delight—"was a Communist!" "You know *what*, Kathleen," she tells me suddenly, "I feel the most comfortable when I'm with that Alzheimer's group."

But then Dad is off the phone and we turn our attention to news from Holland. We return to Mom's Alzheimer's group about fifteen minutes later. The Alzheimer Society of Manitoba runs a group that Mom has been attending since the fall, joining in happily for Thursday mornings of conversation, singing, and games. Dad goes reluctantly at first, only when it's his turn to drive (he and Mom carpool with a couple from their church), but he soon realizes that the spouses who gather in the kitchen are a rich source of information, friendship, and support.

On 28 March 2008, we're running out of afternoon. I check the bus schedule, adjust my plans. "Mom," I say, "tell me about the last Alzheimer's meeting. You were saying how comfortable you feel with that group." When Mom tells me enthusiastically that it's because "We're all the same; we don't have to hide it; everybody *knows* we're forgetting stuff!" we laugh, and my curiosity turns to this new idea of hiding. "Do you find you have to hide it?" I ask and almost before that question crosses the room I add, "How do you hide it when you hide it?" "Well," Mom begins characteristically, "I don't even know how you hide it when you hide it," and then she finds her way. "You hardly say anything, to make sure, for one thing," she explains. "You don't tell something—you don't *talk about something*," she corrects herself, "that you don't know anything about." She pauses. "It's partly also when people asks you—*ask you*—when people *ask you* something and then you forget it again within minutes. That kind of thing."

"And how do you hide that?" I ask. "Well," Mom says, "you shut up."

post secret (11)

In the summer of 2007, before I begin recording our conversations officially, my mother tells me a story that hinges on another of Beppe's friends, not the schoolteacher this time, but a woman who must—I understand now—have been married to a man in the Dutch SS. "We hated going there," Mom remembers vividly, "we *hated* it." I imagine the place shrouded in proverbial darkness, because Mom describes armed men in black uniforms, the ominous presence of German shepherds straining at leashes, an atmosphere of dread. "We went there once," Mom remembers, "and not again. She would often ask Beppe if we could come again, that lady. I guess their kids were lonely. It was hard for Beppe: she knew we didn't want to go and she didn't want to make us go. And then I heard them talking in the store."

"'You can say it, Gepke,'" Mom remembers Beppe's friend cutting through Beppe's careful evasions: "'The children don't want to come. It's alright. I understand.'" I suspect that it might have been the same woman who asked Beppe, when talk in the de Jong household had turned to emigration, about Canada's requirements. "But will they take people like us," Beppe's friend had asked, "people with our *antecedents*?" Mom tells this story in Frisian and uses the Frisian word that is also the English word. *Ûns antecedents:* our background, our history of affiliation, our distorted allegiances. In the winter after Harry died, on one of our long walks in the neighbourhood, on a day whose date I don't remember, in a conversation I didn't record, I asked Mom again about her experiences when she first came to Canada.

"What were the people like," I ask, "the ordinary Canadi-ans?" Mom has spoken frequently about the extreme anxiety she suffered at her factory and office jobs, but I know very little about the people with whom she worked. "Some of them must have been kind," I speculate. "Some of them must have been interested in you?" "Oh yes," Mom responds archly. "People had lots of questions, especially when they heard we were from Holland. 'How did you survive? Were you starv-ing?' I just told them, 'Our family always had enough food. We lived in the north.' That was all they needed to know."

The Canadians Mom is remembering were likely imag-ining that the de Jongs suffered directly during the Nether-lands' *Hongerwinter*, the "hunger winter" of 1944–45. D-Day, on 6 June 1944, had marked the beginning of the Allies' pro-tracted liberation of Holland, and in September, the Dutch national railways staged a strike to support the Allied push. The German administration retaliated with a total block-ade of food and fuel to the densely populated western prov-inces. Although the embargo was partially lifted in early November, an exceptionally harsh winter had set in, and by May 1945, over eighteen thousand Netherlanders had died, either directly of malnutrition or because malnutrition was a contributing factor. Ironically, because the Netherlands was a modern, developed, and literate country, the well-docu-mented *Hongerwinter* has afforded scientists and medical his-torians extensive insights into famine's effects on individual and societal health, including across generations.

By the time the de Jongs arrived in Winnipeg, most Cana-dians knew that the *Hongerwinter* ended as Allied forces—primarily the First Canadian Army and the 1st Canadian Corps—crossed into the country in late March 1945. "I guess they were curious," I suggest to my mother, who maintains her most austere manner. "I'm sure they were concerned for you. What else did you talk to them about?" And though I didn't record it or write about it later, I remember precisely where we were, marching north on Ashworth from Novavista, and the sound of Mom's abrupt response: "Nothing," she tells me sternly. "I didn't tell them anything. It wasn't any of their business," and I suddenly wonder whether the absence in my mother's life of a circle of close, warm, long-time friends is an effect of a protective shield I am only now speculating into being.

It's the austere manner that prompts my intense sense that I'm on to something, an arch attitude that Mom only affects when she considers elite people—"English ladies"—and the disparaging ways in which "English ladies" might look down on people like her. Was this, I wonder now, a pre-emptive form of protection from people who would have reflexively understood "immigrants" to be "lesser"? Might it also have been the tacit strategy an intuitive, highly sensitive young girl would adopt, believing that if she carefully said nothing, ever, about her family's history in the Netherlands, she might successfully protect her parents—especially her father—from the ramifications of their wracked political history?

~~~

Some of the people Mom liked the very best were my friends. Her letters regularly reference visits and telephone conversations; collecting my friends' letters and gifts when an acquaintance was travelling to Uganda; distributing letters and gifts I sent in return; dinners in groups; lunches with individuals; updates when they'd meet unexpectedly at the university or shopping; gifts exchanged for the sheer pleasure of it.

Aware that my correspondence with Luke was accelerating, Mom added Luke to the friends to whom she'd send joking messages. On learning that Luke was considering several international engineering positions, Mom insisted I tell him for her that "there's lots of noble and hydraulic work to be done right here in Canada!" I wrote to Luke about my parents, too, including to explain that the handwriting on the back of a photograph I'd enclosed was my mother's. "Both parentals grew up in Holland," I added, "and at the time, they forced left-handed kids to write with their right hands. Mom loves to use it as an excuse. 'How did you manage to lock the keys in the car?' we might ask, and she smiles one of her ethereal smiles and reminds us in confidential tones, 'Well, you know of course that they made me write with my right hand when I was young?!'" As our correspondence picks up speed, Luke and I regularly update one another on family and friends—

Letter #17 to Luke   *8 September 1988*

Late-ish evening I am laughing out loud again, engaged this time in land claims negotiations with a gecko who's wedged herself ingeniously into the soap dish [. . .] which would basically be no problem except that someone just outside the house, who can clearly hear me laughing, is calling me—

Normally I don't worry too much about the fact that the bathroom curtains are thin almost to transparency: there's a massive cactus right outside the window and beyond that, an enormous poinsettia hedge that hides the whole house and not just the bathroom from the road. This voice isn't coming from behind the cactus, though, and it occurs to me to wonder just how much of me I can cover with a washcloth. "What?" I growl out loud.

"Katherine? How are you?" Isaac from next door, requisite greetings perfectly placed. "How am I?" Good grief. Wet Isaac, I'm wet. "I am all right." I chop out my words just in case he hasn't figured out I'm also annoyed. "How are you?" I've been here long enough that politeness requirements are almost second nature . . .

"Well," he begins hesitantly, "I have a problem." Isaac. Honey. I am sitting in a bathtub behind a very small washcloth and a very transparent curtain, and you're telling me you have a problem? "Are you busy?"

I don't know whether to laugh or yell. "Yes, I am busy, I am bathing." Turkey. And then I do laugh, but very quietly,

*at how many times in three and a half seconds Isaac can
repeat the word "sorry." "I will come back in ten minutes,"
he suggests.*

*"Fifteen," I say. If I move too quickly I'll have to wash
twice to scrub off all the little gecko-type footy-prints.*

*Sixteen minutes later and sparkling clean, I let Isaac
in the back door and learn that the boys have blasted the
bejeepers out of their cooker, supper isn't made yet, and
they're not just hungry but wondering if I have a paraffin
stove they can borrow. Well, I don't, but they're welcome to
borrow the gas burner (though I utter a silent, fervent hope,
as Isaac lugs the tank through the door, that the rainstorm
just beginning doesn't take out the power, because if it does,
it's raw eggs and week-old untoast for breakfast tomorrow).*

Not all my news is funny. With Luke and Cindy both eager for
updates on Ugandan politics and cultural events, I'm regularly
busy sending newspaper articles and trying to keep details
straight, including of the fighting that continues sporadically
and not-so-sporadically in the north and east, and the famine
that rages in the area Luke not very long ago called home. By
early October 1988, aware that the international press isn't
covering these developments, I let Luke know that Oxfam is
drawing comparisons with Mozambique and Ethiopia, reporting the rare phenomenon of *adults* with kwashiorkor,[9] and
describing the current generation of children as so severely
malnourished that their brains will never develop properly.
The next time I write, Frances and I have just returned from
a unit meeting where I've fielded unofficial questions about
Luke's possible return to Uganda. First, though, I report on
the gifted young artist who's recently joined the staff at LIC...

Letter #20 to Luke   *23 October 1988*

*Writing as pungent traditional medicine burbles in the
kitchen. My newest friend Namukasa Beatrice, our recently*

arrived Arts and Crafts tutor, got tired of listening to me cough, and so has done magic with guava tree leaves, mango tree leaves, bottlebrush tree leaves, and leaves from a tree that has red berries but no known English name. Just smelling it makes me feel better and if, as our mothers always told us, the worse it tastes the more good it does, this should cure everything from insomnia to shin splints, never mind the cough . . .

In other news, Luke-babe, that was the meeting that was, and I'm home with approximately 4,893 things on my mind. Jake caught us up on fighting in the north as soon as we were all assembled, beginning with Stan P——'s recent report about the fighting around Gulu, which has even more recently been contradicted because it's suddenly quieter than it's been in months (crazy). Jake's distinctly wound up, mostly because it's so difficult to keep track. "We need to be paying close attention to the way things are shifting in the north," he says. "Gulu area could heat up again overnight, but Kitgum is definitely getting quieter. Church of Uganda people are talking seriously about us getting someone up there soon. Nick S—— (Oxfam head guy) just got back from his trip and he's been to the office a couple of times insisting too that MCC can't be using 'security' anymore as a reason for not getting someone back into Kitgum."

Jake says Oxfam's launching a massive famine-relief program in the north, the full deal, truck convoys, lots of people, good communications-support. He says he doesn't know how he feels about MCC-ers working under Oxfam's auspices, but a chilly little premonition runs up in my spine anyway—whatever form a secondment to Oxfam might take, it's eminently clear that MCC wouldn't put inexperienced people up in Kitgum. [. . .]

The whole next day is taken up with business details, but in the evening, Jake maneuvers a few moments alone. He knows I'm eager for as much detail as possible, so he

elaborates a bit on Stan's report from Gulu, Nick's on
Kitgum, then says very seriously, "I was only half-joking
yesterday. If we put someone in the north, it's not going to be
a fresh recruit." He pauses, then just asks flat out, "What do
you think about asking Luke to come back?"

Well. Since he's asked so directly, I tell him what I know
[. . .]. And I tell him what I think. [. . .] But he hasn't asked
about my feelings on the subject, so I keep those to myself. [. . .]

P.S. 27 October. Beatrice was just by with tree root
her mother gave her when she went home to Kiboga last
weekend. Apparently tree root is what a person wants
for curing muscle pains. Bea's still leery of making me
traditional medicine, but I can hardly wait. If tree-root
tea is half as effective as the leaf syrup she made me at the
beginning of the week, "yuppie flu" has met its match!

Defying entirely BHOIP's strange logic and the weight of sta-
tistical error, all of Luke's letters reach me, sometimes with
remarkable efficiency, sometimes after modest and maddening
delays. By the middle of 1988, our letters are frequent, funny,
flirtatious, and increasingly affectionate. Luke sometimes
includes tapes with his letters, of Canadian comedy shows
and music we both love. In October, he sends a perfectly sized
Cirque de Soleil T-shirt because, he says, the show was so fantastic he wishes I could've come too; he says he cried when
he watched *Out of Africa* for the second time, then reread my
most recent letter.

It's clear to us both that we can't build a relationship just on
correspondence, though, and we speculate on ways to practise
spending time together. He's applied for a job in Boston, not
because it's a good fit, but because he knows I'm interested in
a graduate school there. After acquiring professional certifica-
tion, he sends a business card. "Environmental problems?" he
scrawls on the back. "Just call!" "Do next-door discos count?"
I dash back. "Burst water pipes? Monkeys in the garden, rats

in the attic, sweet-eating ants all over the kitchen and safari ants traversing the college? Nearest phone is Bombo. Hurry!"

In early November, I can't resist using as writing paper the backside of an ad for "Mission to the Hunks," a parodic international development organization ostensibly based in California. "There I was, Luke-babe," my letter begins, "I had my application ready for these clowns, and I mean *r-e-a-d-y*, I mean signed-and-sealed, I mean book-the-flight, I mean bound-for-the-beach"—and over the next several paragraphs, I settle down enough to tell a story that I know will make him laugh . . .

Letter #21 to Luke   *12 November 1988*

Back, though, to yesterday's events which cannot not be recorded somewhere for posterity. See, I had this cheque for a hundred zillion Uncle Sam bucks made out to me (actually, not to me, to someone named "Kathleen Vemema," a slight problem which was, incredibly, not magnified out of proportion in the maze of Kampala's formidable financial bureaucracy) by the Manitoba Teachers' Society (MTS, of which I was, up until my departure for this fair land, a member in good standing) but intended for college use, specifically for a goat project, and I'd had this cheque for what seemed like an eon but was probably only eight months and finally yesterday, finally, we were going to do something about it.

Like, cash it and spend the loot. This, after putting pressure on the powers that be, having received a letter from the good folk at MTS in which phrases like "receipts for items purchased," "auditor's report," and "closing our books," were prominent, and I, occasionally pragmatic, said to myself, "Kath, if you want a job from these nice people again sometime, it wouldn't do to tick them off now about uncashed cheques and unspent loot."

And my pressure was accidentally well-timed: it seems Mrs. Kabaka Katonda had big (to say nothing of devious)

*plans to use someone else's money for goats ("baaa") and to
take my cheque in American dollars out of the country and
use it for other purposes entirely. Hah. Not on your sweet
patootie, Mrs. God. That was definitely not MTS's intent
when they sent this baby (they are very big on use of local
resources etc., etc.), and it was definitely not mine either
when I sweat blood composing the essay that accompanied
the application, which, incidentally, got us twice the usual
amount allocated.*

*So there we were yesterday, William and I, Tweedledum
and Tweedledee, babes in the flippin' woods, off to turn our
very big cheque into very many goats, oh yeah, oh yeah.*

*Oh no, oh no. "You cannot come in with this and get the
money today." That was the not-so-nice-guy at Grindley's
Bank. "If you leave it with us today it will take at least
seven days and maybe two weeks until we can give you the
money." Period.*

*Inside I'm saying, "Damn, I shoulda known, I shoulda
known," but the words the not-so-nice-guy (n-s-n-g) at
Grindley's Bank hears sound something like, "Is there no way
we can speed this process? Can we send a telex to confirm that
the funds are there?" But the answer to that is also no—no
no no no no, and it does not look good for the home team,
especially because William has gone white (always unnerving,
more so when your colleague is African). "We must have the
money today," he whispers to me, "I don't think I can borrow
the vehicle again another day" (we've got Nalinya's new
pickup). "We must get the large items today—"*

*We hassle through the apparently immutable regulations
governing this sort of thing and the n-s-n-g redeems himself
somewhat by suggesting that if we could get permission to
run the cheque through the Mennonite account, we could
possibly use existing funds there to make the most pressing
purchases (he's decided that he recognizes my name and
clearly thinks the world of Jake and Amy).*

Not a bad idea and William is extremely keen to try it (and back to his natural colour, thank goodness), which gets us to MCC's hole-in-the-wall office where we, as local slang has it, "bounce" (though we did find the stack of Ndejje-bound mail I mentioned earlier, your illustrious letter perched on top), and that gets us to the recurring existentialist question, "Okay, now what?" and the realization that William is turning colour again.

To stave off that disconcerting process, we agree we'll consult with Mrs. Katonda, who is now the deputy chair of such an important government organization I cannot mention it by name, with an office right here in town. William thinks it's possible that she could help us orchestrate a similar maneuver using the college account, so we're off again, this time to Crested Towers where, as you know, all the high-ranking bureaucrats live, breaths held in anticipation (we have Nalinya's vehicle and one of their drivers, so I can expend my limited energy holding my breath), but all in vain—Her Eminent Immenseness is nowhere to be found.

Oh no. By this time, I'm turning white on William's behalf, my usual pinky hue diluting to an unhealthy beige (though I've already managed to read your letter once), but:

"There is one other person who may be able to help us," William announces mysteriously when he gets back to the truck; he gives another set of directions to the driver and we're off, catapulted into an espionage ring, I wonder, deadly curious what seedy area of town we'll land in, when we pull up to the very respectable offices of the Mengo Teachers' Cooperative Society.

Aha. Yes. This may finally be the place. At first, though, this fourth alternative also flounders. The lovely older gentleman we're dealing with is tremendously sympathetic and tickled that I'm Canadian (back in '81 he went to a banking seminar in Antigonish), although he takes a

*few moments to berate me kindly for not being able to
understand Luganda after more than two years. (Kale
Ssebo; very sorry sir, but I've done my guilt on that score,
there just isn't any left. Explicating "yuppie flu" is beyond
me.) He's not sure he can help us, but it's at about this point
that intuition kicks in, and intuition kicks in speaking very
clearly. "Just relax into your comfortable chair, Kath," says
intuition, "because this is one of those obligatory delays that
will, in the end, yield results worth waiting for—"*

And it does.

*Oh, granted, at one point William and I are sufficiently
desperate we're speculating on a fifth alternative, which has
me cashing in all my "What-To-Do-In-Case-Of-A-Coup"
traveller's cheques, but it's at about this same point that the
lovely gentleman's attention is drawn to the fact that the
cheque in question is written on the account of a Teachers'
Society. Naturally I play this one for what it's worth, charm
in high gear, and wouldn't you know it, in thirty minutes,
I'm practising signing my name "Vemema" on every
available scrap of paper as the red-tape financial machinery
chugs into motion.*

*I love happy endings. The rest of the day is spent
collecting various of the larger necessary items, but since
I probably know more about hydraulic engineering than
I do about goat-shed construction, my main job now is to
guard the truck while William negotiates and the driver
helps carry. I also manage to read your letter two more times
before we leave town, which means I can concentrate on the
other thirteen when I get home, one of which was mailed in
August but didn't get here till now because it was missent
to Funafuti (Jakarta Post Office is clogged with packages
I guess), and what I want to know is, where in the heck is
Funafuti?*

*It sounds like someplace you'd end up. Please don't go,
okay, until I find out it's politically stable? [. . .]*

*P.S. Extrapolating casually from what my mother writes,
it occurs to me that your Mom has probably not stopped for
one second being glad that you're home. We talked about
this at the business meeting last month, how, in many ways,
the time we're away ends up being harder on our parents
than it is on us. Had written home about Dr. B trying to sign
me up to teach at the International School when, as he put
it, I'm "done with the Mennonites," and Mom sent back a
classic Maternal Unit reply:*

*Isn't it wonderful to be appreciated?! Isn't it wonderful
when your talents are recognized?! Isn't it wonderful to have
exciting opportunities?! But you come home. "We have to
talk," she writes, "and talk and talk and talk."*

Letter #23 to Luke　　*27 December 1988*

*P.S. Okay, so I'm quoting from the very end of your most
recent letter where you mention an Aaron Davis album
and write, "A good Mandela song on that one. Speaking of
which, rumour has it that he could be released soon?" To
which you add, "Sade just came on with 'Why Can't We
Live Together'—how appropriate." Now Luke, sweetheart,
something is troubling me about that last sentence and I
won't sleep till you say for sure: is it Nelson Mandela you're
wanting to live with, or our friend Sade?!*

new meadow (6)

By the end of 1988, my health has improved significantly. I've resumed teaching mathematics for the September–December term and look back on a year of revelations: Carla and Joe's invigorating visit in April, assuring me that I'm still recognized and known and missed and loved; an August jaunt to Botswana where I'm knocked flat by that country's affluence. Gabarone, the capital, looks to my eyes like a prosperous Midwestern North American town (set in a desert). Buildings are new and clean and systems work. State-of-the-art highways run the length and breadth of the country. My MCC friends shop at modern, well-stocked grocery stores; follow South African television programs; choose from a range of movie and theatre offerings; drive reliable, late-model vehicles. I enjoy myself thoroughly, including on a camping trip along the Chobe River where crocodiles swim, and during a misty, Kathleen-paced tour of Victoria Falls. There's a lurking sense of unease, though, right inside this front-line state, just kilometres from the border with apartheid South Africa, and I'm eager to disembark when my return flight lands at Entebbe.

Mom, in the meantime, is enjoying the leisure of being, as she calls herself, "an unemployed university graduate." In September, she reports that a recent church service was led by a former minister, once venerable and bombastic, now much reduced by failing health: "I'm sure I've heard that sermon before. I spent the time meditating on the beautiful wood of the organ." Later in the fall, she works as an enumerator for the upcoming federal election and assures me, "I'm gonna be rich!" In mid-December, she takes up the challenge to join

Sandy's choir for Christmas Eve: "It was quite exciting to take part in such a beautiful service. [. . .] I was surprised at how much I'd picked up in just one practice!" This is in a long letter that Mom writes over the holidays in which she reports more singing on Boxing Day, the annual gathering of the clan: "Eta, her usual exuberant self, suggested we might cut a de Jong family record! Run for cover, music lovers!"

~~~

My exuberant friend Tracey meets Frances and me in Nairobi in early December 1988. We'll be at Ndejje for Christmas, but first we set out for Lamu, one of the original Swahili settlements along the Indian Ocean. My parents' birthdays (late December, late January) provide convenient occasions to record the optimism and energy with which 1988 turns into 1989 . . .

Letter #78 to Mom and Dad   *31 December 1988*

Dearest Dad, [. . .] I think you would have loved Lamu, except for the overwhelming humidity: the day we left, you couldn't move without sweating. I'd been regretting that we didn't have time for one more leisurely wallow on the sand, but everyone we ran into (eyes rolled dull at the sticky exertion of sliding onto a café seat in the shade) announced in listless tones that their companions could do whatever, they were not going to the beach. (The town's built on the seawall and the beach is a good forty minutes' walk south, which translated into an hour's slow plod for us yuppie-types, about three days' worth of energy, so I'd take a motor boat each time!) [. . .]

It's quite a place, profoundly quiet; the only vehicle on the island belongs to "the Fisheries man," who got transferred in from Mombasa, says he loves the life, the pace, sultry as slow blood, says his only worry's that he might get moved again. The guidebooks agree: make this your last stop on a tour of

*Kenya or you may never see Lake Turkana, Lake Naivasha,
Masai Mara; Nairobi's bustle will fade in your memory and
you'll forget the point of catching the flight home . . .*

*We had a front room in a guesthouse on the seawall;
curtains stood horizontal for the first six hours, brisk ocean
breezes beat back threatened mosquitoes, and we slept like
babies, heavy with the bliss of exhaustion, but at six I was
up, and the town was stirring—*

*Dawn prayer-call done, the man at the mosque next
door sits dreaming, eyes half-closed, contemplating rubble,
unperturbed by my balcony bird's-eye view; exchanges
greetings with the khanga-skirted men who pass; buys a cake
from a girl who slides fragile-delicate to kneel by the stone
bench while he finds his coin; tandem donkeys pass on the
waterside; belying last night's raucous braying they turn
seal-sad eyes away and trot—*

*Black-veiled women gauge familiarity, pause, greet, chat
(show us only eyes), and the man at the mosque mutters low,
raising his vendor friend with words that chortle her audibly
into humour, a ripple of real across this unfamiliar screen—*

*It was nice. Two flights of stone steps (count-count-count-
stretch-count-stretch-count), uneven, to our room so I got my
exercise; archways, whitewash, sidle-narrow alleys dodging
sun rays, splinter-ice juice of exotic fruits, and oh, the seafood:
shark steak, lobster, kingfish, prawns in coconut, or tuna, all
fresh from the boat that morning—it was really nice.*

Letter #79 to Mom and Dad   *2 January 1989*

*Wondering what you did to celebrate the New Year, dearest
Mom, because we went dancing! Yup. After bemoaning
a sad collection of facts (three-year terms are too long at
festive seasons; none of the other MCC-ers made it here
for our tentatively planned New Year's unit-party; being
single cross-culturally can be a real drag, etc., etc.) we went
dancing.*

*Rose and Frances had come for supper on New Year's
Eve, a special meal of goat's meat and matoke, courtesy of
the Ssendawula family (Moses had promised to send a goat
for Christmas, but Moses is back in the north fighting rebels
again, and a surprise Christmas Eve attack delayed all kinds
of things, goat transport among them. Hail, though, to our
reconditioned bus system: "Billy" made it to Ndejje in time
for the second-most significant celebrations of the year. What
I hadn't expected was that we'd get some.*

*"Mother and Father are so pleased," said Rose, settling
onto a mat to peel matoke, "to have found something they
can give you." Which startled me—their generosity is
constant—only because I forget we all crave the good feeling
of knowing our gifts are worth giving), and we were a happy
threesome, but hopelessly beat after days of eating and
laughing with the new MCC-ers from Hoima (who had to be
back for their community's New Year's events), and in bed
by eleven.*

*"We'll celebrate tomorrow," we agreed groggily, but that,
as it turns out, is how it works here, the real celebrating
happens New Year's Day night.*

*"People will dance and dance and dance," Rose had said,
her bright eyes, and mine must have lit up too because the
next thing she said was, did I want to come? "Oh yes, you
betcha! As long," this has just occurred to me, "as no one will
be uncomfortable if we come."*

*"No, no," Rose insists, "they will be very proud if you
come." And as far as we could tell, they were; people thought
it was great, even better when we actually danced. Even
Frances danced. When we danced, they gave us money, a
Kiganda tradition when people dance well, and (knowing
full well they were being kind) I'll pitch it to Jake as a source
of income: meet the budget and have fun doing it!*

*I haven't danced since August 1987, at a Nairobi
nightclub with Henry and Dana, and oh, did it feel good.*

I was telling Rose later how much I've missed having that kind of fun and how hard it is, living here, knowing for sure where and when it's appropriate just to have a good time. "Ummmhmmmmmmm," she agreed reflectively, emphatically, "but by now, everyone knows you, you are part of us now, so now you can enjoy and everyone enjoys with you."

holy shipwreck (4)

It seems extraordinary now, with Alzheimer's so regularly in the news, that the disease only entered public consciousness in the late 1970s and early 1980s.[10] During 1988, when I struggled most extensively with "yuppie flu" (also called Epstein-Barr virus and identified more accurately years later as fibromyalgia), I described my symptoms twice in the ostensible terms of Alzheimer's. On 3 September 1988, I announced that to celebrate my parents' thirtieth anniversary I was sending an authentic Ugandan woven tea cozy "and the news that my health is *significantly* improving." "It's true," I added, "that when I write too long my hands shake," and then wondered jokingly whether that might signal "early Alzheimer's" (which I misspelled egregiously). Two months later, I described the several special-occasion exertions that had prompted a mild return of symptoms, but noted that after "soaking my aching Alzheimer's muscles in a steamy bath" and a long visit with my new friend Beatrice, I'd decided "that life right here is *well* worth living."

Long after the diagnosis, Sandy and I tried to pinpoint exactly when Mom's symptoms began, but we found ourselves looking back at a woman who could daydream for hours, who'd spent most of her adult life in unstructured time. Mom was clever, articulate, eager, informed, and passionate in her opinions. She was also quirky, ephemeral, and easily spent. "Maybe I have Alzheimer's," she would counter when one or the other of us would implore her, arms akimbo, to *please* keep track of the car keys, grocery lists, maps we'd drawn, written directions, plans to meet, our last conversation about

Christmas gifts. "No Mom," we'd insist callously, "you don't have anything; you just have to *pay attention*."

For a very long time after the diagnosis, Mom talked about having Alzheimer's on every one of our afternoons together, and she would often talk too about her fear that she might live as long as her mother and her maternal grandmother. Beppe de Jong lived to almost 94, the last ten years in considerable physical and emotional pain. *Her* mother—a formidable and ethically suspect woman who was already bedridden on our first and only meeting—died at 101. For a very long time, my mother knew perfectly well that if she lived even as long as her own mother, she'd be completely incapacitated by Alzheimer's predations.

On Friday 5 December 2008, my mother revisits both her awe at the possibility that she might, at some point in the future, not be interested in the world around her, and her preference to end her life before that should happen. "Sometimes I look out of the window here, for instance," she tells me, "and then I think: would I not know any more that that was a car coming? Would I not know any more that that's snow? I find it actually pretty damn scary, but I don't know what else to do except"—and here she makes a choking sound—"'Give me a sword, I'll fall on my sword!' But who has a sword in the first place and it's too cumbersome; I'd rather have something that's bloodless!" And we can't help ourselves, we burst out laughing.

It's almost one full year since our first official conversation, 11 January 2008, the afternoon we spent meandering across that range of existential issues. "My real existence is here," Mom had said that afternoon. "I live in my mind." Her claim is utterly true and presents the unequivocally most painful aspect of living with her alongside Alzheimer's—the fact that what's slipping away is her defining capacity for intellectual engagement, and her continued awareness that she's losing her mind.

On 30 September 2011, the very bad day with which I began this story, my mother couldn't sustain a thought or a sentence for more than a few seconds at a time. As I wrote to my siblings, "She was working terribly hard to make herself comprehensible, and spent a lot of time with her eyes scrunched closed, sometimes rubbing her face and sometimes rubbing her glasses, as if she couldn't feel the difference. Excruciating to watch. Mom clearly recognized the downturn. 'It's really bad today,' she said at one moment, 'the forgetting,' and at an especially eerie point, after I'd asked her a question, she said, vaguely in my direction but mostly to herself, 'I can't understand what Kathleen is saying to me.'" For the first time that day, Mom kept confusing "I" and "she" and "me" and "you" and "her," as if the differences between herself and others—as if the differences between the two of us—were disappearing.

But it's two and a half years earlier, on Friday 13 February 2009, that I find a note in Mom's handwriting that permanently unravels a piece of my heart. By February 2009, Mom has been speaking regularly about her wish to end her life, but she assures me she won't take concerted action until after her friend Rimi's visit in the spring. Over the past five years, Mom and her best friend from the M.U.L.O. have reconnected. Rimi's husband died last year and now Rimi is thinking about taking a trip to Canada.

It's clear that Mom's written the note after a visit to her geriatric psychiatrist, Dr. Mysore. She's used the bottom third of an upside-down telephone bill and her always clumsy handwriting crawls awkwardly across the page. Given how long it takes Mom and me to compose a letter together by now, I can imagine the exertion Mom has applied to this note. It makes the note's coherence all the more harrowing.

"she called," Mom writes, and then, as if she realizes that "she" doesn't give enough information, Mom adds "Rimmy" after leaving considerable space on the page.

"I have to call her," Mom adds on the next line, and awkward blanks continue to lurch amongst the words:

> her husband died and
> now she wants to visit me here
> in Canada,   but
> my Altzheimer
> is progressing   and [scribble] i cannot [scribble]
> enter tane her properly   DRmysore did a
> memory test

> and I failed

Mom's final three words drop almost off the page.

~~~

Mom retains a cruel and uncanny awareness of what she does not know, even in Alzheimer's final stages. She had a bad fall in mid-July 2013, six months after we'd admitted her into care. Mom was still ambulant at the time, but her compromised vision didn't process her neighbour's wheelchair as an impediment. The fall broke both her upper and her lower dentures and possibly her jaw, though that wasn't ever confirmed with an X-ray. When Gareth and I visited the next day, she was in terrible shape, not just from the pain and the bruising—this time, Gareth's presence seemed both to soothe her and create additional anxiety.

Almost always until then, Gareth's arrival would prompt Mom into a form of humorous scolding that she used for no one else. "I know you," she'd laugh flirtatiously when she saw him, "I know I have to watch out for *you*!" On 16 July 2013, though, Gareth became a placeholder for all the family names and relationships Mom had forgotten, and her distress at this incapacity was wrenching to witness. "I was never dumb like this when I went to school," she almost wept and asked again and again, alternating between English and Frisian: "What is happening to my brain?"

That afternoon I tried for the last time to explain that she has a disease called Alzheimer's and that nothing that was happening was her fault. It was the last time I tried because, for the first time in all our years of conversation, she didn't recognize the word "Alzheimer's." Almost a year later, in mid-May 2014, she experienced what was likely a stroke. Having been out of town, I saw her for the first time afterward on 6 June 2014 and she was desperately reduced, skeletal, but sleeping peacefully.

So I waited, while my aunt Eta's CD of Frisian folk songs played at low volume. Mom woke half an hour later, briefly calm and clear-eyed. She looked happy, I thought, to see me, and almost lucid, but in fewer than five minutes, she clouded discernibly and anxiety took over as she seemed to simultaneously lose connection and retain an awareness that she was losing connection. Just before she did, she looked at me intently and said, with a combination of panic and frustration, "*Ik ferskrei mij.*"

"What is it, Mom?" I asked in response to her stricken look, and she peered more intensely and repeated, wonderingly, "*Ik ferskrei mij*"—or maybe it was "*Ik ferskei mij,*" or maybe "*Ik feskrei mij.*" The words sounded Frisian—more Frisian, at any rate, than Dutch—but when I checked with my Frisian informants at the time, they said it corresponded with nothing they recognized in either language. Grammatically, the phrase is created by a reflexive verb in which the subject acts on itself: "*Ik ferskrei me*" equals "I [something] myself." I forget myself. I lose myself. I destroy myself.

What I *feel* my mother telling me that afternoon is, "I tear myself apart because I no longer know who you are to me." "I tear out my insides at the realization that I am losing my self." One month after my foreign mother wakes up to baffle me with the untranslatably strange reflexive verb "*ferskrei*," she wakes up again, but only briefly, to attempt another communiqué. She tries first in Dutch, but nothing comprehensible emerges. Frisian yields gibberish, but when Mom's eyes open a third time, she speaks fervently. This time, she's completely lucid. "It's so *weird*," she says with perfect English enunciation, her eyes fixed on mine.

"I bet it is, Mom," I tell her, holding her as gently as I can. "I bet it's *really* weird." She closes her eyes, leans back onto the bed, and falls deeply asleep.

holy shipwreck

holy shipwreck (5)

"Dear Mom and Dad," I wrote again and again, on the flight to Nairobi, on the road from Busia, in Kampala, at Ndejje. "Dear Mom and Dad, I'm well over thirty thousand feet; I can't come home at Christmas; I miss you already." "Dear Mom and Dad, everything is magical, otherworldly, surreal; the rare sight of other white people's already unsettling; I worry that no one will know me in three years." "Dear Mom and Dad, how can I feel so far away, when I'm right here?"

And Mom sits down at the kitchen table, looks out at the elm and ash trees lining the house, at the front garden Dad's planted with beans (again), the yard covered for months in snow, traffic dashing down St. Anne's Road, the river's meander encroaching on the meadow by the barn, and writes, "Dear Kathleen, I'm trying to imagine what it's like for you." "Dear Kathleen, we sure have a lot of strawberries this year." "Dear Kathleen, Gerta will also number her letters; I worry about you considerably; I think of you in Africa and then I can't knit right away." "Dear Kathleen, we miss you very much. Write soon."

The letters arrive, weeks late sometimes, or months, or years, and some of the letters get lost, permanently misplaced in the shambles of yet another Canadian postal strike, or detoured through sticky sorting machinery in Manila or Jakarta or Funafuti, or, in February 1988, drenched illegible when Kampala's post office floods. In every one of the letters that arrived safely, you can read the persistence with which my mother and I knit and re-knit our connection and our interdependence:

"I wish you'd seen our house when we first arrived, you'd have been on the next plane, Javex in hand." "I'm doing yoga in the mornings so I'll be in good shape for our trip to Africa." "I hope our students realize when I'm staring that I'm trying to learn their names." "You are always in our thoughts so you can never be really far away." "We don't have glass in all the windows and my bed's getting drenched!" "We're glad the Reads are such good neighbours." "*I'd* sure be skeptical of a half-baked *muzungu* telling *me* about *my* country's agriculture." "The postcards are masterpieces of ingenuity." "I made a *complete* fool of myself in the post office." "I can still hardly believe that you're really all the way in Africa, but I guess the fact that I'm writing to you is proof enough."

Decades later, no amount of proof is proof enough. Decades later, Alzheimer's plaques and tangles proliferate in my mother's brain; confusion, anxiety, paranoia, and fear infect her personality; our conversations are increasingly marked by language loss and miscommunication, and it's my mother, now, who's teetering on the edge of an existential abyss. How can I feel so far away when I'm right here?

~~~

Letters exist because of absence and distance, and every aspect of "correspondence" introduces more gaps—between writing and mailing, mailing and receipt, receipt and response, response and posting, posting and arrival. Letter writers are shape-shifters: they write to become recipients, savour receipt, and then write again, because it is so sweet to be addressed ("Dear Kathleen, Dear Kathleen"). Letter writers often begin by establishing context ("I'm sitting here at the kitchen table"), but time slips instantly, and prepositions lose their grip on the world. When is "now"? How long till "soon"? Is "there" anywhere close to "home"? Reading a letter addressed to you that arrives at the correct address and on time can present challenges in a context of full cognitive capacity. Reading a letter, even one you wrote yourself, years after the fact and while struggling with dementia is almost guaranteed to be an exercise in frustration.

So what made me think that *reading letters* to one another would help my mother and me bridge the distances Alzheimer's is throwing up between us?

I'm hurrying for the bus on Friday 25 April 2008 and pick up letters from a stack of typed transcriptions as I dash. Mom's first two letters, it turns out, so I ask her, again, before we read them, what she remembers about the summer I left for Uganda. She has different answers each time. Today she asks, "Didn't we take you to the airport? Weren't some of your friends there?" Yes, they were (hilarious, disbelieving, none of us able to imagine three years without one another), and we take a moment to conjure up their names ("Carla; and Sharon; and—"), a struggle despite the efforts each one of them made to stay in touch.

Otherwise, the exercise proceeds with a measure of success. "Who is Kim?" Mom has asked, when she reads that "Kim called," and "Where is Baldur?" when she reads where Kim will be teaching. Mom has to work to remember that "MB" is the abbreviation for Manitoba, puzzles briefly over who Elke might be, with all the foster children and "bedlam as usual," but pronounces "penitentiary" perfectly when she reads about Sandy's legal aid work with two of the people incarcerated at Stony Mountain.

She's stumped, though, when we reach the description of the two weddings that she and Dad attended on 16 August 1986. *"Annette walked into the church on her own,"* Mom repeats several times, gathers enough momentum to finish the sentence—*"for which she has my respect"*—then looks up and asks, "Why did Annette walk in on her own?" It's a marker of Mom's cognitive loss that she no longer remembers that in some wedding traditions, fathers "give their daughters away," a further marker that she no long remembers the vehemence with which she once deplored the tradition. But it takes just a few moments of conversation before Mom declares, "So it means, 'Now I'm rid of her and now you own her'!? Good grief, it sounds like slavery."

She pauses and then reflects with considerable humour, "So I said that already then, eh?" She pauses again and adds, "Well, you know me; I was pretty sharp in those days with my pronouncements! Pretty harsh in my judgments." She pauses one more time, unrepentant. "I still am," she says, and we both laugh.

~~~

My project takes shape slowly and slowly acquires clarity. I sort through boxes of letters in the summer of 2007 and emerge with neatly labelled file folders; I begin transcribing the letters myself, but discover I'll be ready to retire before I'm halfway done. My efficient aunt Gerta, one of the project's most enthusiastic supporters, volunteers to help, but after a few weeks, she returns the folder she started with. "I'm sorry, Kath," she says, "they're just too sad." So I hire a series of dexterous young women who are taking time off between university degrees; several have their own stories of cross-cultural living, and two of them transcribe in the face of significant health crises.

Transcribing the recordings, though, presents peculiar challenges. Over the years and on different devices, I record more than 150 conversations with my mother, average length two hours. Extrapolating from shorter experiments, I determine that it takes about eight hours to render a word-for-word, pause-for-pause, accurate transcription of a two-hour conversation. That includes time to record the details as Mom switches amongst languages, and to spell correctly in languages I've never formally learned to read. Gareth urges me to try a word-recognition program, but I look askance. What on earth would such a program make of intermittent Frisian, Dutch, and German, and Mom's multiple attempts to pronounce tricky syllables in English?

I'm the only one who can consistently make out what Mom's saying, and what she's trying to say when she struggles for words, and what we're talking about when our words overlap or get lost in laughter. Besides which, Mom and I sometimes speak candidly and I need to be able to protect her privacy and the privacy of people she speaks about. There's no getting around it: the conversations are mine to transcribe, but I complete the work erratically, sometimes drafting quick versions soon after visits, but usually during breaks in my teaching year. Then I sit for long stretches, creating written records of the audio records that Mom and I have made of ourselves reading from our handwritten records of the relationship we've been nurturing now for decades.

~~~

Late spring 2009, I block out several days to review and add to my collection of first-draft transcripts. On the second day, I select the recording of our third official visit, 25 January 2008, because that was the first time Mom and I read letters to one another. I want to remind myself of our exact words. Headphones adjusted, document open at the precise spot that the transcript begins, I prepare to amend at top speed and press "play." Nine minutes in, I stop typing, hit "pause," and peer at the details I've just added:

M: So where am I now? [pause] Oh. Mmmmm. *"Tuesday August 12. I took Beppe"*—that's Mom of course—*"to her hairdresser. While she was there, I went to visit Elke, where it was bedlam as usual."* [pause] Elke? Who would that have been?

K: Who would that be, Mom, Elke?

M: [pause] Elke Venema of course!

I reread what I've edited so far and review what I drafted the first time through. Mom is reading from her first letter and it's all there, or mostly there and mostly in the correct order: Nairobi, telex, Dad, diary, notebook; Kim, Baldur, Sandy, Stony Mountain; penitentiary (tackled three times, then pronounced perfectly); Beppe, bedlam, foster children, and misogynist undertones in wedding rituals that require fathers to give their daughters away. "I was already pretty blunt then!" Mom says on the recording, admiring, half-embarrassed.

But I've just read this exact conversation somewhere else.

I scramble through the documents I've been creating and refining. Here it is, the transcript for 25 April 2008. I was just looking at this. Mom and I are reading a typed version of her first two letters to me because handwriting is so hard to decipher. This happens exactly three months after the conversation I've just been reviewing and renders a transcript implausibly similar and frequently eerily exact. Word-for-word, pause-for-pause, puzzled-question-for-puzzled-question, Mom and I have almost exactly the same conversation on the twenty-fifth day of both January and April 2008, *and neither of us remembered.*

"Oh my goodness," I type slowly into the middle of the January transcript, "this is so weird."

holy shipwreck (6)

Mom and I read her letters the first time in a world that seems idyllic now because in that world, Harry was perfectly healthy. Exactly three months later, we read them again in the shadow of Harry's cancer.

In the first days after Harry's diagnosis, Gareth and I spend hours making phone calls, answering the phone, answering the door, storing and delivering the meals that arrive, scheduling play dates for Lydia, seeing to the laundry, recording and relaying medical information, drafting visiting schedules, and sending email updates to a constantly growing list of addresses. By 3 March 2008 the blog is up, connecting us to an intricate network of friends and family, teachers and healers from around the world. I steal moments to journal my elation when our friend Bill M——, a brilliant, oddball minister in a predominantly new-Canadian neighbourhood, visits in person.

26 February 2008.

For the moment, I'm ridiculously buoyed, treasuring the image of Bill's reaction when he hears that the survival rate is 20 percent. I've probably said, "the survival rate is only 20 percent," because I've been struggling to describe how I feel. "Surreal" is accurate but not sufficient. "Twenty percent keeps expanding and contracting," I explain, "like Alice in Wonderland, shrinking and growing. Twenty percent isn't much, but I'm so focused, it's taking up my entire field of vision." I wave my hands, don't want Bill to think I'm crazy, it's just that my head hurts, grappling with numbers, and then my vision clears and I can see that Bill is dancing on the furniture—

"There's a 20 percent s-u-r-v-i-v-a-l rate?!" Bill's repeating as he dances. "Kids survive this?!"

He's making it sound enormous. "I know," I say, "I know." I had no idea, but Cynthia explained last night. Most adult cancers are "carcinomas," the result of exposure to a carcinogen. Most kids' cancers are "blastomas," and develop when growing cells don't shut off when they should've, or go off in some wrong direction . . . .

"Oh my God," Bill says, "With 20 percent, we can work. With 20 percent and prayer, we can do this. There's an elderly Muslim woman," he explains hurriedly, "a revered figure in the community, probably the most devout person of any faith I've ever known, and I told her yesterday, 'Asili, I have a baby I need you to pray for.' 'Mr. Bill,' she said instantly, 'we will pray. You tell us, what is baby's name, and we will pray.'"

So I have a new image from the future I'm choosing, in which we bring healthy baby Harry to Asili when all this is done to tell her: thank you. Thank you for loving God and this precious life enough to work miracles, and I will kiss Asili's hands and feet and promise her: we will devote our lives and his to bringing peace.

What engraves itself deepest on my psyche is the image of "20 percent" in Asili's hands and in Bill's and in the fine strong weathered hands of all God's children, "20 percent" eased gently into ever lighter, broader, brighter spacious space for all our healing—

I know, rationally, that Bill stayed seated for our entire conversation, but in my memory's imagination, he bursts to life at the news that children survive and he dances on the table. It's an image that sustains me through the days and weeks that follow, as we re-establish routines for Lydia, set up a meal schedule, coordinate financial support. Predictably, my ability to sleep is decimated by worry. But I'm halfway through my first sabbatical, in the first stages of the project with Mom, and grateful every morning that, however groggy, I don't have to attend meetings or facilitate classes.

28 February 2008. 6:35 a.m.

Gareth's already been on email, so he knows that Harry spent the night in a monitored bed, Henry spent the night on the cot in his room, and Cynthia spent the night at home with Lydia. I love imagining Lydia's face when Cyn arrived unexpectedly to take her home. Heartbreaking, Lyddie's greatest anxiety, that her Mom won't know the way home from the hospital.

Lydia turned four three months before Harry's diagnosis. More than two years earlier, she'd demonstrated her formidable affinity with language, pulling me into their home when we arrived, straight on through to her bedroom where she showed me the plastic magnetic *K* she'd put aside in anticipation and announced triumphantly that this was for me and that I was "Auntie KK."

28 February [cont.]

At the hospital on Tuesday evening, Lydia and I "explored and had an adventure" ("Let's explore and have an adventure, Auntie KK"), which focused on the detailed purple map she made for Cynthia, a tiny circle at the edge of the paper, which is marked with an H for Harry, and connected to a labyrinth of squares and rectangles representing the hospital (which Lydia calls a "museum" several times and laughs at her mistake each time: "Why do you think I keep saying 'museum,' Auntie KK?"). There are probably fifty lines emanating from the circle and the squares and rectangles, representing all the paths her Mom could take. The problem, Lydia explains very seriously, is that some of the paths are the wrong ones. [. . .]

We're thrilled that Harry's absolutely fine after the biopsy, but I'm shocked when Gareth reminds me how it could've gone, and I wonder, am I ready for what we may need to face, cocooned as I am right now with my wise and quizzical nephew in the imaginary safety of something called "20 percent," where Bill danced with angels on the head of a pin?

When the Baylor diagnosis comes through we rejig, downward, because primary rhabdoid tumours have only a 5 percent survival rate.

10 March 2008.

Two weeks without a break, too many late nights, too little sleep, and my system's in overdrive. [. . .] We wake up early on Friday after the report from Baylor and I tell Gareth, "I keep imagining being able to lie down. I keep thinking how nice it would be to lie down. If I could lie down, I could rest. I'm not fussy, I would lie down anywhere, kitchen, sunroom, study, bathroom. If I could just lie down, I'd be okay.

"I have to consciously remind myself," I tell him, "'You are lying down.'"

Henry tells me he hasn't been this traumatized since he visited me in Uganda twenty-one years ago. Cynthia keeps us focused, returns us to a shared image of Harry in the future, healed and well, foremost in all our minds. For the first five weeks, events inside our bleak situation are mixed but mostly positive—and then Harry comes home from the hospital, 31 March, discharged early after two rounds of chemo because he has so utterly exceeded his doctors' expectations.

Gareth and I reach Santa Fe late that evening and spend our week of holidays telling Harry's story to everyone we meet, certain that each one of the artists and visionaries we encounter has the capacity to bring our baby nephew closer to complete health. On 4 April, we mark Harry's first birthday in ancient Chimayó, light a candle for him at El Santuario, site of pilgrimage and healing. And we're home by 6 April, in time to record our family's (delayed) celebration on the blog, Harry and a chocolate cupcake the unrivalled highlight. My parents visit Harry regularly, at home and at the hospital, but they'll never own a computer, so I phone them whenever I update the blog. Each time I do, Mom says, "That's good. That's very good": 16 April, when I report that, even coming out of sedation after a pre-chemo CT scan, "Harry was his usual exuberant self"; 20 April, to celebrate the fact that the scan results are "better than the best we dared imagine"; 22 April, the last day of Harry's third round of chemo, to confirm that, "the treatment plan is working far more effectively even than it was originally intended to do."

Three days later, on Friday 25 April, I reach Mom and Dad's late and struggle to express in person the nuanced message Cynthia's sent me just that morning, just as I'm leaving, for posting on the blog. It's a detailed, poignant message. Cynthia reiterates the last several weeks of astonishingly good news and expresses, again, her powerful, measureless gratitude for the myriad ways in which friends and family are providing support. And it's a heartbreaking message, reminding us that even all this good news still means that what we're working for right now is to get one-year-old Harry well enough to have a liver transplant as soon as possible. When what we really want is for the cancer to be gone. When what we really want is a miracle.

After lunch on 25 April 2008, Mom and I will read and talk about her first letter as if we've never done so before. Is it any wonder, though, that we were sometimes confused?

holy shipwreck (7)

On 10 March 2008, four days after the specialists at Baylor weigh in with the news of a primary rhabdoid tumour, I use my journal to record the fact that "I'm resting but unable to rest, a classic fibromyalgia response. Add in anxiety and shock, denial and disbelief, and I find myself consistently turning in precisely the wrong direction, picking up utensils that complicate the task, choosing absurd ingredients, and blurting out the opposite of what I want to say, as if specific connections in my brain have been unscrewed and re-fastened upside down and backward."

I am, you might say, just like my mother.

21 April 2008.

Woke up early from a very bad dream, all wars and droughts and bad guys and cancer, connected, I'm sure, to thinking about Harry's healing against a background of international events, wracked, knowing there are babies in Baghdad and Kandahar and Harare and Darfur and Mogadishu and northern Uganda and northern Manitoba and the North End who are not getting the attention or the medication or the rest or the rehabilitative care they need to heal, and the daunting imperative to surround each one of them, with Harry, in unwavering, unconditional love. [. . .]

The same unconditional love with which we surround Lydia as she grows and changes. Yesterday, in Harry's room, post-chemo, she was "reading" one of her fairy princess books for her Beppe and Pake's benefit, and in the midst of chanting, in the singsong voice that she knows signals end-of-the-story ("and Princess Mariposa sat out under the stars, dreaming about worlds that don't exist"), she suddenly snapped alert to ask: "Pake, what's the word for when stars make pictures?"

When stars make pictures? Lydia's Pake is stumped. Auntie KK veers into the scientific, wonders whether her niece means the pictures of space that satellites take, and then catches on. "Do you mean 'constellations,' Lyddie?" Auntie asks. "Yes," Lydia says with an appreciative sigh, "'combellations.' I just forgot it for a minute."

"Well," Mom rouses herself to add, "it's a pretty big word to remember," and it's the first time the juxtaposition strikes me, the preternaturally bright four-year-old and the word-loving grandmother losing her mind. Thankfully, Lydia hasn't noticed what's been mostly Beppe's blankness; Lydia's back in fantasyland with Princess Mariposa, letting the story come to an end out under the night sky, watching for "combellations" and dreaming of worlds that don't exist . . . .

My project has me returning to letters I wrote to stave off existential terror. I knew I was alive because I wrote letters and my letters were answered, and I want to use both, letters and answers, as a bridge to my mother. Even untouched in the archive, the letters and the answers ground me, recording experiences that formed the critical centre of my adult identity. So I imagine they might work a bit like maps, tracking the places from which Mom and I have come. Like Lydia's maps in the hospital's playroom, though, these maps, too, don't all show the right way home.

~~~

Winnipeg's summer of 1988 is so alarmingly dry it prompts comparisons with the 1930s. The winter that follows is one of the snowiest on record. Mom is palpably eager for my return to Canada in August, but she refers to snow in almost every letter she sends.

Letter #81 from Mom and Dad   *26 October 1988*

> *If you were here with me, you'd feast your eyes on that most typical Manitoba winter scene: bare trees, branches swaying in the wind, sky a uniform grey, a fairly heavy snow falling steadily, the ground already covered with several centimetres. You remember the sight I'm sure. It is in many ways beautiful and in a strange way comforting in its reassurance that the seasons are repeating themselves with regularity and predictability.*

A few paragraphs on, Mom writes, "I'll bet one thing you won't find hard to adjust to will be the telephone and the easy way it connects you with people," and she explains that she was no sooner off the phone with Tracey (relaying details about her upcoming trip) than Nathaniel had called (to find out what I might like for Christmas). "I can see it now," Mom writes with evident glee, "we'll have to install a second line!"

Mom begins Letter #83 with another detailed account of snow, to which she adds, "I don't really know why I'm telling you about this: it would be considerably more stunning if winter did *not* arrive here." Four days later, she begins Letter #84, which she'll send along with Tracey, with the dispiriting news that the Progressive Conservatives have won another majority, though she's delighted to have bumped into Carla and Joe *twice* while Christmas shopping. "The only reason I'm glad we're not bringing our gifts personally," she writes in closing, "is that we'd have to leave you behind again." Letter #86 is Mom's first letter of 1989 and begins with an extended meditation on snow and snowing. Mom starts Letter #87 on 8 January 1989 while a blizzard rages. The next week, she conscientiously refocuses:

Letter #88 from Mom and Dad   *15 January 1989*

*Let me update on you my latest "social action" activity,
which ain't much but it's something, starting with a letter
to the chairman of the finance committee of Winnipeg City
Council urging that not-so-illustrious body to help finance a
recycling pilot project.*

*"Ha," you think to yourself, "my mother the social action
butterfly strikes again." Well, hold on a minute. Before
I lap up your admiring snort, let me admit that without
prompting at R.A.R., I probably wouldn't have, because I'm
not really the activist type. I lean more to daydreaming and
meditating, although on most important social matters, my
heart (if not pure) is in the right place (which is left, right?).*

*By the way, it is, I know, a physical impossibility to
"lap up" snorts of admiration or snorts of any kind. It may
be what's usually called "a mixed metaphor" or simply a
"malapropism," and you can tell me, since you're the English
teacher. [. . .]*

*We have been saving our empty glass jars and bottles
and plastic soft-drink bottles as well as aluminum cans and
newspapers to take them to a recycling depot, which will be
open on April 1st. There was one last October but I didn't
know in time and had hardly anything to contribute. What
we hope is that the city will jump in and begin a recycling
system with its waste collection. Surely there are better
things to do with land than fill it up with garbage!*

I like remembering that my dreamily non-activist mother
was involved at the very beginning of the long process that
now enables every Winnipeg resident who wants to to recycle
from home. By the end of January, my meditative parent has
received all my letters up to #80, in which I've noted that Luke
has asked about my travel plans home to Canada ("because
he's wondering if he should meet me in Europe!?"), to which
Mom responds, "*ALLRIGHT*," all in caps, surrounded by stars.

Mom's Letter #90 goes permanently missing. Her Letter #91 reports an "avalanche" of mail from me and assures me that she'd "much rather have letters than snow!" It's been too cold to go to a movie, so Mom and Dad watched *The Barber of Seville* on TV. "That was a lot of fun to see (and to hear)," Mom writes. "[. . .] I wish I could sing that way myself. What a liberating thing to release so much sound and breath and make it sound so good!" Mom's fact-checked my claim that Boston (where I was considering graduate school) might be closer to Winnipeg than Vancouver (where I was also considering graduate school). "Now, you know my passion for maps," she writes, "and can therefore understand that I immediately pulled out the atlas to verify. And lo and behold, Vancouver is closer and *much, much* easier to get to!"

Mom's Letter #93 follows #90 permanently into the BHOIP, but a "freebie" she writes on 14 March reaches me with details about a friend's wedding plans, the news that all of my letters up to #86 have arrived safely, and the fact that she's glad, as a result, "to know that there is someone now who's as concerned about your well-being as I am." Mom means Luke, of course. But three weeks earlier, on 21 February 1989, Luke has penned a breezy missive letting me know he's met someone else.

holy shipwreck (8)

Five weeks earlier yet, on 14 January 1989, with the long letter that Luke sends after the holiday, he encloses four photographs: of his family at Christmas, the little nieces he clearly
dotes on, himself reading to a friend's young son, and himself
again, posed with his new car. Among many other topics, the
letter includes a meditation on his wish to do the best job
possible of whatever work he's engaged in, and his eagerness
to know my thoughts about teaching as a career. He clearly
hasn't yet received my response to his idea about travelling to
Europe to meet me ("as long as this isn't just a fetish for neat
handwriting!"), but he urges me several times to take care of
myself, if not for my sake, then for his.

Luke's letter of 14 January reaches me on 1 February and I
begin answering four days later. As his letter has, mine engages
in detailed ways with the broad range of subjects—serious,
tender, funny—we've been exploring together. I've determined that Funafuti is just south of the Marshall Islands, and
suggest that if his (well-travelled) brother's been there and
found some of my missing letters, could he simply hold on to
them for me till I get back to Canada in August?

After the fact, the three letters I send Luke between February and April 1989 acquire a unique poignancy. Even as
far back as October 1988—when we are implicitly theorizing
the nature of love letters and explicitly reiterating our shared
interest in seeing how, as Luke puts it, "things work out with
us"—I include the prescient caveat: "If, for whatever reason,
you decide to stop writing, I'm trusting you'll have the grace
and the gallantry to erase from your memory banks some of

the crazier things that have found their way from my place to yours?!" But when I mail my response to Luke's long, mid-January letter on Valentine's Day, I don't yet believe in erasing.

One month later, facing postal silence, I send a test-probe: "Hey L-babe, you break an arm playin' some kinda mean squash, or are you mailing to Jakarta for the sheer challenge? Or ('ooohoooo') is that new car improving your social life beyond your wildest dreams? On this end, the BHOIP is sucking stuff up at random; you getting *my* letters?" I describe a wild night of machine gunfire and not sleeping in Kampala, but add as a final postscript, "Just back from dinner with Jake and Amy's friends and their adorable kids, who really do say the funniest things. The older of the two is a pretty articulate three-year-old who'd been off charming other patrons while we waited for our supper, but at one point returned, obviously perturbed, to announce, 'Daddy, I forgot my name!'"

Luke's letter of 21 February could have been sucked permanently into the BHOIP, but on 9 June 1989, as I'm marking four full months of his silence, and just six weeks before Frances and I are scheduled to fly out of Entebbe for the last time, it meets me in Kampala, stamped, "*Jakarta Soekarno Hatta.*" Three days later, our car's broken into and we lose all its contents, including one volume of Frances's journal (I imagine jumping off a tall building on her behalf), several boxes of slides, all the writing I've done and collected for our unit's next newsletter, and all the personal letters we picked up earlier that weekend, eight, in my case, including my mother's Letters #100 and 101.

"There's something deliciously ironic about this," I write to my parents five days after the theft. "I can hear myself now: 'Yeah, I got a Dear John letter once. Took more than three months to get to me and three days later somebody stole it!' Uncanny, that it could get lost for so long with so many others, show up by itself so much later, and disappear so soon afterward, forever." I'm not unprepared for Luke's letter. It's been clear for at least a month to even the most hope-filled observer that the romance is over. Prepared, though, doesn't keep my heart from shattering. Luke's letter casts a pall over my remaining days at Ndejje, but if I'd known earlier, it would only have extended the scope of the pain.

holy shipwreck (9)

Mom is busy writing in the meantime, explicitly determined to "stay ahead" of me, by which she means, write more letters than I do. She begins Letter #94 with another weather report and the startling observation that "the swings in the backyard are immobilized by the snow." The letter describes an especially hectic recent Sunday, and Mom explains that she didn't write because, "I had to first of all *bikom in bytsje fan all dy drokte,* and when I had 'become myself again' it was time to start making supper." She adds an asterisk that directs me to the bottom of the page where she meditates in more than usually cramped handwriting on the intriguing similarities of the phrases, then squeezes into the corner the words, "Did I write about this before? Sorry about the repeat!"

In response to my news that neighbours at Ndejje have wondered whether I'll extend my term to make up for the time I wasn't well enough to teach, she writes, *"Don't even think about staying longer. I couldn't take it."* And then she concludes hurriedly, "Elke V just called, asked me to baby-sit her four foster children! I didn't have the heart to refuse." Two letters later, Mom is still writing about winter weather. In Letter #97, though, Mom apologizes for her particularly bad handwriting and explains, "I've just finished signing my name and address to seventy cards to MPs urging them to support disarmament and banning of nuclear tests, cruise tests, and space weapons tests. And I have approximately 230 to do. This is a postcard blitz of Project Plowshares to all members of Parliament. The cards are to be mailed simultaneously on April 9 and according to the latest issue of *Peace Projections* about seven thousand people are taking part."

For only the second time this year, Mom mentions Walter, noting that while he sometimes delivers reasonably good sermons, he quickly falls back into "conservative, supposedly evangelical ideas expressed in fifty- or hundred-year-old jargon. If you were here," she adds gleefully, "we'd be talking about it all morning, exploring all the angles, nuances, implications, etc.! I can't tell you how much I'm looking forward to be able to do that again!" Mom doesn't write again for almost two weeks, but the letter she writes next is unlike any of the others.

Letter #98 from Mom and Dad   19 April 1989

My dear daughter, just this morning I was thinking about how you are like Pake de Jong, in your love of literature and poetry. Perhaps it had something to do with watching an interview on TV last night, Bill Moyers interviewing Robert Bellah. [. . .] Some of that came back to me this morning and then a memory of Pake also came. Came? Appeared?

Exactly how does a memory present itself to a person anyway? I don't know, but I will tell you what the memory was. Pake was reading a poem to Beppe (this was still in Fryslan) out of a magazine he subscribed to called In de Waagschaal, which means literally "in the weighing scale" (a progressive, religious journal it was). The poem was about Martin Luther, the Reformer, and it moved Pake so that he had difficulty finishing it and had to make more than one attempt. I do not remember if there were more people in the room besides the three of us, there probably were, with so many in the family. I do remember that I was rather embarrassed by Pake not quite being able to control his emotions, but in some strange way I loved him for it too.

That wasn't the only time I saw Pake cry; sometimes it happened when he read from the Bible, not often, but sometimes, and I always wondered and wanted to understand what it was that moved him so. I was still quite

young in those days. Later on I understood better.
Then today your Letters #90 and 91 arrived, and I read
your poem and it moved me to tears. From everything you've
sent so far, I think this is the best yet. [. . .] Pake was a lover
of poetry, although to the best of my knowledge, he never
attempted to write any. Perhaps he never even considered it;
I don't know that either. He'd be very proud of you.

It's a striking letter, the only one that discusses Pake or child-hood memories at length, the only one that records Mom's fleeting speculations on how, exactly, a memory presents itself. Mom's recollection acquires additional resonance later, on the handful of occasions I can induce her to speak about Pake's tears while reading the Bible, especially the Old Testament, especially the Psalms, and episodes when he was too overwhelmed with emotion to continue reading. "I think he couldn't believe how wrong he'd been about everything, you know," Mom speculates quietly, protectively, about those times. "The whole war. But especially everything that happened to the Jews."

~~~

When Mom learns that another colleague of Frances's father will be travelling to East Africa and is willing to carry mail, she brings Letter #98 to an abrupt conclusion. It means a great deal to her, though, and she refers to it twice in Letter #99, hoping I'll receive it because it was about her father and how much I'm like him. (She also writes that she's biked to Beppe's to pick up Beppe's laundry and her aluminum cans, and notes that I can now call her "the recycling, cycling, saddlebag lady!") Mom almost certainly refers to Letter #98 in her next two letters too, but they're both stolen when our vehicle's broken into on 12 June 1989.

Irony pervades my postal existence. When it was carried to us directly, mail arrived promptly—the whole point of sending letters with people who are travelling to distant locations is to reduce the time it will otherwise take for the letters to arrive. But Frances's father's colleague, who is carrying Mom's precious Letter #98, makes the spontaneous decision to vacation in Kenya before travelling on to Uganda, so that it takes more than two months—until Friday 23 June 1989—to arrive. On 23 June 1989, I collect Mom's Letters #98, 102, and 103, three letters from friends in Ethiopia and Botswana, and one letter each from Tracey, Nathaniel, and Luke. Mom's #102 and 103 both wonder whether #98 has arrived, but the former expresses her particularly fervent wish that I should have that letter because, "it is a response to your poem and a remembrance of Pake de Jong."

~~~

Letters are always pointing to distance, separation, absence, and loss, and simultaneously embodying a commitment to their opposites: connection, kinship, communication, and remembering. Except for DIY-ers and people incarcerated, almost no one handwrites personal letters any more, although we practise letter writing's dynamics every day, assiduously developing and monitoring our social-media personas, our Facebook posts, our Instagram accounts, and the hundreds of texts and tweets we send, each of which arrives with the subtext, "I'm here; are you there? I'm here; have you registered my existence? If you're there, write me back, text me back, message me back, 'like' me, leave me a comment, let me know that we're connected."

The worst thing is hearing only the sound of your own voice calling: "Has Letter #98 arrived yet?"

~~~

On 23 June 1989 I collect Mom's Letters #98, 102, and 103, three letters from friends in Ethiopia and Botswana, and one letter each from Tracey, Nathaniel, and Luke. Finally grasping that

his February letter—which he now describes as "crappy"—
hasn't arrived, Luke writes again on 1st June and attempts,
in the midst of an engaging new relationship, to understand
what our correspondence was and what it meant. The next
and last time Luke writes, it's to append a friendly note to the
stack of letters he's bundled up at my request and shipped to
Winnipeg. Several weeks after I get back to Canada, he'll be
married, memory banks erased.

There is so much noise in my mind on 23 June 1989 that I
don't appreciate the multiple ironies in the writing and receiving of Mom's Letter #98. Mom began Letter #98 more than
two months earlier by reflecting on how much I am like her
intensely emotional (especially where literature is concerned)
father. She's been prompted to those reflections by watching
Bill Moyers interview Robert Bellah on the effects of individ-
ualism on democracy. A pre-eminent social activist and soci-
ologist of religion, Robert Bellah expounded eloquently on
the need to tackle personal and public problems from within
a community based on moral and spiritual values.

In the interview that gets replayed on 18 April 1989, Bellah spoke about the failure of individual freedom and tech-
nological advances to provide meaningful solutions to social
ills. Bellah's focus was American and it was American society that he identified as needing to recognize, explicitly and
broadly, that it is interdependence that enables all levels of
human engagement with the world. Mom's subsequent reflections prompt what was likely not a rare memory of her father,
but one of the rare memories she puts into writing. What
are the chances that, in the middle of these particular musings, she receives my Letter #91, which includes one of the
few poems I've written, this one for an elderly neighbour at
Ndejje, whose complicated identity as a mother I've been honoured to glimpse?

Letter #32 to Sharon   *10 April 1989*

*Wednesday it will be ten weeks since I heard from the legible
bachelor. I have cried and cried. I am tired of crying. I am
tired of getting my hopes up each time we go into town
for mail. [. . .] The most likely scenario is that Luke's not
writing. It's less likely but possible that Luke's writing and
it's all getting sucked up (with your #35 and several of my
Mom's) into the BHOIP. But I think we need to proceed
on the assumption that I'm being dumped by a formerly
wonderful guy who's scrapped all tentative, vacation-
together-in-Europe options, which is fine, right, because it's
one less organizational headache for you and me?*

In August when my term ends, Sharon and her husband, Lev-
itt, will meet me in Nairobi and we'll travel back to Canada
together, stopping in the Netherlands on the way, to visit my
relatives. Sharon is (inasmuch as international post allows)
up-to-date on the state and pace and tenor of my correspondence with Luke. With little to report on that score, I recount
a medical emergency and evidence that, after two and a half
years, I'm still a cultural neophyte . . .

Letter #32 to Sharon [cont.]

*"It's a good thing I don't have any liquor in the house, 'cause
for sure I'd get schnocked," I tell Frances gloomily last week
when we get back from Kampala with another bag-load of
silence from Luke. A good thing indeed, because not more
than an hour after we're back, but plenty long enough to
have quaffed a beer, or more than one big glass of wine were
you and I together, there's a knock at the door. The little boy
who brings me milk each morning is bringing me a story the
gist, if not the details, of which is clear: a wild dog has bitten
someone in the family, can I please come down to help?*

Earlier that day, over lunch in town, Frances and I listed all the things we'd miss about Ndejje, among them the unhesitating ways in which we always found the help and support we needed. "Of course," Frances added, "it's also assumed that *you* will help, whenever and wherever you're needed." For the months of my illness, my neighbours have been scrupulous about my need to rest. This evening, little Geoffrey's appearance feels as much like community affirmation that I'm well again as it does a request for help.

Letter #32 to Sharon [cont.]

Geoffrey's one of the Mulengas' orphaned grandchildren, the elderly, stalwart churchgoers who befriended Frances and me from our very first day here. Mrs. M is a bit of a character; she slips unpredictably into spells of mental aberration that can go on for days, during which she says and does all manner of odd things, dances without warning, and sings, sudden shrill plaintive bursts of sound. But well, she is kinder than kind. [. . .]

Geoffrey's English isn't up to a clear description of the wound and my Luganda, neglected now for a year, halts over anything more than simple greetings. I don't have access to serious antibiotics or a tetanus shot, but I pack what I have in the way of first aid, remember the torch, switch on the porch light, and give several silent cheers for Uncle Menno's proscriptions on alcohol. Bad enough I should head out on a mission of mercy weaving down the path, but the Mulengas are "saved"—it's possible even a whiff of liquor could shake their faith in "the Mennonites." [. . .]

Geoffrey and I crunch down the rocky, rain-eroded track at a good pace, past the shape of the Butagiras' house, past their cooking fire's glow, past the spindly shadows of cassava, through the gloom of the banana plantation, broad leaves filtering pale slivers as a moon begins. Even in a sweatshirt I shiver slightly. It's like walking into a fairy tale. Almost

*there; a fire behind the Mulengas' house lights up parts of
the compound so I recognize it, but in front, it's all low eaves
and roof runners brushed against shrubs and leaves, and I
see Mrs. Mulenga in my mind's eye as she was on my most
recent visit—*

*It was early evening and the children hadn't come yet for
the milk bottles, so I thought I'd run them down myself and
found Mrs. Mulenga on the steps at the back of the house. I
treasure the picture she made that evening, wide and brown
in a workday busuti, sweater-wrapped against the chill, her
perfectly round, close-cropped head of bright white hair held
erect on her straight neck, and the childlike delight in her
eyes, the gentle way she directed the children in their chores.
If this is a fairy tale, Mrs. Mulenga is the good witch [. . .]*

*Once inside, in the front room, by the light of two
candles, I discover that the dog bit Daphne, the older
granddaughter, twice, once on each thigh. [. . .] Both
wounds are clean; one's not much more than a graze, but the
other looks excruciating, and underneath it, I'm disturbed
to feel what may be infection. When I start in with cotton
batting and iodine, Daphne grits her teeth but doesn't flinch,
and I wish I knew comforting things to say in Luganda. I say
comforting things in English instead, between my own gritted
teeth, flinching as I dig iodine in under bits of skin. [. . .]*

*I don't notice that Mrs. Ssendawula, Mrs. Butagira, and
Mrs. Nsubuga have arrived until Mrs. S slips to kneel beside
me to inspect the damage more closely. Inside, I grimace
ruefully. This is Rose's mother, mother of seventeen children,
who could, with one hand tied behind her, whip together
an effective brew of traditional medicine in moments. We
exchange smiles and she speaks words of shock, chagrin,
and sympathy, asks the question that starts Mrs. Mulenga
on a dramatic tale—gestures, gesticulations, Mrs. M's voice
rises and falls, her head shakes from side to side, a mixture
of horror, anger, resignation, and I realize the mothers have*

slipped into the ring of candlelight to convey their concern and their solidarity, and to query the role that Mirimu has played in this—"Mirimu," "Mirimu," their voices sound—the "small god" who keeps our valley and whose unpredictable anger must be appeased.

Mrs. Ssendawula takes another, closer look at the bites, shudders slightly, and then asks what I imagine translates as "What else can we do?" because Mr. Mulenga answers instantly, "Sabe." Pray. And despite the seriousness of the situation, I have a tiny silent chuckle at myself, again, because I've failed, again, to understand the agile syncretism my neighbours practise. Even the Mulengas, I realize, would not likely have judged me for one glass of wine. [. . .]

I glance up, almost finished. I've done very little but there's not much more to do till tomorrow, when Mr. Mulenga will take Daphne to the doctor in Kampala, including for a rabies shot. For just a few more moments here with the good mothers, I can carry my share of the anger and the pain. I tell Daphne good night, sleep well little one, and I'm off the mat, back to my chair. "I will go now," I say in my halting Luganda, "and wish you goodnight, sleep well." Around the circle, "goodnight, goodnight, goodnight." "Weebale nyo, nyabo, sula bulungi." Thank you for coming, thank you, thank you. "Na we, musule bulungi." You are so much more than welcome; I'm glad I could do a little bit to help. [. . .]

I thought for a very long time that it must've been the war to blame for Mrs. Mulenga's spells of mad dancing, but my neighbour Joseph, Joseph the Erstwhile Peddler of Papayas, about whom you have heard many, many times, is also Joseph, son of Mrs. Mulenga, and the story he told me about his mother's madness broke my heart. According to Joseph, Mrs. Mulenga had hoped and hoped to have a daughter, but when she'd been delivered of her third son, after her third risky Caesarean section, attending doctors had taken action to ensure that she wouldn't get pregnant *again. It was when she learned that she'd never have the daughter she so longed for that Mrs. Mulenga first "ran mad."*

In the poem I write for Mrs. Mulenga, I grapple with what it means to have loved even unknown daughters so much that the end of their possibility drives you to madness.

holy shipwreck (10)

On the various journeys that my story has taken so far, I've plied you with numbers. These have often been the numbers of specific letters, and they've often been dates on which letters were written, or dates on which letters arrived; dates on which conversations occurred and the dates on which events recalled during those conversations occurred. Other numbers measure gaps and space and silence, attempting to say something meaningful about the time between events or letters or conversations, or between events and when they're forgotten—or remembered. I know that the numbers' apparent linearity is an illusion, but there's something comforting about being able to say, "Friday 30 September 2011 and my mother is having a very bad day." "Mom's second letter reaches me on 3 October 1986." "It's 6 March 2008, and the pathology report is in."

5 March 2008.

Impossible, Saturday afternoon, when Gareth and I arrive at the hospital and find ourselves comforting Harry, inconceivable that this beautiful baby, with his soft hair and his perfectly hand-sized head, the tiny, precisely articulated fingers that stroke my hand as I stroke his head, could be ravaged by illness, under siege by tumours, multiple tumours on his liver and his lungs—

No correspondence between the levels of body, between the perfect, physical body we hold and stroke, and the visceral body that science examines, both products, in different ways, of our imaginations, except, crucially, for the discomfort we see the physical body suffer. That's the hardest part, the fact that Harry's in the hospital and suffering. [. . .] The other hardest part, of course, is the waiting, waiting, waiting, waiting for biopsy results. [. . .]

Such unexpected solace, that someone we know is doing spiritual care at Children's Hospital, Ruth S——, my very first best friend. We've been out of touch far too long. "Oh yes," Ruth says when we talk yesterday evening, "your Mom gave me a big hug and told me, 'I have Alzheimer's. It's such a pain in the neck!'" I laugh out loud. Mom apparently also said, after she'd asked how Ruth's kids are doing, "I know I'll forget, but tell me anyway, okay?" Such reserves of graciousness. "Good for her," I say, "good for her."

We realize early on that we can't allow either of the two numbers, 20 percent or 5 percent, the power to determine what happens next, so we focus instead on how profoundly *well* we always feel when we spend time with Harry, how thoroughly Harry's life force—even compromised by chemo treatments—fills the room and—for the time we're with him—releases our anxiety. Gareth and I concentrate on the blog, calmed by the need to maintain a conduit of information for, and a connection with, all the people around the world who are praying and drumming and chanting and meditating on Harry's behalf. We send digital messages into the ether and tell one other several times a day how grateful we are that we can see Harry in person.

Often, when I hold him, Harry takes one of my hands in his and rubs the top of my thumb. I guess at the time that it's simply one more facet of Harry's heart-clenching sweetness, the way his thousand-watt smile lights up a room, but when I check months later, no one else remembers this particular gesture. The day Harry died and many times afterward, I imagine a moment in the future when someone will take my hand and rub the top of my thumb and I'll recognize Harry in the new form he's taken . . .

Because Harry died. Despite our prayers and our chanting, our meditations, our drumming, and the candles we lit, despite the vivid futures we envisioned for a healthy family, despite Harry's excellent health going into the ordeal, despite all the advantages of being Canadian and coming through five rounds of rigorous chemo with colours flying, despite the expertise that doctors from around the world brought to bear, despite the love Harry showered on us and the love we showered on him, "lethal" caught up with "childhood" and Harry died.

On Friday 18 July 2008, Cynthia and Henry are scheduled to receive the results of the CT scan that followed Harry's sixth round of chemo. This is the scan that will confirm that Harry's liver is sufficiently free of cancer to qualify him for a liver transplant. In the future that we imagine—and despite the wracking realities that render organs available for transplant—we will accept another child's donated liver, Harry will grow into the person he is meant to be, and we'll slowly resume our former lives, buoyed by eternal gratitude. The CT scan on 18 July shows that the cancer has returned and has not only spread throughout Harry's liver but has re-entered his lymph nodes and both his lungs. Harry's medical team is heartbroken at the news. Harry is discharged with a palliative program, but Cynthia and Henry are not done believing in his capacity to live. After several days of research and stock-taking, they transfer their full confidence to the naturopathic healer in Arizona who has, until now, been working collaboratively with the allopathic experts.

On Monday 21 July 2008, Gareth and I see Harry looking well for the last time. We find the family sitting down over supper with neighbours who've been bringing their medical and spiritual wisdom to the journey since Harry was first diagnosed. Lydia and her friend Bethany are slipping off their chairs as we arrive, keen to resume their play outside.

I'd spent the previous afternoon with Henry and Harry, so it wasn't surprising that Harry immediately held out his arms, eager for me to carry him around the house and to practise his words. Harry's language learning has been delayed by the intensity of his health crisis, but he has recently begun to say "bye-bye."

Just twenty-four hours later, on Henry's forty-third birthday, Harry is so listless that Gareth and I visit only long enough for a whispered flourish of the cake we've remembered for the occasion. The next nine days are a blur of homeopathic remedies and terror. Gareth and I are scheduled to leave on Saturday 2 August for the cottage in northern Ontario we rent every summer. The ten days we spend at Coutts Camp constitute one of the highlights of our year, but we consider cancelling, Harry is that sick. We talk through the night and determine that not to go would be to break faith with Harry's spirit, to imagine that we know in advance what the future will hold.

5 August 2008.

The presentiment arrives at 5:41 p.m. on the drive to Coutts Camp. I cry more on that trip than I've cried since February, and then Chris Smither's heartbreaking "Cold Trail Blues" comes on ("I could use / Any kind of sign / That you're still on the line"), and I'm suddenly gasping for breath, certain that something has smashed through my body leaving a fist-size hole. I grab at my chest, I can feel the hole, glance across the windshield—were we hit by a rock?—intact, glance down at the clock, 5:41, and moan incoherently. "Oh," I say, "oh," like an animal in pain. I can't put it into words but the thought floods my mind: "Harry has died?"

I lean up against the door of the cottage when we get there. No note taped to the glass; no message from Winnipeg. I was wrong. Thank God. I let myself breathe

and imagine we'll last out our stay. It's a short reprieve,
though. My premonition was off by just 27 hours.

Harry jumped from this life into what comes next at nine in
the evening on Sunday 3 August 2008, one day before his six-
teen-month birthday, in a brief rare instant in which neither
his mother nor his father was in the room.

> *18 August 2008.*
>
> *I cannot believe how literally sore my heart is, how tight*
> *and heavy and painful, as if it's been sealed up a hun-*
> *dred years in an iron chest without air, exacerbated every*
> *time I'm obliged to last out other people's chatter, suck-*
> *ing out the oxygen I need to survive. [. . .] Two weeks*
> *ago we were driving in from Coutts Camp and I cried*
> *even more than I'd cried on the way out. How to write*
> *about finding Harry still at home as I'd hoped we would?*
> *Beautiful, limp, waxen doll of Harry. In the pictures he*
> *looks ancient and wise, like the oldest Buddhist monk of*
> *a half-forgotten legend, while the "real" world distorts*
> *and bends, folds and cracks, as if it can't hold itself steady*
> *now that Harry's gone, Harry's gone and there's a crater*
> *left by the explosion that took him, jagged, dangerous,*
> *broken things rain down all around us, I'm flattened*
> *under a fallen boulder, and Mom's illness is suddenly vis-*
> *ible again, bearing down like a massive mining truck, me*
> *immobilized in its path.*

After Harry died, it became impossible to continue reading
letters with Mom. Because of grief and because of Alzheimer's
"progressions" and because of both, Mom was suddenly unable
to do the extra cognitive work that letter reading requires—
identifying "voices" for instance, or following the looping narratives woven into letters' strange, contextless spaces.

22 August 2008.

*Remembering the days very early on, just after the diag-
nosis, during the first round of chemo, at the hospital one
evening just as M—— was finishing a Reiki treatment
and the way Harry let me know, "Sorry, Auntie KK, I
don't want you rubbing my head right now." Balanced by
all the times and times we'd hold hands and he'd gently
tap the top of my thumb. Months later, Monday 21 July,
the last time we saw him well, the way he lit up when we
walked in and held out his arms, the way he waved bye-
bye to everyone as we walked around the house together
that evening. "Bye-bye Lyddie, come home soon. Bye-bye
Bethany, thanks for playing with me; come again soon!"
I guessed. "Bye-bye kids on the sidewalk." "Bye-bye Lisa,
bye-bye Shelly, come again soon," I guessed. "Bye-bye
bus. Come again soon." We were running out of things
and people, but Harry still wanted to say bye-bye.*

*Now it's hard not to imagine that he was also try-
ing to say, "Bye-bye, Auntie KK, I have to go soon." How
much do I want him to have also been saying, "I'll try my
best to come again." [. . .]*

*I have no idea how I'll finish my book. Mom's behav-
iour right now—her illness, I remind myself—makes me
so fretful and anxious and annoyed, I can't bear to be with
her. I can hardly get that legibly onto paper, I'm breathing
so quickly, as if this writing were a full-contact sport.[1]*

perfect correspondence (10)

My mother was, in the small world in which she orbited, famous for her radiating empathy. It was a force, a gravitational pull, and it worked on no one more powerfully than on me. Listening as if listening were an Olympic sport, my mother gave me the unparalleled gift of her time and attention, her keen insight, her thoughtful questions, her profound kindness, her unshakeable confidence in my capacities. In 1989, Mom had been available for every crisis in my life, large and small, lifting me up, sometimes literally, reassuring me, encouraging me, believing in me, and she was—despite our separation in literal space—no less utterly present for me when Luke's disappearance left behind its abyss of silence and uncertainty . . .

Perhaps that's what I miss the most as Alzheimer's proceeds, the retreat now of my most ardent fan, my most conscientious supporter, my readiest listener and reader and mentor and friend. On Friday 30 March 2012, I yawn through most of the afternoon, vastly underslept, struggling with perimenopause. I've been mourning for months the fact that I can't compare notes with my mother, determine which of my experiences match hers, learn from her. But she surprises me by noticing, and asks me, kindly, why I'm so sleepy, so I give it a try, detail my symptoms in the simplest language I can think of. And Mom listens carefully, sweetly, nods in all the right places, makes all the reassuring sounds she was always so good at, and says, when I finish, deep concern in her voice:

"Oh honey, that sounds awful. Have you talked about it with your mother?"

〰〰

Letters from my last months at Ndejje measure silence from Luke, but they also track my developing friendship with Namu-kasa Beatrice, which blossoms, including literally. At the end of February, Bea—whom I describe variously as "a godsend" and "very cool"—recruits me to help with nature arrange-ments for a district-level arts exhibition. "So today," I wrote to Mom and Dad, "we spent a few hours organizing feathers and birds' nests, seashells (I know Uganda's landlocked; these seashells turn up anyway), sticks, leaves, and rocks into our various pots. Photo opportunity lost to encroaching dusk when we use a broom to deliver several mighty *thwacks* to the front compound acacia tree and successfully dislodge more of the dried pods we've found particularly beautiful. Deeply con-tented sigh. (And just in case it's all wrong, Bea's friend, the art teacher from the secondary school, will come tomorrow to fix our mistakes!)"

A few weeks later, while musing to Lil and Roxanne about patriarchy's pernicious effects, I write about the trip Frances and I have taken with Rose while Rose is on a school break, to visit MCC friends in western Uganda. I know Lil and Rox will share the stories with Mom, who'll love Rose's theory (that *muzungu* women neglect their husbands, based on the very dirty feet that some *muzungu* men sport) and news of my various "grandmothers" here . . .

Letter #15 to Lil & Roxanne   *23 March 1989*

We duel regularly, my fierce traditionalist feminist friend and I, score points, argue, concede, give ground. Her grandmother came to visit again after Christmas, and while we prepared supper one night, the conversation turned to Grandmother's stories, Grandmother's curiosity, Grandmother's questions. "She was asking," Rose struggles to keep a smile down, "'Does Katherine have a husband? Is she going to get married? Will she have children?' She is a bit worried."

It's a conversation Rose and I have had before, but on this evening, she explicitly outlines her priorities for my life: children ("but only two," she says, patting my belly tenderly, still concerned about my health); as much more schooling as possible (but not if it means no children); and then a husband, but only a very good one (that Luke fellow, say, if he comes through with another affectionate letter).

Letter #15 to Lil & Roxanne [cont.]

"Okay Boss," I tell her, "and this will be the plan we'll tell to Grandmother!" And we both laugh. [. . .] Rose's grandmother invites me to believe she's also my grandmother, and she forms, with several others, a kind of grandmother collective that surrounds me with a store of wisdom and concern. Nearest by is white-haired Mrs. Mulenga with her sweet eyes and her smooth, child's face, and her spells of madness: unpredictable bouts of aberrant behaviour that I attributed to war shock until I learned, when I knew how to ask, that they'd begun when she was told that she'd never get pregnant again. Joseph, her last son, who sells me pawpaws and anything else for which I'm willing to exchange cash, is the one who tells me: "It was when she knew she would never have a daughter that she first ran mad." [. . .]

Nalongo Catherine is a great contrast, fierce, impetuous, matriarchal, proud of her title, given to mothers of twins; she's a big woman, used to getting her own way, and her voice is especially impressive, imposing, gravelly like a jazz singer's; she commands the community's respect, but it's also Nalongo whose gritty barks and raunchy rebounds explode her audience into laughter. (It happens again and again, and in all this time, I still haven't convinced anyone to explain. People literally burst with laughter, then quickly cover their smiles and decorously avoid full translations). [. . .]

Mrs. Muwanga is younger than the first two, reserved, dignified, wise. Shy of the halting English that keeps us from

*communicating deeply, she nevertheless visited several times
while I was sick to urge me to go back to Canada and return
when I'd recovered. "We want you to be well, Miss Katherine,"
she repeated fervently, "we want you to be well." [. . .]*

*And Tolofina, the ancient beloved bent-double crone
whom Rose always calls, "your friend who loves you very
much." When Tolofina rides with us to Kampala, her
thanks come in the form of banana-leaf-wrapped produce:
a pumpkin sometimes, purple gleaming eggplants, sweet
potatoes, or new, fresh-scrubbed "Irish," but mostly hands
and hands of perfect, sweet, finger bananas. Tolofina
and I exhaust our store of mutually understood phrases
seconds after she's creaked into the room, but we visit
nevertheless, through the creaking, the settling, the greeting,
the groundnuts, the glass of cold water, and Tolofina's gift
of the day, her thick stumpy ground-dirt fingers fumbling
with tightly tied banana fibres as she keens, a low-throated,
timeless, blessing-lament. [. . .]*

*And there is Julia, deep in the village, whom I don't
know by sight, who sends greetings and "messages"—hands
of bananas, a pumpkin. "She is a very old woman," says
Sekijobba Tomas, one of the college porters, a gentle, simple
man still harrowed by the war. His mother stays in that
same village and he is often the one who brings the message.
"Julia has never visited you," Rose explains, "but she knows
who you are."*

*And, of course, there's Rose's grandmother, who laughed
deeply and broadly and again and again at her joke when we
first met, that when I married she would be the one who sat
in the grandmother's seat. "And everyone will say, 'How did
that muzungu bride get an African grandmother?'" Rose's
grandmother, whose husband took a second, younger wife,
and who is regularly abused by the co-wife and the co-wife's
children. Rose's grandmother, who only ever had three
children, who knew Rose had considered ending her second*

pregnancy, who didn't censure the possibility but talked instead with Rose about the children she might never have. Rose's grandmother, who danced for us on New Year's the dances once danced for the Kabaka. [. . .]

"She says," Rose said that night, kneeling close to catch the old woman's words, "that if you could visit her at her home, you would leave with so many gifts they would fill the whole car." [. . .]

Julia, whom I've never seen, visited me last night in a dream. When I reconstruct her features they seem familiar in the way of dreams. She is tall, not particularly gainly, not particularly beautiful. She wears a plain faded-red busuti; her intelligent eyes face me directly. She speaks impeccable English and comments matter-of-factly that she's come to find me to see if I will go with her to church. It's not always easy, she explains, to find someone to go to church with. [. . .]

I'm glad for the comfort of my Julia-dream. Otherwise, these days, after talk and talk with Rose, I've been having nightmares, versions of the time Rose had to take her daughter to the hospital during the war: "If Obote's soldiers came, they would rape the mothers waiting with their children." The time she ran with the other daughter, the three-month daughter, sixteen miles under a drought-ugly sun, on foot, unable to carry much more than the baby: "I was so sure she would die." All the nights they left their homes, to sleep but mostly to not sleep in the bush, to hide from the soldiers who came regularly to loot and ransack: "the ones with babies were always most afraid; they always had to go furthest away." The time the soldiers came for her mother and her mother had gone for water and they said that she wasn't there, they didn't know where she'd gone, they didn't know when she'd come back, and, thank God, thank God, the soldiers shrugged and left them in peace.

At the end of March, Frances and I—who've been jointly responsible for the Drama Society since halfway through our first year—organize and direct our students' Easter play ("dress rehearsals appalling, and then the girls pulled it together overnight and rendered me speechlessly proud"), which prompts my realization that, though I've written about it extensively to Cindy, I've never described our Christmas play for my parents:

Letter #91 to Mom and Dad   *1st April 1989*

[It] was a stage version, courtesy of Frances's careful adaptation, of Henry Van Dyke's The Other Wise Man, a story that imagines a fourth Magi and his thirty-three-year search for the One he knows has come, three splendid gems secured as gifts for the end of his pilgrimage. At the story's heart are the Magi's choices along the way, when he sacrifices the jewels, one by one, each time to alleviate the human suffering he encounters . . .

[. . .] Rehearsals were gruelling (I was still unwell), particularly exhausting on the days I forgot to remember that I shouldn't be jumping up to demonstrate a gesture, a facial expression, mimic a tone of voice. Our trousers were, as always, a hot costuming commodity, and on performance night, the girls were marvellous. Particular showstoppers were the two-woman, blanket-draped, banana-fibre hoofwrapped "horse" and the Bethlehem baby-slaying scene—

The scene itself happened offstage: wild backstage pounding, smashing, and hysterical screaming by the sound people ("The soldiers are killing our babies! The soldiers are killing our babies!"), and then the sudden appearance of those very soldiers, ingeniously and formidably arrayed, a stellar example of our students' understanding of the story's drama. In Van Dyke's story, the soldiers are placeholders; the crucial business of the scene is the Magi's decision to use the second of his three jewels to ensure the safety of the child hidden in the house where he's found lodging.

*Not so in our production: the girls cast as soldiers were
having none of this non-part-part business, and after some
extensive extracurricular costuming efforts and numerous
consultations and set-design changes, they built themselves
starring roles. Because I'd seen them stride on several times,
epaulets emblazoned, bayonets at the ready, I watched the
audience instead:*

*Absolute rapt attention, like one heart beating through
each body in the room and a whispered, "the banyanya,"
that criss-ed and cross-ed in tight tense waves around the
chairs. Each person here, I thought, knows exactly what that
is like, midnight military visits, soldiers who wouldn't flinch
at killing everyone and the babies too. I knew, of course,
how the scene would end, but I didn't breathe again until
the crowd roared its approval—the banyanya marching off
stage, greedily flourishing the Magi's second gem, oblivious
to everything else including, upstage, lit by candles, the
mother and child, safe, unharmed.*

A few weeks later, I muse extensively on what the past three
years have meant and enclose some of my thoughts in a Mother's Day card:

Letter #93 to Mom and Dad   *16 April 1989*

*In this last year, the past six months, these latest weeks I've
felt so much more like my old self, and in the meantime,
we've watched the community re-form, re-root, recover the
energy and the momentum to work for a future that's farther
off than tomorrow's meal, and it seems I'm only beginning
to understand, and only in a tiny way, how much of nothing
people here had when we first arrived, how absolutely from
scratch they were rebuilding their lives . . .*

*[. . .] Wondering ruefully if I could've survived so much
loss and continued. Especially now, when, along with the
re-forming, re-rooting, and recovering, come deeper levels of*

*remembering. I'd wondered if this would happen, and if it
happened, how it would happen, the way the stories might
change with repeated opportunities to tell them, which they
seem to do, almost as if previous tellings form protective
scars that allows other memories to rise to the surface. [. . .]*

*Rose was back from Ggaba for just a few days two weeks
before Easter. With Moses's battalion stationed there now
and Jake's recent trip, it was inevitable we'd talk about Gulu.
Same story. Same ugly, hateful story. Let them starve and etc.
Not good timing, I was having a very bad day, exhausted,
and my eyes ached. Covered 'em with my hands. Wished I
was someplace else. Felt like a battle I'd fought a hundred
times. Felt like the last thing I wanted to fight again.*

*"Rose," I finally said, defeated, "I don't understand you.
I watch you with people you know and with people you've
just met, and I think, 'There is someone who is interested in
people, there is someone who cares about other people.' You
say, 'Let them starve, let them die,' but if you met them, if you
knew them? You would care about them too." A hundred years
later when I look at her, she's watching me and smiling a bit.*

*"It's true." She says it with a bit of a laugh. "We have
these easterners at Ggaba and these ones from the north?"
She's begun to clear off the table. "And we are friends; we
work together, joke, help each other. But sometimes I look at
them and I think, 'Their brothers are the ones who killed us.'
And yet, we are friends."*

*She pauses. Starts again. "These ones at college—" She
searches for words and ideas. "We can be friends and then—"
She looks up. It's important that I understand the subtleties
of her dilemma. "Then we find ourselves remembering things
we thought we had forgotten about the war."*

*She's standing by now, heading for the kitchen, deep in
thoughts that stop her just at the doorway. "Maybe bygones
should be bygones?" she wonders, but there are volumes of
uncertainty in her voice.*

[. . .] Later that night, getting ready for bed, I was in a lot of pain and Rose knew it and was determined to heat milk for me to drink before I tried to sleep, which got her thinking, and that got her talking. Before the war, she told me, she'd been teaching in Semuto and a friend was working on a nearby farm—

"*Aaaaaay,*" her voice lilts in the half dark, "*that was so nice; we had milk whenever we wanted it—*" She sits on her bed, quiet, thinking. We both sip milk and I watch Rose remembering.

"*You know,*" she chuckles part of a chuckle, low, abbreviated, "*in that school in Semuto we were on the BEIIRD (Basic Education Integrated Into Rural Development) program. It was very interesting. We learned all the names of the trees and the flowers and the insects. And the children would bring things they had found—in that program the emphasis is on learning from real things in the environment.*"

"*One day,*" she scrapes out the other half of the chuckle, "*a man brought us a skull he had found and we were terrified.*" There is something like astonishment in her voice. "*No one had seen a skull before. We were all terrified. And that night, when the skull stayed at school, no one could sleep because we were all so afraid.*" She pauses.

"*The headmaster came back the next day,*" she goes on. "*He made the man remove the skull. One skull,*" she wanders with her voice across the Luwero Triangle that would sprout them later like weeds, "*and we were terrified.*"

Six months ago, Frances and I believed we shouldn't be replaced here at the college. Enough has happened since that I'm now equally adamant that if MCC is serious about listening to the voices with which this country speaks, we have to keep someone in Luwero. Two years ago people had not healed enough to tell the stories they're remembering now.

holy shipwreck (11)

On the first day of November 2007, Gareth and I take Mom to the Winnipeg launch of *Amish Grace*.[2] *Amish Grace* tells a story about the astonishing, almost immediate collective decision the Amish community of Nickel Mines, Pennsylvania, made to forgive the man who invaded their schoolhouse on 2 October 2006, shot to death five young girls and seriously wounded five others. Donald Kraybill, one of the book's three authors, presented that evening, contextualizing the community's rapid decision in the deep culture of forgiveness that Amish history and theology have enabled.

Forgiveness is a complex notion and process, no less complicated for people within faith traditions than for people who aren't. I was intrigued by the presentation, devastated by the stories of individual survivors and stories about the little girls who were murdered, but not convinced, even at the end, that such rapid public expressions of forgiveness were appropriate to the event's horror. And yet. Kraybill's final point was that forgiveness is certainly an altruistic act but it is, much more centrally, the act with which one frees oneself from what might otherwise be servitude to hatred and vengeance.

2 November 2007.

On the drive home, Mom agrees entirely when we remark on the power of Kraybill's anecdotes, so it makes me crazy that the very first thing she does, when he finishes talking, is turn to me, with her face practically in mine, and announce belligerently, self-righteously, and without leaving me any space to respond, "I could never do

that. I've never forgiven the man who molested me. Why
should I? I don't. Why should I let him off the hook? I
don't. I hate him. I'd like to kick him."

Three months later, on the first day of February 2008, Mom
and I are in the Millennium Library, where she tells me the
story about sticking her tongue out at the pretty little girl
in her pretty little hat, which reminds her of the delicately
poetic birth announcement (*"Een lente-kind is ons gegeven in
een dochtertje"*) whose debatable theology she had to defend.
We've been talking since lunch, but I only begin recording once
we've settled in at the library.

To relaunch the conversation, I ask Mom if she remembers
when she first wondered whether she might have Alzheimer's. In the conversation that ensues, we cover considerable
ground, including Mom's frequent visits over the years with
a friend from church who was clearly in the throes of dementia ("I'd sit with Margaret and think, 'This could happen to
me'") and a time in the vague past during which she remembers increasingly frequent attempts to pin down details ("I
ran up and down the stairs more often to look for something,
like a book or a date; like your birthdays"). I ask if she was
already worried fourteen years ago, when she would've been
babysitting her oldest granddaughter every day ("Not when
I was babysitting Gwyneth"); if there was a family history of
dementia ("Noooooooo. Those siblings of Beppe and Pake,
they were pretty much on the ball"); if she imagines long-term effects from the head injuries she suffered in a car accident in 1970 ("I've never had a head injury").

I would like a definitive answer to the question, "Why does
my mother have Alzheimer's?" More than that, I'd like my
anxious, readily self-blaming mother to know, permanently
and forever, that having Alzheimer's is not the result of something she did wrong. "I don't know either," I admit about my
speculations, "but the important thing is to realize that the

disease is not your fault." "No, no," Mom agrees, "it was not something that I was so stupid to...to catch, you know." And then she pauses and her voice drops. "I've never told this to anybody," she says, almost in a whisper. "You know, what happened to me when I was a little girl, and how Pake came, and Beppe came flying out of the house? Because Pake, you know, he, he, he—how do you say that—he caught him in the act."

Mom says, "I've never told this to anybody," but she's told this to me and she's told it to my sister and she's told it to her sisters and to at least one of her brothers. She has, in fact, told me a version of the story earlier today, over lunch, a version so vivid I didn't dare interrupt to retrieve my iPod. What she tells me now is, by comparison, scrambled, halting, and bereft of logic, but the conclusion is absolutely clear: "I've always hated him after that. I've never forgiven him."

I'm trying to understand how the story fits into our conversation so far, so I ask, "And you see that experience as connected to your illness, Mom?" "I don't know," Mom says, "I don't know if there's a link." But it's clear that she's wondered. "Have you wondered if there's a link," I ask, "between having been sexually abused and developing Alzheimer's disease?" "Yes I have," Mom says clearly. "Absolutely I have. Certainly. Maybe that doesn't make very much sense. But who's to say?"

At the time, the theory strikes me as highly implausible. At the time, I'm blinkered by the compellingly visual model that medical science describes, the story about plaques and tangles interfering with neurons' messaging functions, but I've since welcomed alternative explanations. Mom's experience of having been sexually abused comes up again the next week, on an afternoon I spend with my aunts Eta and Gerta. They've been helping me round out a picture of my mother as a younger woman, and they, too, have tried to pin down the time at which Mom began manifesting dementia's symptoms. When Gerta expresses her fervent hope that memories of the abuse don't come back to haunt Mom, I tell them about the

November book launch and Mom's grating insistence afterward: "I do not forgive that man. I hate him."

"You know, eh," Eta says at that, "at least ten years ago, prior to all this Alzheimer's jazz, your Mom went to some sort of workshop about forgiveness and atonement, and there was a service at the end of it all, and everybody had a stone or maybe it was a piece of paper, and that stone symbolized whatever it was the person wanted to be done with, whatever they were atoning for, or forgiving, and everybody was supposed to put that stone—no, I guess it was a piece of paper—in the fire." She pauses briefly, gathering up the details.

"I don't know, exactly, I can't remember, but she said to me after—your mom, that is—she said: 'You know what, Eta? I couldn't do it.' And that was ten years ago, I'd say, so what was that, 1998 or around then. 'I had it in my hand,' your mom said—and I'm pretty sure, you know, it had that guy's name on it—and she said: 'I couldn't do it.'

"Or maybe she said, 'I didn't do it.'"

new meadow (7)

Almost exactly one month after the book launch for *Amish Grace* prompts intractable thoughts about forgiveness, Mom and I have our first conversation about *Merijntje Gijzens*. Three days later I steal time to record what we've said.

3 December 2007.

An astonishing afternoon Friday, the tape recorder regrettably absent. Because she knew I was coming, Mom memorized a Dutch poem from a thick novel that she's often spoken about, always with enormous affection. "I've memorized it," she tells me when she greets me at the door, "and I want to see how much of the Dutch you understand." I didn't think it at the time, but what a good metaphor for the work Mom and I are doing, relearning as much as we can of languages we once knew fluently. [. . .]

Mom launches into her recital before I'm finished lunch, and when she falters repeatedly at the poem's third line, I suggest that she get the book so I can follow along. The truth is, I'm terrified. So much could go wrong. "If she's faltering so early," I think, "this could be disastrous." Add to that all my usual nervous questions when she goes in search of something: 'How will she possibly find that magazine/book/letter/card in all this muddle?' And 'What are the chances she'll find it before she forgets what she's looking for?' Mom produces the surprisingly fat novel with alacrity and deftly locates the correct page. I can follow the Dutch well enough to prompt her through the early stumble and am astonished to hear her recite the rest of the poem flawlessly. She uses the wrong prefix for one word on her first two attempts, but when I correct it, she gets it right from then on.

I deliberately don't get too excited, but this is an astonishing feat isn't it, for someone with Alzheimer's? That Mom would be organized enough to plan this work in anticipation of my visit and follow through is amazing enough. That she would bring it off flawlessly is almost miraculous. We talk about how an English translation might go and get several sentences in. When I suggest that Mom write it in the journal I've been encouraging her to keep, I mean the English version, but she begins in Dutch and I don't stop her. I'm learning not to give too many instructions. It's been touch and go whether she'll even get/find her journal.

"Oh," she says airily, when I ask where it is, as if she's covering irritation, "somewhere upstairs." Perhaps she's annoyed or disappointed that I haven't entered more fully into the poem, that I haven't appreciated the emotion of the final line—she gets choked up reciting it, which is surprising and a little unnerving because Mom almost never gets choked up.

For the next several weeks, Mom and I will discuss this poem, and we will again a year from now, when we inventory her Dutch and Frisian books. And then, two years from now, Mom will phone me at my office and, as soon as she hears my voice, she'll say, "I was thinking about that poem." I'll know immediately that she means "*De Goede Dood*," and I'll be able to picture the poem, which appears almost exactly halfway through the 1,171-page novel, near the end of its fifth segment, "*De Grote Zomer*." I still won't know what my uncle John helps clarify years later, that *Merijntje Gijzens* is a coming-of-age novel, tracking its protagonist's growth and maturation through crucial years of adventure with his devoted companion, Flierefluiter. Flierefluiter, I understand from Omke John, is a deeply appealing character, a drifter, devoid of ambition but compelled by a questing, existential spirit—a man who regularly ponders God, but whose freethinking ideas offend everything their traditional community holds as true.

Years later, Omke John describes the existential crisis with which *"De Grote Zomer"* ends, the wine-fuelled debate between Flierefluiter and the Vicar—Merijntje's other powerful moral compass—during which the Vicar reveals himself to be a freethinker too, if not an outright agnostic. Merijntje is in his teens by this point and out of sight and only accidentally overhears this unexpected exchange between the two people whose opinions he values most. It's near the end of the exchange that the Vicar recites the poem that thoroughly confuses Flierefluiter, devastates Merijntje, and almost reduces my mother to tears.

6 December 2007.

I've rarely seen Mom cry and I'm not prepared to start now. So I concentrate on the poem, which begins (in poem-speak) with an apostrophe. "It's as if the speaker in the poem is addressing Death," I suggest to Mom, and that seems to make sense to her. We wrestle together with the translation of the phrase "de Goede Dood." It's far more textured than the literal, "good death," even begins to encompass. It's perhaps something more like "loving Death" or "tender Death," but even those aren't quite it, there are intimations of something deeper, some surpassingly compassionate wisdom in this apostrophized Death that the stark English "good" or even "Good" only barely approximates.

It may be exactly that all-knowing, foreordained, wise, and gentle inevitability that draws Mom again and again to the poem, because I think that's how she's also

*understood God, a Romantic sensibility, or maybe an
Indigenous one, of the continuous, uninterrupted presence of the Divine or Spirit, literally in every blade of
grass. [. . .] I'd give a lot to know whether and how what
Mom's loved about the poem has changed over the years.
How does she understand the idea of "de Goede Dood"
now, at almost 72 and struggling with a disease that will
rob her of her identity before she is dead in any common
sense of that word?*

Merijntje has placed his faith so fully in these two men that
what he hears in the poem's abstract language and apparent
bleakness threatens to dismantle everything he believes about
life and the world. But, Omke John explains, in the chapter
that follows, the narrative slowly bringing Merijntje—and the
reader—to a readiness for Flierefluiter's mortality and passing.

～～～

In the gruelling, grief-grey winter after Harry's death, my
mother mourned in part by planning her own life's end. On
5 December 2008, almost exactly one year after she first recites
"*De Goede Dood*," in a conversation at her kitchen table about
an acquaintance with dementia, now in care, she was especially
clear. "I'd rather die, actually," she announced bluntly. "If you
sit there like a human being but you're . . . you're not exactly
lifeless, but—? [. . .] I cannot imagine that, that I would not be
interested in anything anymore, you know. [. . .] Sometimes I
look out of the window here, for instance, and then I think [. . .]
would I not know any more that that's snow? I find it actually
pretty damn scary, but I don't know what else to do except just
to"—and here she makes a choking sound—"'arcghhhhhh.'"

This isn't the first time and it won't be the last time that
my mother speaks about doctor-assisted death, but on this
afternoon she frames it as a clearly ethical issue. When I ask,
"Would you really want that, Mom?" she replies sternly. "To

die? Kathleen," she says, "if *nobody*—if I could not communicate with anybody and that was obvious to you. If I couldn't
have a conversation with you...if I wouldn't know who
you were, or who Dad was, or my grandchildren...what is
left then, tell me that? [. . .] Being sick is one thing but this
is...it's...it's as though your life is by a little bit, is just dwin-
dling away and it's gone. And you're going to have to die some
day anyway. I've said that many times: I hope I don't have to
live as long as *my* grandmother or even Beppe, and certainly
not in this condition!"

Astonishingly, she remembers then that we've read together
from the "Alzheimer's Disease Bill of Rights"[3] a few minutes
earlier. "I have an idea," she says; "maybe in that Rights of
Alzheimer's people, maybe they could...should also add one
thing in: the life to...the right to die." "If people want to make
a war," she adds passionately, "then it doesn't matter how many
people are getting killed; [. . .] and maybe people sign up for
war, they die, the strong fall, [. . .] but there are also people that
do not want to have that war, and they can say, 'No, I'm not
going to go to war,' and I should have the right to say, 'This is
a dead-end circumstance.'" I underscore the illegality of what
she's proposing but haven't finished my sentence before she
retorts, "It's not legal now, but when you think about it from
my position, then it should be. It should be."

Over that long winter, my mother returns to the possibility
of ending her life almost every time we visit and almost every
time I phone. I come to dread our conversations that winter:
Mom is increasingly fixated on the possibility, increasingly
serious about making a plan, increasingly unable to carry out
the necessary operations. What I dread most is that she'll ask
me to promise to help.

perfect correspondence (11)

Over the years that I record our conversations, Mom and I often speak candidly and sometimes we speak very candidly. To protect her privacy and the privacy of the people we talk about, I take on the work of transcribing our conversations, but it's worth asking, how much of Mom's privacy have I protected? On 11 January 2008 Mom signed the permission form that allowed me to record and use her words and then promptly announced that she wanted to be "anonymous," because, she explained, "I am not the woman I used to be." It took all that afternoon to convince Mom to reconsider anonymity, but by the time I left—for a Project Peacemakers visioning meeting— Mom had agreed. She still remembered Project Peacemakers, too, and her years of volunteer support, so I asked, as I was leaving, how she thought the organization might reposition itself in the future. "Well," she told me after a brief hesitation, "it will be crucial to identify people who think the work is important, and to say, 'Exactly what is your aim? What is your purpose?'" I told her she was absolutely correct and then I made her laugh: "See Mom," I said, "you can't be anonymous, because then I'll take credit for all your best ideas!"

Four months later, I review with Mom the paper I'll be giving at an upcoming conference. I tell her I'm planning to speak about the fact that she was sexually abused as a child, and about Pake's initial support for the German cause in World War II. Do I have her permission? To my surprise, given the secrecy with which it has been shrouded until now, Mom readily consents to including material about the sexual abuse. "If it will help other people," she has said earlier, about the Alzheimer's narrative generally, and she reiterates that permission now: "It will help people understand what that is like." About her family's politics during the war, though, she is adamant: "Nobody needs to know. Nobody needs to know that."

One year later, on 1 May 2009, Mom and I have a long conversation in which we range over a multitude of topics. In the context of the pope's expression of sorrow to Canada's Assembly of First Nations, Mom talks again about her experience of having been sexually abused. When we consider Canada's engagements in Afghanistan, Mom reiterates her strongly pacifist convictions, a position she immediately identifies as originating with Pake. Memories of Pake prompt memories of an aunt to whom Pake was especially close, including in intellectual temperament, and then Mom also remembers, fleetingly, stories Bertha told about a failed love affair involving this aunt, stories I'm eager to hear.

"Oh," Mom says, after a few moments of muddled narration, "I don't even know exactly; I wish Bertha was here. What I can tell you are just bits, and you have to make of it what you can. Like the Mennonite women," she proposes, and explains, "the Mennonite women make all those little pieces and they sew them together, right?" "Do you mean a quilt, Mom?" I ask. "*Jah*," she says, "it's like a quilt. You have to make a quilt of it in your head, and you can put it all there." She gestures toward the iPod.

"And what should I quilt together from the pieces, Mom?" I ask. "Well," Mom says, "you'll probably make one or two books or maybe more, God forbid!" And she laughs. "But Mom," I say, "if I have only fragments, I'm going to have to piece them together with something. People will read this story if it's a *story*, but I'll have to make up the pieces in between the fragments. What if I get it wrong?"

"I don't know," Mom says and repeats herself. "I have no idea. I've thought about that too, because it's all so complicated. People will tell you stuff, but still—you've not experienced it.

You've heard it, but you haven't experienced it, so it can never be totally true." "Exactly," I say, "and this is my problem. How do I get the true version of something?"

"Well," Mom says, "truth is a fleeting thing. Maybe it's truth at the moment, but what went before, or something that happens afterward, changes that truth, and it becomes something else." "That's *very* interesting, Mom," I say. "You're saying that what's true at any given time changes as we learn new information, as we see things differently." We ponder this for a moment and then I say, "Mom, I'm going back to the question I started with: how can I be sure that the story I tell, at the time I tell it, is the truth?"

"Oh," Mom says, "I think we better stop, my brain is working overtime, I can't keep up." She pauses. "I have to consider my brain," she repeats; but then she adds, "You have to decide what kind of story you want to make out of it. Maybe you make a true story, but maybe So-and-So didn't understand the story that way. Or maybe it's true but somebody else misreads it. Well then I say, folks, I can't keep track of all this, my brain doesn't allow it." We sit back and think.

"I'm glad I'm not a judge," Mom offers, "the possibilities are endless, whether the truth or not. But, you know," she adds, "you can do with all this rambling whatever you want. I don't think you'll lie."

〜〜〜

I suspect that several factors predisposed my mother to develop Alzheimer's, and one, I think, was the accumulated silence Mom imposed on herself. I think my mother learned early not to say some of her most important truths out loud. I believe she expended enormous energy staying silent for decades about events that damaged her permanently—the sexual abuse she experienced as a vulnerable child, her father's murderous anger, her parents' decision to emigrate, and, more than any of these, her parents' grotesquely wrong allegiances during World

War II. I loved my grandparents. It's not my place to forgive their mistakes, but it is my place to grieve those errors, and so, in this book I've quilted about my mother's life and mine you can find truths my mother didn't want told, papers she'd urge me to burn if she could. Much as I love her, though, and I love her deeply, these are truths I can't relinquish to the fire.

~~~

The last letter I send to North America is addressed to Nathaniel, who'll find me one week later in transit in the Toronto airport and be the first of my friends to welcome me back to Canada. "Nathaniel," I write wonderingly on 5 August 1989, "tonight, late, I leave Africa. It hardly seems possible that three years have passed. I'm determined to return, though I'm not yet sure when or how. Painful silence. Let's just say that that determination didn't make farewells in Ndejje any less wracking."

The last of the letters I write to my parents reflect a community gathering momentum as it gets back on its feet. Beautiful Nakazibwe Cate returns early from Ggaba and begins teaching traditional drumming and dance to all those of us who want to learn. When Rose finally gets back permanently a few weeks later, I'm able to resume living as my whole self. Shortly after our students' impressive Easter play, our local Resistance Council women's group launches plans to raise money through a Variety Show—*the very next week*. Frances and I (and our much-coveted trousers) are drawn into the celebration in various capacities:

Letter #92 To Mom and Dad   *11 April 1989*

So we dressed up with everyone else in busutis and sang the welcome song; had a brief, pious, crowd-pleasing walk-on in one of the traditional pieces, representing the missionaries who converted King Mutesa (not every RC can boast their own muzungu); co-opted Namukasa Beatrice and Mrs. Nsubuga

*(the only alto for miles able to "cram" so many English
words in such a short time) for an a cappella version of the
suffragette classic "Bread and Roses"; and then, near the
very end, Bea and I delivered a country-revival duet worthy
of Dolly Parton and Crystal Gayle (though Dolly would
likely have remembered all the words and Crystal would, no
doubt, have hit the high notes!?).*

In May, Frances and I begin casting for the pièce de résis-
tance of our producing-directing career, a double bill of Wole
Soyinka's *The Trials of Brother Jero* and *Jero's Metamorphosis*
for the district-level drama festival. Deft and acerbic, the plays
mock duplicitous preachers who grow fat on their parishioners'
credulity. Our students relish the scripts' richness and collabo-
rate to extract from Soyinka's words every devastating ironic
possibility. They didn't take first prize, but they should have.
In early July, when a travelling Red Cross blood collection unit
parks at Ndejje for several days, Bea and I celebrate the fact that
I'm well enough to donate—

Letter #102 to Mom and Dad   6 July 1989

*Bea and I decide suddenly over tea to go. We get in line
amongst a troupe of Nalinya's older students, and I can't
understand why they're watching us so closely. Me they've
seen a million times and Bea's been here for months. [. . .]
It's not until I'm settled, needle in my arm, collection bag
filling beside me that I understand what the girls are so
wildly curious to know: "Is Miss Katherine's blood red like
ours!?"*

And then Cate's students at Nalinya win a place in the national
dance competition.

Letter #103 to Mom and Dad   *15 July 1989*

They won the zone and district competitions and head today to Kampala for the finals. That will be an incredible show— music and dance by schools representing every area of the country. Last night's rehearsal blew my mind. Laughing back afterward, late through the dark, under the stars, I tell Bea and Rose: each time I hear the music and the drums and see the dancing, I wish I'd been born in Uganda—

I can't think how hard it's going to be to say goodbye.

postscript: *waiting for you here*

You know how the story ends,
so I tell you stories to defer the end.

~~~

Frances and I both pursue graduate studies after we return to Canada, though I delay for a year to practise managing the symptoms of fibromyalgia in high-speed North America. At schools just a hundred kilometres apart, we continue our friendship through the next decade, then laugh at our luck, hired into tenure-track positions at sister universities in Winnipeg as a new century begins.

Five months after moving back to Winnipeg, I'm late and slide into a back pew at the church I've begun attending, where I sit beside an attractive but sorrowing man I haven't seen before. My mind reels through scenarios that might explain his presence and his palpable sadness, the way he refuses when I offer him a hymn book ("I don't sing"), the way he hurries out at the end of the service. Just before he does, though, he joins in on the final hymn, and when he sings, he sings beautifully, the tenor line first, bass for the second verse, and then he repeats the pattern, tenor, then bass; perfect harmony.

I don't know exactly what I've witnessed, but I know that whatever "church" is supposed to be, "church" has happened for the stranger beside me. I experience the transformation and my proximity to the transformation as gifts. Our encounter that November morning knits itself into both our memories, but we don't learn one another's names until we meet again four months later. A few weeks later yet, Gareth and I spend hours over a first lunch revelling in the mutual friends we've discovered, many of them connections through MCC, so that it's clear, all these years after Dr. B's question in Kampala—I'm still not done with the Mennonites. In five more months, Gareth and I will be unofficially inseparable, something we celebrate with a wedding in August 2003.

Frances is also on sabbatical the year Harry is diagnosed, doing research in sub-Saharan Africa—

24 March 2008.

Early Saturday morning, I catch up on "Harry-logistics" email and in the midst, take a carefully choreographed call from Frances, who's at Ndejje for Easter celebrations. [. . .] Despite radical changes to communications technology, long-distance calls are still a comedy of errors, mostly because of the transmission lag (which makes them seem, like everything in my world these days, "just like" Alzheimer's). Because of the lag, there's silence where there should've been a response, and if you aren't remembering the lag, you're certain your interlocutor's disappeared or the line's been cut.

And that means that almost a third of long-distance conversations still consist of the repeated question, "Are you there?! Are you there?!" And if even one of the parties can't accommodate to the awkward rhythm, another third of the conversation is incomprehensible because one person is talking when the other one's voice arrives. "Pardon?" we say, "Sorry," in our outside voices, because it's all the way to Canada after all, all the way to Uganda. And if that weren't bad enough, I've lost my facility with

Ugandan English, Rose's voice is even throatier than it used to be, and we both answer questions with the simplest available version of truth: "Baby Harry is progressing"; "The crops have been very good"; "Canada is fine, but [glance out the window] there is too much snow."

A month earlier, just three days before Henry and Cynthia rush Harry to the hospital, I've been reminded that my project is always balancing distance and proximity:

19 February 2008.

My heart almost burst yesterday when I reread the last two letters Carla addressed to me in Uganda, the last letter Sharon sent before she and Lev set off for Nairobi, the sheaf of letters Rose mailed in the first year after I'd left Ndejje. "Hey Kathleen!" Rose begins her Christmas card that year, and my whole self compresses again in pleasure. It's this informal intimacy I long for, the easy living-alongside on a hot, bird-sung, laughter-punctuated, diesel-drifting afternoon ("Fuel is now so expensive," Rose writes, "that the school mistress has ordered the old lorry back into use")—

The love in the letters from Canada is palpable. "Hey toots, I'm counting the weeks," Carla writes. "I don't know how I'll get out of the habit of writing you," says Sharon, "it's as if my heart is coming home." "Don't worry about missing Ndejje," Carla adds, "cause I've already started—"

For the first year I'm back in Canada, Rose and I write one another almost every month. I've left Rose all my remaining stationary and a sheet of international stamps, gloriously expensive for someone earning a salary in Uganda shillings (especially when the salary isn't always paid). As our lives get busier, we write less frequently, but we always send cards at

Christmas. We sometimes telephone, but that requires careful coordination: Rose phones me first, briefly, to let me know what number to dial, on which day and when, carefully taking time zones into consideration. The first time Rose sends an email, I exult, thinking *this* will let us resume detailed communication about our lives. But Rose can only email when she's back at Ndejje, and only via the family friend who keys in polite platitudes from a computer at the community's new university.

Communication technologies have reached dizzying levels of sophistication and it sometimes seems there are no ways left to *not* be connected, but Rose and I manage. In 2011, she gets a cellphone, and for a short while we talk regularly, but only when she's back at Ndejje visiting her family. By now, Rose is headmistress of a small primary school in a district about a hundred kilometres from Ndejje, where cellphone coverage is sporadic and reception is poor. I acquire a cellphone a few years later and regret the delay when I realize I could've been texting Rose all this time. Except that, for reasons of contract and reception and cost, she can't text me back.

I longed for Canada while I lived in Uganda, and now I long for Ndejje and Rose. I want back our slow afternoons of easy conversations and easy silence; I want to dream again, together, about women's lives and women's possibilities; I want to debate, again, which one of us loves the other one more; I want to write to anyone who'll read me: "Rose was over for ages yesterday; we laughed so hard we had to sit on the floor." Rose and I get at some of this in our infrequent conversations, but the rareness and the difficulty limits the breadth of the concepts we tackle. When news of Uganda's proposed anti-homosexuality legislation reaches me, I want to discuss it with Rose but dread misunderstanding one another long-distance. American missionaries, discredited in the US, have brought an extreme form of homophobia to Uganda. Worse, they leveraged disproportionate influence on this explicitly

Christian country's parliament and shifted a society traditionally but tacitly anti-homosexual into one that stops just
short of condoning the murder of LGBTTQ* people.

Like Julia, the Ugandan grandmother who appears in my
dreams, I keep going to church because I have no idea who
the universe might want me to meet there. Sunday 19 January
2015 marks thirteen years and two months since a handsome
stranger first didn't and then did sing beside me. Gareth and
I have been married for eleven and a half years and, with his
grown-up children and their partners, form our own version
of a happily blended family. When our granddaughters are
born—Nora Autumn in October 2011 and Adeline Clover in
July 2013—I add "Nana KK" to my list of identities and step
into the blissful space of a grandparent's fathomless love.

And then a young African woman slides into the pew
behind me. Over the next hours and days and weeks, Gareth
and I will learn that Yiga arrived in Winnipeg alone in mid-
November 2014, knowing no one, a gender refugee from
Uganda. Back in the early 1980s, half a decade before the
United Church made it official policy, our congregation was
the first in Canada to accept LGBTTQ* members. We have a
reputation in the city as a progressive Christian community,
so when Yiga asked at the Rainbow Resource Centre about a
church where she'd be welcome, we seemed a likely answer.

I can tell by her English that she's not Canadian-born, and
the moment the service ends, I turn to greet her and ask where
she's from. When she tells me Uganda, I almost fall over.
When I tell her I lived in Uganda for three years thirty years
ago, she's just as surprised. Over coffee afterward, I ply her
with questions. "Do you have family in town? Friends? How
can they have put you here without anyone to help? Where
are you living? How much money do they give you? Who is
looking after you? Who is helping you find a job? Where will
you go to school? How old are you? How will I contact you?"
I finally stop my barrage. "Sorry," I tell her, slowing down.

"None of this is my business. You don't have to answer any of my questions. I'm not your mother!"

"It's okay," Yiga says with a shy smile. "Maybe you can be my Canadian mother?" Gareth and I are about to begin climbing two steep learning curves, one called "supporting a refugee in Canada," the other, "helping a transgender woman of colour live safely." But on 19 January 2015, it's still simple delight that compresses my heart, the chance to return the generosity friends in Uganda extended to me when I was just a little older than Yiga is now. If my mother were well, she'd be thrilled at our meeting, and I think Rose's grandmother would be too, the generous, affectionate old woman who imagined herself in the future, the honoured guest at my wedding: "And everyone will ask, how did that *muzungu* bride get an African grandmother!?" Three decades later, everyone wonders quietly instead: how did that stylish, charismatic young Ugandan woman get a *muzungu* mother?

~~~

We never recover from Harry's death, we never get over it. At our best, we make accommodations, improvising new selves around the chasm left behind when Harry jumped from this life to what comes next. Harry's absence and Alzheimer's ravages exacerbate Mom's anxiety about unattended children, and on Christmas Day 2012, no amount of reassurance assures her that her 33-month-old grandson is safe on his own. Late afternoon, supper about to be served, I find little Sebastien's Beppe crouched in the front hall, holding up a cautioning finger, urging him to be careful. But my nephew Sebastien (mathematician, magician, athlete), who was here a moment ago, is gone, chasing Uncle G in a hilarious bit of pre-supper mirth. "Sebastien's fine, Mom," I tell her, "he's with Gareth." When we gather with the others at the table, Mom wants to ask nine-year-old Lydia (wise and clever, already a graceful, passionate writer, already bitten by the travel bug) a question, but angles her face far too low. "It's okay, Beppe," Lydia says, placing her hands gently on Mom's cheeks, tilting Mom's head upward. "I'm right here."

~~~~~

We admit Mom into permanent care on 18 January 2013, three weeks after Christmas and six days before her seventy-seventh birthday. Mom still recognizes us by name, walks without support, forms some complete sentences, engages in simple conversations, and feeds herself. She'll never know our "little girls," Nora and Adeline, and she'll never know our "big girls," Yiga and Jasmine, the delicate South Asian transgender teenager seeking refuge in Canada whom Yiga recognizes as a sister and adds to our ad hoc family.

Mom receives excellent care and nevertheless falls several times. After a stroke in May 2014, she declines precipitously, but until that August, when she gets up abruptly and walks away from the piano in the multi-purpose room, we still reach her through music. I visit Mom without my iPod now and look back on the project I began seven years earlier. In the original plan, the letters Mom and I exchanged when I lived in Uganda are a pretext for our weekly conversations—a pretext for the text we'll quilt together of Mom's life and mine. Desire fuels the original plan and unfulfilled desire discovers that, even in conditions of optimal cognitive function, letters are difficult to understand outside of their original context. And yet—sometimes simply by their presence—the letters prompt the meditative excursions Mom and I make every week, examining political events, remembering family histories, and musing on the nature of mind, brain, body, and spirit, the business of being alive, the possibility of death.

Freed up now to revisit our archived conversations, I'm regularly startled by what I've forgotten, our conversation on 15 February 2008, for instance, one week before Harry goes into the hospital, when Mom and I talked for hours but didn't ever get to the letters I'd brought along, when she told me, in a long conversation about biblical interpretation, "I can't get rid of the idea that we're making our own God. We imagine our own God."

After a lifetime committed to what she's understood to be Christian principles of loving-kindness, compassion, peacemaking, and work for global and economic justice, Mom often expresses uncertainty now about God's existence. On 15 February 2008, she adds, "I think it's not so important to think there *is* a God, or maybe there *is not* a God. I think what's important is—for human beings anyway—to survive together—that they treat other human beings alike." "Like the Golden Rule?" I ask, and Mom says, "*Jah*. The Golden Rule. If you live by the Golden Rule, I think, then you pretty well have everything covered what you as a human being are due to other creatures."

I love Mom's claim and am baffled by it. What did she mean, I wonder, listening to her recorded voice? Maybe not. "*what* you as a human being are *due* to other creatures," but "*that* you as a human being *should do* to other creatures"? Or maybe "*that* you as a human being *owe* to other creatures"? What I want Mom to have meant is all this and a radical, poetic expression of trans-species interdependence: "what you as a human being are, due to other creatures."

On 15 February 2008, our discussion of shared and mutual responsibility prompts Mom to consider, too, the passionate desire of life for life, and to remember the atomic bombs that were dropped on Hiroshima and Nagasaki. "I remember thinking," she says, about that destruction of life in all its forms, "if it is like that then—then you're better off running toward the—" she pauses, searching for the word. I suggest "centre." "*Jah*," Mom says, "the centre." "You think," she explains, "'You're not going to get alive out of here.' But still," she adds emphatically, "you would try to run away from it. *You would not run toward it.*"

~~~

By January 2015, Mom no longer speaks recognizable words in any of the five languages in which she was once fluent. She vocalizes only to communicate her almost constant distress, irritation, or anger. She often sounds like an animal in pain. Confined to a wheelchair, she's fed her meals of puréed food, and registers only the barest awareness of others around her. On Fridays I find Mom bent almost double over the tray attached to her chair. I lay my face beside hers, hold my head to hers, massage her arms, and tell her that I love her, hoping to balance off at least some of the distress. Because I can't help thinking, every single time, that it's anger she's expressing, at us, for not helping to end things before they got to this point. She so clearly did not want to get to this point.

〜〜〜

On 21 September 2015, Omke John responds promptly to another of my urgent emails asking about Frisian phrases. "I'm amazed," he writes, "at how accurately you interpret your mother's expressions and the words. Based on what you provide, I am quite sure she said, '*Ik ferskuor mij*,' literally, 'I tear myself apart,' or 'I tear myself up.'"

〜〜〜

Musing inside our archived conversations, I discover that grief and mourning and dread filled my mind so completely in the winter after Harry's passing that I missed my mother's complicated ethical courage—willing to hold in tension the deeply felt empathic truth that, even in the midst of nuclear calamity, one would run toward the possibility of life, and the firm conviction that someone facing the consequences of Alzheimer's should have the right to choose her own death. With time to reflect, I notice too that, contrary to my fears, Mom didn't ever ask me to make promises I couldn't keep. So I massage her arms now on Friday afternoons, hold my head to hers, stroke her hair, and tell her, "I love you. You're a wonderful mother."

And then, near the end of my visit on Friday 27 November 2015, Mom exerts unexpected effort, raises her head, turns in my direction, and dazzles me with a smile. She tries twice to say something, but it's incomprehensible both times. "I'm right here, Mom," I tell her, basking briefly, "I'm so happy to see you."

~~~

I want singing at the end, a choir of angels.

~~~

"*De Krystreis fen Broder Iwersen*" is a story in the old style, one for reading aloud on candlelit winter evenings in a long-ago time. My mother loved this story even more than she loved *Merijntje Gijzens*; Pake read it every year on Christmas Eve and little Geeske revelled in each telling. The story's set amongst the tiny islands that constitute North Frisia and run along the coast of Germany, where small groups of people live robust, precarious lives, bordering the sea that sustains them and that sometimes rises without warning to inundate their low-lying lands and drown them. It's a hard life, and Broder Iwersen, the story's protagonist, supports his family by working half the year on ocean-going ships. He spends winters on the island, though, with his beloved wife, attending to repairs and reading and singing through the long cozy evenings with their six cherished children. Broder is uniquely adept at reading the sea and the tides, reading the pathways that emerge amongst the islands when the tides are out, and in the winter Broder works as a "water walker," running errands to the mainland.

The story's suspense begins two days before Christmas, when a young neighbour arrives to ask if Broder can make an emergency journey for medicine that the boy's mother suddenly needs. Broder's wife urges caution; the children will be heartbroken, she reminds him, if he's not home by Christmas. They've been practising their carols for weeks, she says; you cannot disappoint them. Broder, though, is wonderfully confident: look at the sky, he says, it's perfectly clear; the weather will be fine. I'll reach the mainland tonight, run the errands tomorrow, and be back on Christmas Day, in time for our delicious supper and a celebration with the children.

But the weather turns on Broder's journey home, the dreaded fog rolls in, and Broder—who's been meditating with satisfaction on the extra gifts the errand has paid for—fails to notice in time that the light of a far northern Christmas afternoon has turned unexpectedly dark. The sea rolls ominously all around, the tide is coming in, and Broder is lost just one or two right—or wrong—turns from home. At home, Broder's wife notices the fog before he does and her anxiety deepens. The children, who've been playing in the yard, notice too and return to the house with worried questions that she can't answer. We'll go down to the beach, she tells them, we'll wait for your father there. On the beach, they hear the sea's roar, can feel the tide's imminence, call their father's name. "We're here," they call, "we're here," as loudly as they can, and then Inge, the oldest daughter, thinks to sing, and all the children and their mother join in, singing in the harmonies they've practised, the Christmas songs their father loves.

Broder hears, of course, just in time, just before the tide. Just before the tide, Broder turns to the sound of the singing and finds his way home through the fog. It's an adventure, the narrator assures us in conclusion, that Broder and his wife tell many times in the years that follow, and no one, in all those years, can dislodge Broder's conviction that angels joined his children that dark and dangerous evening to sing him safely home.

~~~

My mother dies quietly on the morning of 15 February 2017, exactly nine years after she endorses an ethic of "surviving together" and just minutes after Dad leaves the room. I sit with her for the last time on the night of 14 February 2017, knowing it's a good and a welcome death that approaches. At first I don't recognize the music I hear when I hold my head to Mom's for a final farewell. And then I do, Geeske and Bertha, biking to the M.U.L.O., laughing and talking and singing, together again...

~~~

On 16 November 2012, seven years and four months after the Alzheimer's diagnosis; more than one year after the very bad day with which I began my story; two months before we admitted Mom into care; and four years and three months before her death, I send my siblings an update on my most recent visit:

I don't take the iPod on our walks, which is, ironically, where Mom says the most interesting things. Last week I went back to our word games, which are much diminished from our previous accomplishments, and now involve me simply throwing out a word and asking Mom what it means. She balked at "enterprise," so I reminded her that it isn't a test of any kind, which relaxed her enough that she could tell me, after a long pause, about "vacillate": "If you're waiting for someone, and they said they'd come then, but they don't come and they don't come, and you wait, and maybe you're with other people and you say, 'Now where is he?' and he doesn't come and doesn't come and it's very late. That's vacillating."

I told her she was right, then asked about "correspondence," and that one Mom answered without hesitation: "That is when, say you have something and then something else. And you have something and you say, that looks like the same thing." I told her she was exactly right, that if one thing corresponds with another, it means that the two things are quite alike. "Jah," Mom said, "and then if, say, you are living here and someone else is living there, and if you want to communicate with them, maybe you send them something, like a message." Which was pretty amazing, that within the space of just a few sentences, she could, without prompting, produce both main meanings of correspondence.

I told her she was right and that when I lived in Uganda, we would send each other letters and those letters were our "correspondence." Interestingly, and unlike a few years ago, when telling her that often made her anxious ("I sent you letters?!"), she seemed pleased with the information. "We did, eh?" she said, beaming one of her rare contented smiles, "That's good."

Notes

Part 1   *perfect correspondence*

1 Some names in this memoir have been changed.
2 Or *mzungu*, a term in Bantu languages for people of European descent. Depending on whom you ask, it originally meant "freak of nature" or "someone who roams aimlessly."
3 Cooking banana, a staple in southern Uganda.
4 *Busutis* (also called *gomesi*) are floor-length, usually colourful dresses, with a distinctive square neckline and short, often puffy sleeves.

Part 2   *crosswords*

1 My parents have supported the CCPA, a leading voice for progressive public policy on social, economic, and environmental justice issues, since the early 1990s.
2 "Being with the Lamb" originally appeared in a 1981 issue of *Sojourners*. *Sojourners* has been published since 1975 by Sojourners community, an American Christian organization committed to convening, building alliances among, and mobilizing people of faith in action for racial and social justice, life and peace, and environmental stewardship.
3 *(Meer) uitgebreid lager onderwijs,* which translates literally as "(further) extended primary education."
4 Salty black licorice, a popular Dutch candy.
5 As an agency of the Canadian Council of Churches, Project Ploughshares provides analysis and advice to governments and civil society on Canada's role in preventing war and advancing human security in conflict zones.

6 The Greenham Common Women's Peace Camp began in September 1981 at the RAF base in Berkshire, England, to protest the decision to house cruise missiles.

7 I use "progressive" and "conservative" to distinguish the denominations in terms of (i) their allegiances to traditional Protestant theologies and (ii) their openness to social issues related to women's roles, environmental concerns, human rights, global economic justice, and non-traditional sexual identities.

8 Literally, a spring child has been given to us in a little daughter.

9 Approximately, "Holy heck, that's Reverend de Haan!"

10 Though my mother didn't keep up with the expanding acronym, she would have celebrated its inclusion of lesbian, gay, bisexual, transgender, Two-Spirited, and queer, and appreciated the asterisk, standing in as it does for other minority sexual orientations and gender identities.

11 Since retiring in 1994, my father has been extensively involved in Save-Our-Seine (SOS), a community environmental group dedicated to restoring and preserving the Seine River that runs north through Winnipeg and my parents' property.

Part 3   post secret

1 "Madam," a term of respectful address, as is "Mama."

2 Plural of *muzungu*.

3 It's not obvious, but here I mean the children I got to know while I was a student teacher in inner-city schools.

4 After a long search for caregivers, I find Vivian, a young midwife with an almost miraculous knack for planning activities that Mom enjoys. Grace's claim here may be accidentally accurate: the psychiatric hospital in which Beppe de Jong worked before she married likely also housed people suffering from dementia.

5 Uganda's international airport.

6 Resistance Councils were a form of local, elected government, initially established during the war to support Museveni and his NRA combatants, and implemented in every district after the NRM's victory.

7 Multi-purpose cloth wrapper.

8   Uganda's official language.

9   MCC proscribed the consumption of alcohol unless its volunteers were under what it called "strong social pressure."

10 "Broder Iwersen's Christmas Journey."

11 Alice Lakwena led the Holy Spirit Movement against NRA forces from 1986 to 1987.

12 My aunt Line and her family lived in Stony Mountain, a small town just north of Winnipeg. As a child, I experienced our late-night rides home from Stony Mountain as eerily, deliciously magical.

13 A literal translation renders "kicking him up," which is surprisingly accurate. The sense is of one person very roughly manhandling another, including by using his feet.

14 Ans H—— was a long-time friend of my parents.

15 My mother's youngest and oldest sisters weigh in.

16 Mom means "by," and I've let her error stand.

17 Despite all the ways in which our collective understandings have *not* changed—

Part 4   *new meadow*

1   Dutch and Frisian are the Netherlands' two official languages. Fryslân is sometimes called West Frisia to distinguish it from its ethnically close neighbours, East Frisia and North Frisia.

2   Dutch- and German-speakers regularly claim that Frisian is an incomprehensible dialect and sometimes joke that it isn't even a dialect but the result of a speech impediment.

3   At a surprisingly early stage, my mother no longer remembered that she'd completed an honours undergraduate degree with a major in French. Despite my encouragement, she rarely resorts to French to make her points.

4   While I investigated grad schools in Boston, Luke was employed in various communities around southern Ontario and considering a job in Mozambique.

5   *Nijemardum as It Was.*

6   O. Van der Groot, M. de Jong-Beucken, and J. Bosma-de Jong, eds., *Nijemardum sa't it wie* (Easterein, The Netherlands: Van der Eems, 1985), 11.

7 "The Linnet's Secret," by Sir Henry Rowley Bishop. Decades later, I'm glad young Geeske didn't realize—at a point where it would've made a difference—that the song she associated with beauty in Canada was an English song.

8 Uganda Electricity Board.

9 Caused by a protein deficiency, kwashiorkor typically affects young children.

10 Alzheimer Society Canada and the US-based Alzheimer's Association have been active since 1978 and 1980, respectively, raising awareness of and advancing research into the disease.

Part 5   holy shipwreck

1 Gareth and I maintained Harry's blog until September 2008. In January 2009, Harry's mother, Cynthia, took over the blog as a permanent memorial.

2 Donald B. Kraybill, Steven M. Nolt, and David L. Weaver-Zercher, *Amish Grace: How Forgiveness Transcended Tragedy* (San Francisco: John Wiley & Sons, 2007).

3 In Virginia Bell and David Troxel, *The Best Friends Approach to Alzheimer's Care* (Baltimore: Health Professions Press, 1997), 39–42; http://www.alzsupport.org/uploads/AN_ALZHEIMER _bill_of_rights.pdf, accessed January 4, 2015.

Acknowledgements

My heartfelt thanks go to the many people who have helped in small and large ways to make *Bird-Bent Grass* possible:

- Gareth Neufeld, Carla Keast, and Gerta de Jong, without whose unwavering support there would not be a book;
- Gareth Neufeld, Carla Keast, Deborah Schnitzer, Cathleen Hjalmarson, Sharon Doerksen, and Steve Noyes, who read early versions of the manuscript and encouraged me anyway, and who, with Bruno Cornellier, Catherine Hunter, Miriam Meinders, Heather Milne, Kate Ready, Ruth Rempel, Ruth Schultheis, Marty Slyker, Margaret Sweatman, Gertie Wakuraya Wanjohi, and Jenny Heijun Wills, have, over the years, offered combinations of insight, advice, encouragement, meals, laughter, and, best of all, memories of my mother;
- my colleagues in the warmly collegial English Department at the University of Winnipeg, for their personal and professional encouragement; the University of Winnipeg for institutional support in the form of sabbaticals and travel grants; and all of my students over the years, each one of whom has stretched me and helped me learn;
- Nakato Rose Ssendawula, sister of my heart; the Ssendawula family; my friends at Ndejje; the MCC Uganda unit; and all of my correspondents, named, pseudonymous, and anonymous;
- the R.A.R. group, the community of Augustine United Church, and Augustine's Just Living group, especially as we work together to be better allies to our Indigenous friends and neighbours and hosts here in Treaty 1 territory;
- Hilary Bergen, Jasmine Budak, Meghan Kizuik, Camille Krahn, Ali Millar, Kristin Millar, and Robyn Van Inderstine, for their deft research and transcriptions; Carol DeBoer-Langworthy,

editor of *Lifewriting Annual*, whose warm encouragement at a crucial point in 2014 helped me find *Bird-Bent*'s shape and form; the encouragement of anonymous readers for Wilfrid Laurier University Press; and my wise and perspicacious editors, Lisa Quinn, Siobhan McMenemy, Robert Kohlmeier, and Margaret Crammond, who sent perfect and perfectly timed editorial advice and safety ropes;

- Noreen and Glenn Duncan for the gift of seven weeks in their glorious sunroom, writing in view of the Assiniboine River;
- Theresa Meinders, Vivian Unger, the Alzheimer Society of Manitoba, publicly funded Home Care, and the staff at River Park Gardens, for the various, loving ways in which they cared for Grace;
- Lynne Braun, MaryAnne Hembroff, Gilles Noël, Indira Rampersad, Josef Silha, Libby Yager, and Amel Zaki, who keep me healthy, balanced, tuneful, and alive;
- my terrific family of Neufeld in-laws; the Venema clan in Canada and in the Netherlands; my raucous de Jong cousins (and the three quiet ones); and my aunts and uncles: Line van Solkema, Hinke Polet, John (Omke Jan) Kruizenga (for energizing conversations about language and literature, and for unlocking the mysteries of *Merijntje Gijzens*), Lou de Jong, Pauline Fia, Jess and Douwe Bosma (including for getting me my own copy of *"De Krystreis fen Broder Iwersen"*), Henk Meinders, and, especially, *de lytse famkes*, Eta Meinders and Gerta de Jong, including for the unstinting support they provided Geeske in her final years;
- my family: Alexandra Venema (intrepid collaborator in strategies of care), Gary Hornby, and Gwyneth Venema Hornby; Henry (Hank) Venema, Cynthia Neudoerffer, and Lydia and Sebastien Neudoerffer Venema; Simon Neufeld and Judith Klassen; Sara Neufeld, Matthew Broeska, and (heart's delight) Nora and Adeline Broeska-Neufeld; Yiga Arafat and Jasmine J; and my father, Dave, who lets me know in a hundred quiet ways that he approves of what I do and what I write;
- and, at the first and at the last, Gareth Neufeld, to whom I owe a hundred thousand thanks, and with whom my heart and I are, fully and completely, safely home.

Books in the Life Writing Series
Published by Wilfrid Laurier University Press

Haven't Any News: Ruby's Letters from the Fifties edited by Edna
Staebler with an Afterword by Marlene Kadar • 1995 / x + 165 pp. /
ISBN 0-88920-248-6

"I Want to Join Your Club": Letters from Rural Children, 1900–1920
edited by Norah L. Lewis with a Preface by Neil Sutherland • 1996 /
xii + 250 pp. (30 b&w photos) / ISBN 0-88920-260-5

And Peace Never Came by Elisabeth M. Raab with Historical Notes
by Marlene Kadar • 1996 / x + 196 pp. (12 b&w photos, map) /
ISBN 0-88920-281-8

*Dear Editor and Friends: Letters from Rural Women of the North-
West, 1900–1920* edited by Norah L. Lewis • 1998 / xvi + 166 pp.
(20 b&w photos) / ISBN 0-88920-287-7

The Surprise of My Life: An Autobiography by Claire Drainie Taylor
with a Foreword by Marlene Kadar • 1998 / xii + 268 pp. (8 colour
photos and 92 b&w photos) / ISBN 0-88920-302-4

Memoirs from Away: A New Found Land Girlhood by Helen M. Buss /
Margaret Clarke • 1998 / xvi + 153 pp. / ISBN 0-88920-350-4

The Life and Letters of Annie Leake Tuttle: Working for the Best by
Marilyn Färdig Whiteley • 1999 / xviii + 150 pp. / ISBN 0-88920-
330-x

Marian Engel's Notebooks: "Ah, mon cahier, écoute" edited by Christl
Verduyn • 1999 / viii + 576 pp. / ISBN 0-88920-333-4 cloth / ISBN
0-88920-349-0 paper

Be Good Sweet Maid: The Trials of Dorothy Joudrie by Audrey
Andrews • 1999 / vi + 276 pp. / ISBN 0-88920-334-2

*Working in Women's Archives: Researching Women's Private Literature
and Archival Documents* edited by Helen M. Buss and Marlene
Kadar • 2001 / vi + 120 pp. / ISBN 0-88920-341-5

*Repossessing the World: Reading Memoirs by Contemporary
Women* by Helen M. Buss • 2002 / xxvi + 206 pp. / ISBN 0-88920-
408-x cloth / ISBN 0-88920-410-1 paper

Chasing the Comet: A Scottish-Canadian Life by Patricia Koretchuk •
2002 / xx + 244 pp. / ISBN 0-88920-407-1

The Queen of Peace Room by Magie Dominic • 2002 / xii + 115 pp. /
ISBN 0-88920-417-9

China Diary: The Life of Mary Austin Endicott by Shirley Jane
Endicott • 2002 / xvi + 251 pp. / ISBN 0-88920-412-8

The Curtain: Witness and Memory in Wartime Holland by Henry G.
Schogt • 2003 / xii + 132 pp. / ISBN 0-88920-396-2

Teaching Places by Audrey J. Whitson • 2003 / xiii + 178 pp. / ISBN
0-88920-425-x

Through the Hitler Line by Laurence F. Wilmot, M.C. • 2003 / xvi +
152 pp. / ISBN 0-88920-448-9

Where I Come From by Vijay Agnew • 2003 / xiv + 298 pp. / ISBN
0-88920-414-4

The Water Lily Pond by Han Z. Li • 2004 / x + 254 pp. / ISBN
0-88920-431-4

*The Life Writings of Mary Baker McQuesten: Victorian
Matriarch* edited by Mary J. Anderson • 2004 / xxii + 338 pp. / ISBN
0-88920-437-3

*Seven Eggs Today: The Diaries of Mary Armstrong, 1859 and
1869* edited by Jackson W. Armstrong • 2004 / xvi + 228 pp. / ISBN
0-88920-440-3

Love and War in London: A Woman's Diary 1939–1942 by Olivia
Cockett; edited by Robert W. Malcolmson • 2005 / xvi + 208 pp. /
ISBN 0-88920-458-6

Incorrigible by Velma Demerson • 2004 / vi + 178 pp. / ISBN
0-88920-444-6

Auto/biography in Canada: Critical Directions edited by Julie Rak •
2005 / viii + 264 pp. / ISBN 0-88920-478-0

Tracing the Autobiographical edited by Marlene Kadar, Linda Warley,
Jeanne Perreault, and Susanna Egan • 2005 / viii + 280 pp. / ISBN
0-88920-476-4

Must Write: Edna Staebler's Diaries edited by Christl Verduyn • 2005 / viii + 304 pp. / ISBN 0-88920-481-0

Pursuing Giraffe: A 1950s Adventure by Anne Innis Dagg • 2006 / xvi + 284 pp. (photos, 2 maps) / 978-0-88920-463-8

Food That Really Schmecks by Edna Staebler • 2007 / xxiv + 334 pp. / ISBN 978-0-88920-521-5

163256: A Memoir of Resistance by Michael Englishman • 2007 / xvi + 112 pp. (14 b&w photos) / ISBN 978-1-55458-009-5

The Wartime Letters of Leslie and Cecil Frost, 1915–1919 edited by R.B. Fleming • 2007 / xxxvi + 384 pp. (49 b&w photos, 5 maps) / ISBN 978-1-55458-000-2

Johanna Krause Twice Persecuted: Surviving in Nazi Germany and Communist East Germany by Carolyn Gammon and Christiane Hemker • 2007 / x + 170 pp. (58 b&w photos, 2 maps) / ISBN 978-1-55458-006-4

Watermelon Syrup: A Novel by Annie Jacobsen with Jane Finlay-Young and Di Brandt • 2007 / x + 268 pp. / ISBN 978-1-55458-005-7

Broad Is the Way: Stories from Mayerthorpe by Margaret Norquay • 2008 / x + 106 pp. (6 b&w photos) / ISBN 978-1-55458-020-0

Becoming My Mother's Daughter: A Story of Survival and Renewal by Erika Gottlieb • 2008 / x + 178 pp. (36 b&w illus., 17 colour) / ISBN 978-1-55458-030-9

Leaving Fundamentalism: Personal Stories edited by G. Elijah Dann • 2008 / xii + 234 pp. / ISBN 978-1-55458-026-2

Bearing Witness: Living with Ovarian Cancer edited by Kathryn Carter and Lauri Elit • 2009 / viii + 94 pp. / ISBN 978-1-55458-055-2

Dead Woman Pickney: A Memoir of Childhood in Jamaica by Yvonne Shorter Brown • 2010 / viii + 202 pp. / ISBN 978-1-55458-189-4

I Have a Story to Tell You by Seemah C. Berson • 2010 / xx + 288 pp. (24 b&w photos) / ISBN 978-1-55458-219-8

We All Giggled: A Bourgeois Family Memoir by Thomas O. Hueglin • 2010 / xiv + 232 pp. (20 b&w photos) / ISBN 978-1-55458-262-4

Just a Larger Family: Letters of Marie Williamson from the Canadian Home Front, 1940–1944 edited by Mary F. Williamson and Tom Sharp • 2011 / xxiv + 378 pp. (16 b&w photos) / ISBN 978-1-55458-323-2

Burdens of Proof: Faith, Doubt, and Identity in Autobiography by Susanna Egan • 2011 / x + 200 pp. / ISBN 978-1-55458-333-1

Accident of Fate: A Personal Account 1938–1945 by Imre Rochlitz with Joseph Rochlitz • 2011 / xiv + 226 pp. (50 b&w photos, 5 maps) / ISBN 978-1-55458-267-9

The Green Sofa by Natascha Würzbach, translated by Raleigh Whitinger • 2012 / xiv + 240 pp. (5 b&w photos) / ISBN 978-1-55458-334-8

Unheard Of: Memoirs of a Canadian Composer by John Beckwith • 2012 / x + 393 pp. (74 illus., 8 musical examples) / ISBN 978-1-55458-358-4

Borrowed Tongues: Life Writing, Migration, and Translation by Eva C. Karpinski • 2012 / viii + 274 pp. / ISBN 978-1-55458-357-7

Basements and Attics, Closets and Cyberspace: Explorations in Canadian Women's Archives edited by Linda M. Morra and Jessica Schagerl • 2012 / x + 338 pp. / ISBN 978-1-55458-632-5

The Memory of Water by Allen Smutylo • 2013 / x + 262 pp. (65 colour illus.) / ISBN 978-1-55458-842-8

The Unwritten Diary of Israel Unger, Revised Edition by Carolyn Gammon and Israel Unger • 2013 / ix + 230 pp. (b&w illus.) / ISBN 978-1-77112-011-1

Boom! Manufacturing Memoir for the Popular Market by Julie Rak • 2013 / viii + 249 pp. (b&w illus.) / ISBN 978-1-55458-939-5

Motherlode: A Mosaic of Dutch Wartime Experience by Carolyne Van Der Meer • 2014 / xiv + 132 pp. (b&w illus.) / ISBN 978-1-77112-005-0

Not the Whole Story: Challenging the Single Mother Narrative edited by Lea Caragata and Judit Alcalde • 2014 / x + 222 pp. / ISBN 978-1-55458-624-0

Street Angel by Magie Dominc • 2014 / vii + 154 pp. / ISBN 978-1-77112-026-5

In the Unlikeliest of Places: How Nachman Libeskind Survived the Nazis, Gulags, and Soviet Communism by Annette Libeskind Berkovits • 2014 / xiv + 282 pp. (6 colour illus.) / ISBN 978-1-77112-066-1

Kinds of Winter: Four Solo Journeys by Dogteam in Canada's Northwest Territories by Dave Olesen • 2014 / xii + 256 pp. (illus.) / ISBN 978-1-77112-118-7

Working Memory: Women and Work in World War II edited by Marlene Kadar and Jeanne Perreault • 2015 / vii + 243 pp. (illus.) / ISBN 978-1-77112—035-7

Wait Time: A Memoir of Cancer by Kenneth Sherman • 2016 / xiv + 138 pp. / ISBN 978-1-77112-188-0

Canadian Graphic: Picturing Life Narratives edited by Candida Rifkind and Linda Warley • 2016 / viii + 305 pp. (illus.) / ISBN 978-1-77112-179-8

Travels and Identities: Elizabeth and Adam Shortt in Europe, 1911 edited by Peter E. Paul Dembski • 2017 / xxii + 272 pp. (illus.) / ISBN 978-1-77112-225-2

Bird-Bent Grass: A Memoir, in Pieces by Kathleen Venema • 2018 • xiii + 340 pp. / ISBN 978-1-77112-290-0